A MANUAL OF BUDDHISM

FOR ADVANCED STUDENTS

A MANUAL OF BUDDHISM

FOR ADVANCED STUDENTS

MRS. RHYS DAVIDS

GYAN

Published by

GYAN

Gyan Publishing House
5, Ansari Road
Daryaganj, New Delhi-110002
Phone: 011-47034999, 9811692060
E-mail: books@gyanbooks.com

Distribution Network
gyanbooks.com
India, USA, Canada, UK, Australia, France

ISBN : 978-81-212-3753-6 (PB)
First Published, London, 1932

2nd Impression 2020

Printed at: Gyan Press, Delhi.

A Manual of Buddhism
Author: Mrs. Rhys Davids

TO

HUSBAND AND SON

PREFACE

EIGHTEEN years after Spence Hardy had published his *Manual of Budhism* [sic], mainly a translation from late Sinhalese sources, the Society for Promoting Christian Knowledge published, as the first of their Non-Christian Religious Systems, a *Manual of Buddhism* by Rhys Davids. This was fifty-four years ago, and the book has been reprinted twenty-three times and yet lives. It has wrought a most useful work, first, by diffusing knowledge about the history of a great and long-lived institution; secondly, by at least checking, in its historical sobriety, the growth of erratic impulses, arising out of a very little learning about that institution and materializing in much well-meant but misleading assertion.

Rhys Davids *believed* in viewing a subject historically. A religion, he would have said, is not a ready-made, reach-me-down set of notions and conduct, evolved, with no past and no change, from the inner being of any one man, however great. That this is not fully grasped is evident from the many writings on what we have lately come to call "Buddhism," which have appeared in spite of the example set by his book. Yet but for that example, who can say how many more, how much worse we might have seen! That his Manual has not been an even stronger check may be because he was himself unable to profit more by all the materials that, mainly through his scheme of purveying, have followed on the appearance of his Manual.

This scheme was the completion of the issue in roman letter of editions, together with a Dictionary and Translations, of the oldest literature of Buddhism which has yet been found: the Pali Canon and affiliated literature.

Printing exigencies made it impossible for him to rewrite or even recast any of his book, and ruefully does he write, in a Preface to a later reprint, of the growing need for rewriting it. Compared with most of our special sciences, the study of Buddhist sources is very new. A scientific manual is superannuated in a decade, even though the science date from a couple of centuries back. Equally and more so is a Buddhist manual superannuated after fifty-four years. Had it been possible for Rhys Davids, with youth renewed in place of a suffering old age, to have set about the recast of his own views, rendered possible through his own persistent labours, the present work had been less needed. If I say "less" rather than "not," that is only because he is he, and I am I.

Nor do I claim to have in every way reproduced all the kind of information that is packed into his Manual. In the first place, it is now less needed. So much more is now accessible to the reader that it is rather guidance in his reading than a substitute for his reading that is needed. A long, very little-chronicled history of the many changes in the life of a religion is a very baffling problem, and no easily got citation of formulas rightly embodies it. In the second place, the present Manual is relatively less concerned with the external history of either Founder or "Church."[1] It is primarily out to inquire into the history of how to fit a certain nucleus of ideas into the history of Indian religious ideas; to show in that nucleus an attempt at an expansion in that history, followed by a number of contracting changes, with—merely by a glance—a re-expansion of a distinctive character in the Far East. But no outline of Sakyan descent will explain the man Siddhattha Gotama. It is *he* who is the explanation of the Sakyan emergence in the religious history of India; it is the life as a whole

[1] I have, *e.g.*, refrained from reproducing my husband's very guarded statistics of, not "Buddhists," but *Buddhist Influence*. I have too often seen his care in this matter disregarded.

of this man, and not our "heredity" (as we now see it) which could explain that. Similarly, it is the ideas swaying opinion at this or that period which made the history of Buddhism the decadent change that I see—not the ideas *as such*, but the ideas as being held by an increasing (and therefore influential) number of men. And it is the Man himself, his message and these ideas, that form the subject of my Manual, far more than his domestic or topical history, or the external superstructures that his fundamental work underwent after he had gone. The verbal superstructures, the formulas are often being held up as what he taught. Buddhists are curiously complacent about being free from "creeds," but they are the very votaries of the formula. I have striven to lead the reader behind and beneath the formula. The formula takes a long time to evolve; and in it the very Man is lost to view. It is the man in his upward growth that is for me the one fit subject of a world religion. The very Man—India called him "man," "self," we have called him person, soul, spirit—as becoming the More that is in him potentially: here the More presupposes the real being-in-becoming of that very Man. If we blot out the very Man as unreal, then that More becomes just a serial bunch of ideas built up around a nonentity, or at best round a dummy man called "mind." Now in Indian religion the reality of the man was vital. That vital reality lives in the original message of the first Sakyans: a message concerning the More in the very Man.

That I should have been permitted, by the courtesy and generous enterprise of the Society for Promoting Christian Knowledge, to supply a successor to the Manual my late husband wrote for them in 1878, forms for me the happiest termination to my many years of labour in the field to which, fifty years ago, he first directed my steps. This successor has been written with no idea of revising or amending any word in the book he wrote. I have not once consulted this in writing it. Between it and his manual there lies the pile of a world-literature he had spent himself since 1878 in giving to the world—the issues of first editions, prepared by men of devotion and disinterestedness,[1] published by the Pali Text Society, which he founded, contributed to and administered for his remaining forty years of life. It was from surveys of the growing pile that he, as he told us, would have rewritten his Manual, had it been practicable. I am confident, from my long and happy association with him, that he would wish, now that this has become practicable, that I should take his place. Until his last years he read and annotated all that his Society was bringing out. But between these and the forming an ever-maturing judgment on the historic growth they were gradually revealing, there bulked, huge and yet inchoate, the Pali-English Dictionary of his dreams. Here was detail in and surveying of words rather than historic purview in ideas. And on that now-completed Dictionary he worked till the day ended. He had dreamed and schemed an international collaboration of scholars for that Dictionary. But a will like his is given to few, and he found himself, at seventy, left alone to compile it. Achieved it was, through a devoted co-editor,[2] but the consequent revision in ideas suffered too long a postponement.

I am not claiming that, had he lived in vigour another decade and made that revision, it would have tallied at every point with the view presented by me. I am not able to assume that he would have got past the conviction, born of just the need of that later revision, that what we find reiterated and emphasized in those Pali scriptures is truly the original gospel; that he would have come to see in them ecclesiastical superstructure. This is what I see in them; I no longer hold his conviction. Whether, in supplanting his early work by my own later belief, my Manual will be judged the less or the more worthy to deserve the honour of its position, the man of the coming

[1] Pre-eminently the late Edmund Hardy. [2] Dr. Wm. Stede.

day will decide. I knew Rhys Davids well enough to say this much : his acquiescence in such emphasis of monasticism grown, as the Pali records show, preponderant, never amounted to approval. It is true that, as a child of his generation, he lent himself the more easily to see as true the man-as-unreal taught by the monk. But, as a believer in world-melioration, he never took "dukkha," the world-ill of the monk, to heart; he clung to the Way of Gotama to the end, even though he did not see it in its original setting. If he put aside too much as mere myth, which, for me, is true, here again it was our culture of yesterday that hindered him. Pioneer he was, and such cannot always see to what they are hewing a way.[1]

[1] His collections for a Pali Names Dictionary are being edited by Dr. G. P. Malalasekera.

C. A. F. Rhys Davids.

Chipstead, Surrey,
April, 1932.

CONTENTS

PRONUNCIATION

Vowels in Pali and Sanskrit as in German or Italian. All unaccented vowels are short, save *e* and *o* when ending a syllable. Thus : Peṭakopadesa = Pay-ta-koh-paday-sa ; Go-tama ; but mĕt-tā, Mŏg-gallāna. *Ai* as *eye*; *au* as in *how*. The *ṃ* (a badly chosen sign) is the guttural nasal = *ng*. *C* always as *ch* in *church*.

Cadence. In tri-syllables, you will be usually right in following the modern English tendency to throw the accent early. As we now say bal'cony, con'template, so in Go'tămă, Jā'tăkă. (Gotama becomes Gautama in Sanskrit.) Long vowels will, of course, modify this rule, *e.g.* Dham'ma-din*nā*. In doubled consonants follow the Italian way, *e.g.* *kam'ma*, like *mam'ma*, *buddha* like the staccatos in *sud'det'ta*. Do not let the ṭ, etc., baffle you. It means that the letter is pronounced as in English, not the pure dental, as in Italian.

CHAPTER I

HOW AND WHEN WE CAME TO KNOW

THAT my reader has got and has opened this book means that he has at least heard there is something called Buddhism; that there is or has been a cult or belief or religion so called; that—well, maybe this is as far as I need go after what he knows. But had he lived a hundred years ago, he would most likely have not even known this much. This is not because there was just nothing he could have read, had he gone out of his way to seek for it. Had he lived, for instance, in the seventeenth century, he might possibly have come across Robert Knox's *An Historical Relation of Ceylon,* and have there read about "a great God whom they call Buddou, to whom the Salvation of Souls belongs. Him they believe once to have come upon the earth. And when he was here, that he did usually sit under a large shady tree called Bogahah." And could he then have read French, he might have learnt more than this scrap of curiously recorded information. For he might have also read *A New Historical Relation of the Kingdom of Siam,* by the envoy sent there by Louis XIV. of France, De la Loubère, in which are passages about this "Buddou," translated from palm-leaf MSS., written in a language purporting to be of India and called Pali: the "Row," or Text.

He might also have read Alexander Hamilton's comments on the religions of Southern Asia in his *New Account of the East Indies,* 1688–1723, wherein, amid much account of religious externals included under the cult-name "Pagan," Ceylon is said to find religion in the "worship a monkey's tooth," and, in Pegu, where beside the names of Samaṇa Gotama and Brahman, disguised as Somma

Cuddom and Prawpont, he tells of the great sleeping image in a Kiakiack (god of gods) temple, whose awakening will synchronize with cosmic dissolution.

But four centuries before this, Europe had come to hear of a great man as somehow belonging to Ceylon, and called Sakyamuni Bhagvan. Marco Polo, Europe's informant, writes it Sagamoni Barcan. This man, he says, was called "the first great idol-founder," but was a moral teacher so good that "if he had been a Christian, he would have been a great saint of Jesus Christ, so good and pure was the life he led."

Yet this date, 1200–1300, is not at all the earliest yielding us a record about this man. We must go back about a thousand years, to the day of Clement of Alexandria, the Christian apologist, to the third century A.D. In his Miscellanies, called *Stromateis* ("Patchwork"), he refers to "Indians who obey the precepts of *Boutta*, whom through exaggeration of his dignity they honour as a god." About the same time quite different sources record a connection between this man and Mani, the founder of the cult known as Manichæism. In one, Mani associates himself with this "Boutta" as one who had been his own primal predecessor. In another (fourth century A.D.), one Terebinthos, a slave-secretary to Skythianos of Judæa, an immigrant from Egypt, went on his master's death to Babylon, and "there gave out that he had mastered the wisdom of the Egyptians, was no longer Terebinthos but Bouddha, had been born of a virgin, and had been nourished in the mountains by an angel." This legend of virgin birth served in its turn to associate the Buddha with the "Gymnosophists" of India in the records (of the fourth century) left by St. Jerome. And such vague and incorrect allusions to matters Indian were derived from Greek chroniclers, Megasthenes and others, who wrote some three or four centuries earlier, after Alexander the Great's invasion of India had opened up in new ways that unknown world to Europe.

We have, then, a European tradition that there was a wonderful and saintly teacher known as Boutta, or Buddha, Sakyamuni Bhagvan, who lived "long ago" in India. This tradition we have traced back to the third century B.C., *i.e.* some three centuries after he, as we now know, may be said to have lived. For our forefathers—that is, for a few scholars among them—there was at least available, in apologetic and exegetical manuscripts, this scanty record, a record which little by little the European traveller endorsed by revealing the notable Man of old as still worshipped in this Asiatic country or that. But no longer, the reader will note, in India.

India, it is true, had her own records, both carved and written, but we had to wait till the nineteenth century before we came to learn how remarkable these were. During the eighteenth century, when Britain's commercial influence in India was growing, and when its political influence was exercised in support of that commerce, the main thing, in matters surviving from the past, that we came to know was the wonderful fact of kinship between our languages and the traditional and yet spoken languages of India—the fact that those and these were branches of an originally common tongue we called Aryan. But in the nineteenth century much more came to light, through these cognate tongues, about the man Buddha and his influence, both in India and also further north, through a very different tongue, the Tibet'an. A civil servant, Brian Houghton Hodgson, who served twenty years in Nepal, in North-east India, took an intelligent interest in the culture of the country, and collected over 400 MSS. written on palm-leaves in "Sanskrit" (lit. well-, or co-made), the literary diction of mediæval and modern India, and presented them to learned societies in England, France and India. Among these were works written by votaries of a cult of "the Buddha," florid compositions in verse and prose revealing, not living memories so much as poetical idealized conceptions of what a superman leader, living in an indefinite past, surrounded by a host of disciples, might say, might foretell, might decree.

One of these, given to a French library, the *Saddharma-puṇḍarīkā*, "The Lotus of the Very Religion," was translated into French by Eugène Burnouf, the doyen of European Buddhist learning, in 1852, and it may be consulted in the Dutch scholar Kern's English translation of thirty-two years later, in No. XXI of the *Sacred Books of the East*. Another, which may be seen at the Royal Asiatic Society's library, to which Hodgson presented it, is the *Ashṭa-sahasrika-prajñā-pāramitā*, "The eight-thousand-fold Perfection of Wisdom," and bears a date which has been equated with A.D. 1165. A specimen of it is reproduced in my *The Milinda Questions*, p. 25.[1]

Meanwhile other sources of knowledge about "the Buddha" had been opening up. Missionaries had revealed Tibet as a "Buddhist" country having scriptures, which we have come to know as the *Kanjur*, and the *Tanjur* (this being a collection of commentaries and miscellanies). That these were found to have been translated into Tibetan from Sanskrit sources was due to such pioneers as Alexander Csoma de Körös, a Hungarian, followed by F. A. von Schiefner, P. E. Foucaux, vom Schlagintweit, Köppen, Rockhill, all of them at work during the early, central and later portions of the nineteenth century. That which was for some time the most outstanding source of our crude knowledge about the Buddha was the poem called *Lalita-Vistara(-Purāṇa)*, "The Lovely Details (-legend)," to which Edwin Arnold mainly owed the sources of his poem *The Light of Asia*. This was translated from the Tibetan (Sanskrit original) by Foucaux into French.

At the same time, we were coming to learn what the cult of the Buddha, lingering on in India, centuries after he had

[1] Published in *Oriental Series*, Kegan Paul, 1930.

lived there, had come to mean for China. This was due to the translation of travel-diaries, written, from the fourth to the seventh centuries A.D., by certain pilgrims making their slow, sometimes difficult way overland from China to India, either to visit that which had become the cradle of their own faith, or to procure scriptures of that faith. These men were Fa-Hien, I-Tsing and Hiuen Tsiang, or Yuan Chwang, introduced to Europe by the French pioneers Rémusat and Julien, and since then in such English translations as those by James Legge, Samuel Beal, H. A. Giles, T. Watters and others.

I now come to another source, which has as yet been more fertile than any in yielding us information about the rise of the Buddha-cult in India. This was discovered in Ceylon. Hiuen Tsiang wrote about Ceylon, when travelling to the south of India, and refers to its conversion to his own faith long before by one Mahendra, and to what Buddhist monks had told him about it. But a generation before his records came into our hands, our knowledge of and interest in Ceylon were opening up and beyond the scanty reports of the travellers mentioned above, owing to the Treaty of Amiens in 1802, in which the capture of Ceylon from the Dutch a few years previous was confirmed to the British. From about that time we may note, in English works of research, a growing knowledge about Ceylon and the Buddha-cult of the island. And, so far as I can see, it was then that the words Buddhism, Buddhist came into use. It took time before the spelling of these terms was settled. If in a good library you will consult the Oxford Dictionary (not, of course, the abridged edition) under those words, you will find many varied spellings: Bhoodha, Bhoodhist, Boudhist, Bhuddist, Bhudist, Buddhite, Buddhic, Bauddhas, the last being the form in which Sanskrit mediæval works used to refer to Buddhists, together with the other terms, Saugatas, *i.e.* well-farers, and Śakyas, or believers in the teaching of the Sage of the Śakya tribe, the Śakya-muṇi. Those varied spellings are quoted from a learned journal of that day called *Asiatic Researches*. A generation later, in 1836, George Turnour of the Ceylon Civil Service published for the first time a complete work from the literature of Ceylon. This was a poem about the history, mainly the religious history, of the island, entitled the *Mahāvaṃsa*, or Great Chronicle. But he did not translate it from the Sinhalese language, but from the island's religious language, that named already as Pali (Row or Text), occupying the same cultural relation to the scriptures of Ceylon as Latin used to occupy to the vernaculars of Christian Europe. Besides this poem, Turnour both edited and translated certain Suttas (Sanskrit: Sūtras) said to have been uttered by "the Buddha."

Interest in this language and scripture began to grow in other Ceylon civilians, ardent to come to know what was supremely worth knowing. These, to name only two, were notably Robert C. Childers and Thomas W. Rhys Davids. I have many letters from the former to the latter bubbling over with zest in this pursuit. Childers (who as a boy had taught himself Arabic) was an enthusiast for languages as such, his interest in *what* they said being secondary. His life was cut short by consumption, but not before he had, virtually single-handed, compiled a Pali-English Dictionary, not to mention translations of one or two short texts from Pali. Rhys Davids's life was long, albeit his career in Ceylon was cut short by misfortunes not due to want of honourable will in himself. His interest in Pali literature was started by a suit brought before him as magistrate concerning the advowson, as we should say, of a "cure" of souls in a village, arising on the death of the resident monk or "bhikshu" (incidentally the village children's teacher). Should, namely, the "curate," the assisting monk, or another man succeed him? Reference was made to the "Canon law," the Vinaya. Into the study of this

Rhys Davids plunged, a senior monk, the Unnanse Yatramulle, coming to teach him. A touching and affectionate tribute to this man, a man who made a similar impression on both these ardent young pioneers, is paid in the *Hibbert Lectures*, 1881 (p. 186). In Rhys Davids's copy of his Lectures is affixed, opposite the dedication to his father, to whom he was a devoted son, another written dedication, "To the memory of Yatramulle Unnanse, the kindly friend and earnest scholar, this little work with tender regret is dedicated." And in the tribute he wrote: ". . . he was sinking into the grave from the effects of a painful and incurable malady. I had heard of his learning as a Pali scholar . . . and was grateful to him for leaving his home (?) under such circumstances to teach a stranger. There was a strange light in his sunken eyes, and he was constantly turning away from questions of Pali to questions of Buddhism. I found him versed in all the poetry and ethics of the Suttas and was glad to hear him talk. There was an indescribable attraction about him, a simplicity, a high-mindedness, that filled me with reverence." (I regret I do not know in what language the two conversed, but Rhys Davids had quickly made himself conversant with Sinhalese, the better to understand the people whose disputes he was called upon to adjudicate.)

Of the work which Rhys Davids lived to accomplish I have spoken earlier. One of the chief problems in the field of that work was the explanation of the scriptures of the religion of Ceylon being written in an admittedly Indian tongue, which was not the language of Ceylon, though this had much in common with it, while in India this language—known as Pali—was not found. There was for any European thinker the possible parallel, in religious and ecclesiastical usage, between Latin and, say, Italian. Religious conservatism would go a long way to retain scriptures in the tongue in which they had been written and spoken, ever since some central *ecclesia* had systematized and distributed the sayings or books of the doctrines. It would depend on the historical relations between such a central *ecclesia* and the lives of the founders of the religion, whether this tongue had actually been spoken by the founders. Now we can carry this parallel a little further. We used to have our scriptures written and taught in Latin, not in English—still less in the Aramaic spoken by Jesus and his first men, or the Greek spoken by St. Paul and the second men. And this went on long after Aramaic and Greek had died out from Palestine and the Hellenic churches of Asia Minor. Had, then, the "Pali" of those Ceylon books come over, as we find it, on the tongues of missionaries from India—come over, it is said, before, in India, men wrote any books whatever—or had it been a "literary diction" (our own English is just such a literary diction) which only took shape in Ceylon, partly from the oral teaching of successive teachers, partly from the language of Ceylon?

This is a problem of languages; with such this book is not primarily concerned, nor am I a fit person to go into it. But I am very much concerned, and I would have readers very much concerned, with the problems of religious history closely bound up with this matter of a religion which, as we may say, has lost its native home and taken root in other and various alien soils. Thus: how far is the religious teaching in those Pali books a growth of and from Ceylon? How far can it be called Indian?

Is there, then, nothing of early Pali writing found in India? This brings us to another important source of our further knowledge of teachings ascribed to "the Buddha." This is collectively known as the Asoka (Sanskrit Ashoka) inscriptions. Under the eyes of our civilians and soldiers scattered about India, from north to south, there had been noticed very old inscriptions, carved in characters and language not understood, on rocks and on pillars. The first of these to be reduced to print in England was on a pillar at Delhi. It was reproduced from drawings by a Captain Hoare in the *Asiatic Researches* (to which I have referred) in 1801. But it was not till thirty-seven years later that James Prinsep, ardent archæologist, *aided by George Turnour with his knowledge of Pali*, ascertained that in these inscriptions we had various dialects of what has come to be known collectively as Prakrit (the "made-plain")—that is, the old vernaculars of North India. These were to the relatively polished diction of the Ceylon *Mahāvaṃsa*, and its cruder prototype the *Dīpa-vaṃsa*, the "Island-Chronicle," somewhat as the English of the twelfth century was to the Jacobean English of our translated Bible. This you can compare, *e.g.* in such a passage as that from the MS. of Homilies, Trinity College, Cambridge, *Dominica Palmarum*, on Matthew xxi, 1 ff.

> "Silof dauides bern blesced bie he þe cumed a godes name"

with

> "Hosanna to the son of David! blessed be he that cometh in God's name."

Here, for instance, is a line from an Asoka inscription, compared with its version in Pali:

(*Inscription in a Vernacular*)

Devanampiye piyadasilaja hevam aha: dhaṃme sadhu kiyam chu dhaṃme ti apasinave bahu kayane daya dane sache sochaye chakhudane pi me bahuvidhe dinne . . .[1]

(*Pali, or literary diction*)

Devānaṃ piyo Piyadassi-rājā evam āha: dhammo sādhu; kīva tu dhammo nāmāti? Appâsavo bahukaḷyānāni (katāni) dayā dānaṃ saccaṃ soceyyaṃ; cakkhudānam pi me bahuvidhaṃ dinnam . . .

The English of which will be: "He who is dear to devas, who perceives what is dear (or precious), the king, has thus spoken: *Dharma* is excellent, now how much is "Dharma"? (It is) to have little sin, many good things

[1] From the Delhi-Topra Pillar Edict.

done, kindness, giving, truth, purity; and for-me (by it) gift of vision in many ways is given." [1]

Now the Asokan idiom here sampled is near enough to Indian tongues not to offer insuperable difficulties to Indianists, once the curious *script* of the edicts was deciphered. At the same time, when further light came to be thrown on it by a man versed in the Pali of the Ceylon literature, a literature unknown in India when Prinsep was at work, the help rendered thereby must, it is clear, have been very great. What, then, have the edicts shown us about Pali, and about "Buddhism" in relation to India?

In the first place, the critical reader of this little book can rest satisfied that the "raja" of the romantic name, which is repeated on practically every edict, has been identified with the historical figure of the Mauryan king, third of his house, Asoka, or Ashoka (a name tantamount to "Felix"). This, for long a virtual certainty, was confirmed by an inscription only discovered in 1915, on a granite boulder in a cave at Maski (once Masangi), near Raichur, in Southern Hyderabad, by C. Beadon, a gold-mining engineer. It begins: *Dev . . na . . piyasa Asok . . sa . . . . dh . . t . . ni vash . . am sum . . Bu . . . sake* . . . This half-effaced opening, experts, comparing it with other inscriptions, take to mean: "He who is dear to devas Asoka hath thus spoken: Upwards of two and a half years am I (a) Buddha-Sakyan." The last two words more probably were *upāsake*, that is, a lay-disciple, a term used of such in Buddhist books and parlance to this day. Now we know *that*, and *when* this, the first general sovereign of India, lived—namely, between the beginning and latter half of the third century B.C. (he reigned 271–32 B.C.). We know also that in the Pali poems and Commentaries of Ceylon he is associated with the conversion of Ceylon to the cult of the Buddha, and is even reported to have let a son and daughter

[1] I cannot agree with the "by me" of translators. "*Me*" as "for me" is frequent in the Piṭakas.

go as missionaries, and to have sent a branch of a certain holy tree, which disciples had come to associate with their Founder, to Ceylon as a proof of sympathy. This Embassy of the Branch can be seen in pictures of the Sānchi Tope carvings, to which a date about the third century B.C. has been assigned.[1]

We have, in the second place, the strong presumption that the yet unwritten sayings of the "Buddhist" *Sāsana*, or teaching, were conveyed from India to Ceylon, and did not originate there. And this being so, we may look in those "sayings," as preserved, and so far as preserved, in written form in Ceylon, for a teaching bearing signs of its Indian, not its Sinhalese origins.

In the third place, the Edicts themselves reveal traces, that certain of those sayings, and the ecclesiastical vehicle by which they were or might be taught, were known to the writer of the inscriptions. Thus, reference in one of these is made to a triad which came to rank as a holy Trinity in the Sāsana: "Known to you, sirs,[2] is the degree of my reverence and faith in budha dhamma sangha." And he goes on: "Whatever, sirs, has been spoken by the bhagavan budha, all that was well spoken; but, sirs, it would appear to me (in this):—verily thus the very 'dhamma' will long endure—this verily I do believe. These expositions of 'dhamma,' sirs: the *important things in the Rules, the worthy worlds, the fear as to the future, the verses on the sage, the sutta on sagehood, the Upatissa-catechism*, also the *Rāhula-admonition concerning lying spoken by the bhagavan budha*: these 'dhamma'-expositions, sirs, I wish what? That many groups of monks and (that) nuns may both frequently hear and meditate upon (them) so also laymen and laywomen. Wherefore, sirs, I cause this to be written that they may know my disposition." Now the phrase on "dhamma long enduring" is a characteristic saying in

[1] See *e.g.* Rhys Davids, *Buddhist India*, Fig. 54, etc.
[2] On Asoka see further Chapter XV.

the suttas. And of the prescribed "expositions" some may unquestionably be found in the Suttas, especially the last and the second and third, which may now be read in English. The remaining four references are of probable identification only.

We have enough therefore to show us that both the institutions of the Buddhist "church," known as Sangha, as well as certain identifiable passages of the Pali scriptures revered as such in Ceylon, and in South Asia generally, were known, the one as actively existing, the other as being taught, in the time and the realm of Asoka.

You, reader, may say: This shifts our problem without solving it. It is now this: Was this religion brought from India to Ceylon, or from Ceylon to India? As to that, we have on the one hand the evidence, such as it is, of tradition, that the former was the case. On the other hand, there is much contributory evidence, favouring this conclusion, in the Pali Piṭakas. The environment these refer to is one of mighty rivers and distant snowy mountains, a land where the word "Ar(i)yan" is held as an epithet of human worth, a land where the man has evidently been held in extraordinary worth—by "man" I mean the self, the unseen spiritual man. In the little island of Ceylon there are no such mighty rivers or great heights, no such Ariyan tradition, nor had there ever been a mighty religious teaching and tradition, which saw divine worth in that inner world of man under just this word "self," yes, and in just the word "man."

Had the opposite been the case, had Ceylon converted India to her own faith, we may be sure she would have proudly preserved the tradition of this in her religious "epics." In these she gives full credit to India, notably to Asoka for his patronage, and to Mahinda for having converted her. It is not the details in the chronicles that weigh with me as historic truths; they seem, many of them, poetic fables. It is the credit attached to an alien state, and not claimed for the poet's own race and state, that leads us to infer they had a true tradition.

You may discern this contrast better when you have read this book. You will then in some degree be able to judge of the value of internal evidence as throwing light on the external history of a religion or a scripture. So far, that is, as knowledge at second hand can serve.

Knowledge at first hand serves, of course, much better. And it was this knowledge that has been, and is still, occupying workers in the field of Buddhist history for the last sixty years. In other words, these Pali books, found in Ceylon, if not in India, had to be read and translated. And more, these years revealed these same Pali scriptures as existing in palm-leaf MS. form also in Burma and Siam. The characters in each case were very different, more so than our "roman" characters are different from the Greek ones. But the language in each case is practically identical, the differences being almost wholly in a word or part of one here and there.

Manuscripts of these scriptures had to be procured; copies of them by native scribes had to be ordered and bought. Such a scribe, seated on the ground, would take a strip of the palmyra palm, which we here know only in dwarf specimens, and with a notch cut in his left thumb-nail scratch the copied characters with a brass style. When the strip on one side was full, with margins left and two vacant spaces in which holes were to be cut for the cord to hold the leaves, he would smear Indian ink over the polished surface, the fluid leaving no trace on the blank parts, but remaining in the incisions. By the year 1880 catalogues drawn up of Pali MSS. in the libraries of London, Paris, Copenhagen, Oxford, Cambridge and Stockholm revealed the possession, somehow acquired, of a fair number of these MSS. of the Pali scriptures, but nowhere a complete collection. Rhys Davids published a list of the lacunæ: "Good MSS. of these books are wanted at once," and begged the learned among the Ceylon monks, whose monasteries might have any of them, to lend or sell or let them be copied for purchase.

These MSS. when got had to be edited in book form, and whereas it was customary for editors of Indian MSS. to retain, in book editions, the Indian scripts, the pioneers of Pali editions decided to transliterate the various national characters into roman letter. No other course was reasonable, since Buddhism was not of one country, hence of one script, only. And more: this work was from the first intended to be a gift to the world as world-literature, and especially to the Western world. In that world, if we discount the world-shrinkage inflicted upon themselves by Czech and Slav in retaining a national script, the only characters that count are those of roman letter.

On this work of transcribing, collating, and selecting, with subsequent printing, which we call editing, one man, by 1850, had got to work. This was the Dane, Victor Fausböll, and on it he spent the leisure hours of forty-seven years. A man of original will and temperament, he is not to be looked upon as a historical "freak." A pioneer, he, too, had his inspirers, and his own account of their influence is worth quoting to you. To the Index of his chief work, compiled by his pupil the eminent Pali scholar, Dines Andersen, he in 1897 wrote thus:

"Born in a country parsonage I, until my twelfth year, associated much with peasants, and listened with attentive interest to their legends and stories . . . to the legend of the sunken church lying at the bottom of the lake, where it might be seen . . . when it was clear and calm, and whose bells might still be heard in the evenings . . . to the story of the treasure-seeker who at sunset, in perfect silence . . . sought to bring the long-buried treasure up to the surface. I also laboured and strove for years digging silently, until I could bring the treasure forth to the light of day. Here we have it! . . .

"What induced me with eagerness to begin to work at the Jātaka Book was particularly three utterances I met with: The first I found in Spence Hardy's *Manual of Budhism*: 'The Sinhalese will listen the night through to recitations from this work without any apparent weariness, and a great number of the Jātakas are familiar even to the women.' The second I read in Clough's *Sinhalese Dictionary* under 'Jātaka-pota,' where it says: 'This book is so sacred amongst the Buddhists that they will offer to it and worship it.' And the third I noticed in the *Ceylon Friend*, 1837, where it says: 'The more I think of Buddha the more I love him.'

"In 1849 I had commenced transcribing parts of the Jātaka, but I did not seriously take it up until I had finished my edition of the Dhammapada in 1855. The further I got into the book, the clearer I saw its importance, not only in a linguistic sense, but also from a culture-historical point of view, and in order to awaken interest for it in the literary world, I began publishing specimens of it in 1891. Prof. Westergaard was not at first in favour of a complete edition; he would have preferred an analysis only. . . . Later on he altered his opinion and supported the work. It was, however, principally the encouragement I from the very beginning received from Prof. A. Weber that kept up my courage. And when material failed me, it was especially the Rev. Subhuti's untiring perseverance in sending me a transcript in parts, and Colonel Duncan's present of a complete Burmese copy of the Jātaka (at the instigation of Missionary C. H. Chard) that made it possible for me to finish my undertaking.

"I now trust that the fact will not be overlooked that I have had but little material to work from, also that when I began the study of Pali, the language was nearly uncultivated."

I have not quoted Fausböll at such length to leave in you the impression that in the 551 Jātaka (or Rebirth) stories we have what might be called the New Testament of original "Buddhism," or that you should misunderstand the so-called "worship" of the MSS. of them. I want you to see this man, nearly a century ago, led by this and that source of inspiration to plough for the rest of his life a long and lonely furrow in, not a field but a "clearing," in the faith that he was digging up treasure for which the knowledge of the world might be the better. It is to say the truth to tell you that Victor Fausböll, by these six volumes of the text and commentary of the Jātaka, brought us by a flowery and pleasant way into the inner ring of the Pali scriptures. Into that ring he himself penetrated by his editions of the two venerable anthologies Dhammapada and Sutta-Nipāta, and a Latin translation, usually closely accurate, of the former.

He also translated the latter work, but into English, in which, as we can see, he was not at home. The result may not unjustly be called "wooden," yet with the companion translation by another man of ardent and far-seeing will, Frederick Max Müller, the volume was a very notable event for Buddhist studies in this country, in that most notable decade of burgeoning, 1875–1885. In these years, Max Müller, checked in his Sanskrit studies when not chosen for the vacant chair at Oxford, spread his boundless energies over a larger field—that of the comparative study of languages and religion—and began to edit the fifty-nine volumes now so well known as Sacred Books of the East. In the series this twin volume is No. X.

In the following year, T. W. Rhys Davids contributed No. XI., entitled Buddhist Suttas, a selection of seven, chosen, he wrote, with difficulty from the stores of a nearly unknown literature—a difficulty arising from the embarrassment not of poverty, but of wealth. Here was another man willing and destined to give half a century of work to the unfolding of what this "buried treasure" might contain. With him it was less peasant lore that lured than the religious needs of man. He had himself lost his way in those needs, but in seeking to refind it he was ever mindful of the quest of man, at all stages of world-history, to do the like. A channel for the expression of Buddhism, as one of such quests, was opened to him soon after his return to England. I do not know whether Max Müller's great series was the example, but the Society for Promoting Christian Knowledge, of London, began a series of Manuals on Non-Christian Religious Systems, and the first was that on Buddhism, by Rhys Davids. This little book became in time the classic English work on the subject, and it can scarcely be doubted that, to what extent there can be said to be now a more intelligent acquaintance with what is called Buddhism among English readers all over the world, it is chiefly due to this work. Written at a time when the Pali scriptures were for the most part in MS. form only, and revised in successive impressions only within the narrow limits allowed him, its author could write, already after fifteen years, "Had the manual been written now, it would doubtless have assumed a different form." He could then, he explains, have quoted original texts and ignored European pundits.

But these were not the only openings for making accessible to English readers the new-incoming Pali sources. In its own way Nicholas Trübner's publishing firm [1] was also a Constantine in the establishment of such studies, and its "Oriental Series" of translations and treatises was intended "to give in a comprehensive form all this mass of knowledge to the world," in which such "immense strides had been made in the last century." Starting in 1878, volumes were rapidly issued, so that the series, which all but began with Samuel Beal's *Dhammapada from the Chinese*, in 1878, had already issued some fourteen volumes when, in 1880, Rhys Davids, following up Faus-

[1] Now Messrs. Kegan Paul, Trench, Trübner & Co., Ltd.

böll's Pali Jātaka volumes, began a translation of the Jātaka in the Oriental Series.

Meanwhile a new and efficient worker had come to this country, with a backing of financial support from the Royal Academy of Berlin and the Government of India. This was Hermann Oldenberg, editor of a complete text of the first third of the Pali scriptures, called Vinaya Piṭaka, viz. the list, with historical episodes, of the Rules of the Sangha, or Order of Buddhist monks. MSS. were placed at his disposal by the India Office and the Paris National Library, and in 1880–83 the work was published by Williams & Norgate in five volumes. Oldenberg's activities in Pali did not stop there. In 1882 he had handed to Rhys Davids a prepared edition in MS. of the 1279 lines, composing the anthology of poems by monks, among which were names ascribed going back to the first generation of the Sakyan movement. And Max Müller gave to both of them, in collaboration, the opportunity of publishing, in the "Sacred Books of the East," three volumes of translation from the Vinaya, the portion called Major and Minor Sections, which include quasi-historical accounts of the beginnings and of the early Congresses of the young church.

But Rhys Davids's will was directed with stronger desire to the—I use his own words—far more valuable and interesting Suttas (sayings, discourses) on the religious teaching, which were lying "buried and unpublished" in Pali MSS. In the lectures on the origin and growth of Indian Buddhism, which the Hibbert trustees had asked of him in 1881, he confessed to having formed, backed by generous offers of help from Pali scholars, a society for the purveying of critical editions of the books of these Suttas, as well as of "the whole of these curious and ancient books." Following the example of his friend Richard Morris, editor of the Early English Text Society, a scholar whom he lured into Pali research, he named his effort the Pali Text Society.

Just the organizing will of this one man was needed to set the ball rolling. Holding on for fifty years, the great war notwithstanding, his society has completed first editions of all the remaining scriptural books, has published a dictionary, mainly from his own collections (compiled by himself and Dr. W. Stede, then by the latter alone), and a great portion of the ancient commentaries on those books, with many minor manuals of a somewhat later date. And this undertaking should be completed in about eight years. He did more than this. Max Müller's death in 1901 had led to the closing of his great series, but he had set on foot another more special series: "The Sacred Books of the Buddhists." He took this departure because while on the one hand offers to translate certain Buddhist texts had been made him, the then King of Siam, Chulalangkorn II., had promised, in the interests of his faith, to give financial support to both the translating and the printing. The first in this series was one of the Buddhist Sanskrit texts of which Hodgson had presented copies to the Asiatic Society and to Paris. It was *The Garland of Jātakas* (birth-stories) translated by the Dutch scholar, J. S. Speyer, then of Groningen University, and published in 1895. The next work appeared four years later, and with it began the translation of those Suttas at the head of the second division of the Pali scriptures so much desired by the translator Rhys Davids—the Dīgha-Nikāya, or Long Collection. To these *Dialogues of the Buddha*, the English title which he selected, not without careful thought, for the first two of these four great "collections" or "groups" (*nikāya*), I shall refer later. The second, which he did not live to translate, was carried out by his former pupil, Lord Chalmers. The third collection, begun by myself, has been completed by F. L. Woodward, now of Tasmania, who has also begun the fourth, these two coming into the series of the Pali Text Society's translations.

This is a very meagre sketch, but it may be enough to

leave you better acquainted than you were with the how and the when we of Europe, we of to-day of the English-speaking races, have come to know what, as yet, we do or may know about the "Buddha" and the religion which has been called after him.

A word here about an important historical question, for a discussion of which this Manual affords neither scope nor range. In the two religions, Christianity and Buddhism, where amid more that is unlike there is a less that is like, the question has arisen: Has the one directly derived from the other? Has the younger gospel been influenced by the traditions of the older gospel?

I think it was not. In both cases there is this main resemblance: a helper of the Many, revealing a something More in the nature and destiny of the Man (the very man, not just body and mind), and teaching this, not as seeking to upset the religion of his land and day, but as a New Word in it to give it quickening power of stronger vitality. Around this main common feature cluster many details swept in by scriptures of a later day, and in these *derived influence is possible.* But the New Word in either gospel is not derived from the other. The reader can study the "parallels" in *Buddhist and Christian Gospels*, by A. J. Edmunds, edited by M. Anesaki, 4th edition, Philadelphia, 1908, together with a critical and sagacious discussion by Rhys Davids, *Journal Pali Text Society*, 1920–23. These are not works easily available to all. I therefore give here the conclusion arrived at, after years of research, by my venerated friend Edmunds, and published as a postscript to his work: "Both religions independent in the main, but out of eighty-nine chapters in the Gospels, the equivalent of one (mostly in Luke) is coloured by a knowledge of Buddhism. The transference was made possible by recently discovered versions of the Buddhist scriptures in vernaculars of the Parthian Empire. Parthians were present at the founding of the Christian religion (Acts ii. 9). Of direct borrowings I maintain but " . . . three phrases, and five "narratives as coloured by Buddhist influence." I wish I could also give in its wisdom and beauty the peroration of my husband's article.[1]

[1] I printed this, dated 1877, after his death, copying his title. This had more fitly been: What has Christianity derived from Buddhism? instead of the converse.

CHAPTER II

WHAT IT IS WE CAN KNOW

"HERE you have it!" said Fausböll of his completed seven volumes of the Jātaka. We can now say the same of not one only, but of all the twenty-eight distinct works constituting the Pali scriptures or Canon. Pali religious literature of a "classic" kind consists also of a commentary to each of the twenty-eight, and there are sub-commentaries of respectable age. Of the former we can, for a few years yet, say only: "Here you *are getting* them," for only about two-thirds are yet edited in Europe. Nor, as we have seen, is Pali scripture the whole of Buddhist scripture. If within the limits of this manual I am telling you what it is we can know in the Pali scripture, and am mainly putting the Sanskrit Buddhist scripture on one side, this is for two reasons. First, because in the former I know my way about relatively well, but not in the latter. Secondly, in the study of a world-religion, I seek to make you share my view, that the thing most vital to our knowledge about it is its birth. It is in the birth, the foundation of a religion, that we must look to find what it meant and was to mean for mankind, irrespective of what it came to mean in this or in that land and period. Now a "scripture" is a much later thing than the birth, and it is not always justifiable to say this and that in it is the real "birth"-message. Yet it is justifiable to say this much: "In the Pali books we have a nearer approach to what that birth-message may have been than is yielded by the Sanskrit Sūtras."

We infer this in two ways:

(1) The matters given in the Pali Piṭakas are worded in a peculiar artificial way, betraying that they were

spoken in both metric and in prose fixed forms before they were set down in writing. This leads us to believe that they were first uttered, and repeated as uttered, then redacted in a fixed form, verse or prose, all of it oral, before there was any writing of what some man had wanted to say. When these oral sayings came to be written down, the forms found in the past most effective for memorizing had become too fixed, too "sacred" to be altered to suit the style found most effective in writing. So the fixed ways of the matters were written down relatively unaltered. But when the Sanskrit Sūtras were first composed, writing had apparently come in, in Central Asia, for the style is not crude or stiff, but flowing, and at times very florid. This suggests a relative lateness for this field of Buddhist literature.

(2) In these Sūtras the "Buddha" appears as one worshipped as if he were a very God upon earth. The Pali Suttas show him not yet so worshipped, but in process of becoming so. I cannot justly show you this by picking out sentences here or there from Sūtra or Sutta, for the Pali books are of many dates, both as books and as to portions of any of them, and the same may be said, but to a less degree, of the Sūtras. Both sets of books must be read, or at least carefully looked into, if you would see the difference which prevails in either as a whole. You may hear it said, for instance, that a Pali name for the "Buddha" was Dev'âti-deva—that is, god-beyond-god(s). This is true, but it is first found, not yet in the scripture of the Piṭakas, but in a later Pali book,[1] begun about 90 to 80 B.C., and in the last part of it only, which dates from some years later than that. In the Pali Suttas, on the other hand, the Founder is said to have replied to the question: "Are you deva?" "No, I am not."[2] There

[1] Translated by Rhys Davids as *The Questions of King Milinda*, S.B.E.

[2] *Gradual Sayings*, II., p. 44 (the Fourth "Nikāya").

are contradictions in all scriptures, but this reply you would not, I believe, find in the Sanskrit Sūtras.

In the Pali scriptures, then, we are, as we believe now, getting back to an older stratum of teaching. But we may live to see—you may be here to see it—disclosures of a yet older vein. Fragments of a book of poems belonging to those scriptures, written in, not Pali, but the earlier Prakrit—that is, one form of Prakrit—were discovered only three decades ago. They reveal some differences. We may yet find more—mainly, perhaps, from Chinese translations, made, for all we yet know, through the work of men of the Buddhist church in India, who came to be turned down for their views, views which a changed ecclesiastical authority had come to regard as "heretical." Scholars are now getting to work in this field, and we must watch for results. I can only show (*a*) what we have as yet, (*b*) how I judge we must read it.

Herein we have two things to consider: "the Buddha" and the religion named after him. What are these Pali scriptures which speak of it and of him?

They are divided into three Piṭakas—a word meaning merely a "basket," as we should use the word, but with the secondary meaning of a thesaurus, a casket, of valued contents. The two first, called respectively Vinaya and Sutta Piṭakas, contain what had been, as they reveal, called Vinaya and Dhamma—that is, in their form, the Rules (namely, of the Order of the monks), and the Sayings, fixed in wordings of metric speech and prose. The word Vinaya is of curious characteristic interest. It means *vi*: away from; *naya:* guiding. As used for a withdrawal from a simple unity, it means "details"; as meaning abstaining from this or that, it means "discipline." So we get in these two combined a system or method of monastic details or rules, wherein heed is chiefly paid to what a man in monastic life should not do.

In this Piṭaka are three divisions: the Pātimokkha,

the Khandhakas (being the Main, or Older, and the Less, or Later); and the Parivāra, a summary. The first is a list of 227 rules, tó each of which there came to be attached an exposition about it. The second means (belonging to) the whole body (of worded teaching), the *-ka* at the end meaning what we used to express in a title by the initial word *De*, e.g. *De Animā*. The third is a synopsis (lit. a surrounding, including) of the preceding two. You can read the first, without the expositions, in S.B.E. Vol. XIII.; the second in this and the two other volumes (Vols. XVII. and XX.), called together "Vinaya Texts." The third and the expositions to the first are not yet translated. The article "Pātimokkha" (by Rhys Davids) in the *Encycl. of Religion and Ethics* is very informative.

In the second, or Sutta Piṭaka, Sutta, again, is of curious characteristic interest. Sutta is literally a thread or string such as—to quote the Sutta-Vibhanga, the Exposition itself—you would put round a bunch of flowers to prevent the wind scattering them. Books constituting such binding strings there were none. The bond had to be sought in the theme, the connected set of words, were they homily or saw, as uttered (and repeated) by the speaker. Hence the Vinaya rules themselves were Suttas, no less than doctrinal talks and homilies. These were at times called Suttanta (*i.e.* end, value, object of the Suttas), in opposition to Vinaya; in these the "end" of the discipline was merely subsidiary to that of the doctrine. The older term dividing, with Vinaya, the corpus of teaching was the word Dhamma. You will often find these two so used in the Vinaya Texts. To Dhamma we shall return. The "Suttas" in the Sutta Piṭaka are a very large number of connected sayings, bound up in larger bunches. The latter are called the five Nikāyas, or collections. Of these five the first four, entitled also and later Āgamas—a word meaning "coming in" or "incorporated"—are known as Dīgha, Majjhima, Saṃyutta and Anguttara Nikāyas, *i.e.* literally, Long,

Medium-length, Connected, and Further-Parts. They are now, I repeat, translated into English. Beside the *Dialogues of the Buddha*, by Rhys Davids, assisted in Vols. II. and III. by myself, and *Further Dialogues of the Buddha*, by Lord Chalmers (2 vols.), the third is called the *Book of the Kindred Sayings*, and the fourth, *The Book of the Gradual Sayings*, now in course of publication.

The Fifth Nikāya is a varied collection of anthologies, in some of which are prose portions; and one book in prose only, the Paṭisambhidā-magga, or Way of Analysis. The anthologies are as follows:

Khuddaka-pāṭha, or Text of the Short Sayings (translated by myself in S.B.B.).

Dhammapada, or Verses on Dhamma (translated many times, most recently by myself in S.B.B.).

Udāna, or Outbreathings (emphatic "winged" words).

Iti-vuttaka, short sayings.

Sutta-nipāta, or The Bunch of the Threads (translated by Fausböll, S.B.E., Vol. X., and by Lord Chalmers in H.O.S.).

Vimāna-vatthu, or The Mansion-Stories.

Peta-vatthu, or Stories of Those Gone Before.[1]

Thera-Therī-gāthā, or Verses of the Elder Men and Women (translated by myself as *Psalms of the Early Buddhists*, Pali Text Society).

Jātaka, or Birth-Stories (translated by Cowell as director and four fellow-workers: R. (Lord) Chalmers, W. H. D. Rouse, H. T. Francis and R. A. Neil).

Niddesa, Main (Mahā) and Sequel (Culla): Expositions.

Apadāna, or Episodes by or about Buddhas, Pacceka-Buddhas, Monks and Nuns.

Buddhavaṃsa, or The Lineage of a Buddha.

Cariya-piṭaka, or Basket of Deeds.

There thus remain only eight of the fourteen works of this Nikāya to be translated. I should, indeed, say only six, for Udāna and Iti-vuttaka have been translated into English, but the former is out of print; the latter is scarcely to be recommended. I am hoping that within this decade both of them, and also the two "Vatthus"

[1] Mr. H. Gehman is preparing a translation of these two for *S.B.B.*

will be published in the S.B.B. The remainder may well find translators and purveyors in those who come after me.

The Third, or Abhidhamma Piṭaka, is admittedly of later origin. Books of the Vinaya Piṭaka refer here and there to " Vinaya, Dhamma and Mātikā." And at the beginning of the Third Piṭaka one comes upon a first section called Mātikā (consisting of a dual list of subjects: so many coming under " Abhidhamma," so many under " Suttanta "). And it is presumably out of these mātikās of the former kind that the Abhidhamma-Piṭaka was in part developed.

Both " mātikā " and " abhidhamma " have an interesting history, of which we know very little. *Mātikā* (Sanskrit: *mātṛka*) means " maternal," but it had in our present connection long ceased to have anything to do with " mother." Before the coming of the " letter "—i.e. *a*, *b*, *c*, etc.—the mark or sign had a more pregnant significance. It stood for a " something more "—for instance, it might indicate a space on a surface, within which alone a " more-will " might be brought to bear in what we call magic. It thus meant " generating," and hence, maybe, the term " maternal." " Matrix " has undergone a similar, if more limited, evolution in meaning. *Mātikā*, with a slightly shifted emphasis, came also to mean " water-course," *i.e.* opening or channel for the " something more." In the visible records of speech it will have been used as a significant letter or other symbol, indicating some content. And for the monk in pre-book days the Mātikās will have called up a list of topics which he knew more or less by heart.

The word " abhidhamma " I cannot here take into consideration, for it cannot be understood without examining " dhamma." This is a word of first importance and with a history. Here let us simply see in " abhidhamma " " super-doctrine," and in that see only the partial meaning " supplementary teaching." The " more " in the "super" I cannot deal with here. The Piṭaka consists of seven books, as follows:

Dhamma-sangani, or Compendium of Things, or Mental Experiences (translated by myself as *Buddhist Psychological Ethics*, Royal Asiatic Society ed.).

Vibhanga, or Dividings, *i.e.* exposition of subjects specially inquired into.

Dhātu-kathā, or Talks on Elements.

Puggala-Paññatti, or Designation of (Kinds) of Men (translated by B. C. Law, Pali Text Society ed.).

Kathā-vatthu, or Bases of Talk or Teaching (translated by S. Z. Aung and myself as *Points of Controversy*, Pali Text Society).

Yamaka, or The Pairs-book.

Paṭṭhāna, Vols. I.–III., or, as we might say in golf idiom, the Forward Stance: a book on relations between the agent, as cause, and some mode of producing an effect.

Thus less than half of this Piṭaka has been translated. Nor would the untranslated items be found very readable, with the possible exception of the second book. All are in catechism form. This might involve very readable results, but we have to remember two things. In them we are yet in the pre-book world, when the real book was the *live teacher*, and the matter, fixed in wording only, was merely a memorandum for him to expand. Secondly, it had become a rule of "abhidhamma" procedure, when this later book was added, to follow strictly the way of the general proposition, without discussing individual cases. And this, you will admit, makes very dull reading, as would a list of proverbs, where we get only a number of very general sayings. I have given above but the barest outline of the nature and contents of the Pali Canon or scripture, so that you might know what are these books "sacred" to the Buddhist of Ceylon, Burma or Siam, and to what extent they are as yet accessible to the reader of English only. Some are also translated into German, and a very few into French and Italian. Information as to these is always obtainable from the Pali Text Society, through the Oxford University Press, London.

Each of these canonical books possesses its Commentary. In the commentarial literature there is this added interest—that in a few cases, whereas we cannot assign an individual author, we can say the individual *editor* emerges, who has in some cases been also the translator. As a matter of fact, the editors have been too much credited, in the several Commentaries, with the achievement of original composition, even though such credit was not granted them by the old chroniclers. By these the work of the most famous of them—the man known by the cognomen of Buddhaghosa (voice of Buddha)—is said to have been the translation into Pali, called Magadhese (just as the new standardized diction of Rome's successors came to be called Italian), of the Sinhalese Commentaries. These were renderings into Sinhalese of the traditional Prakrit expositions of the "Sayings," which had been brought to Ceylon by oral teaching. And this is the way in which the next most famed commentator, Dhammapāla, tells of his work:

Verses they spoke whose the true Dhamma was,
They of the Master very sons and heirs . . .
All these the leaders of the Order took
And in one ordered serial compiled,
The Theragāthā-Therīgāthā named.
T' elucidate the import of that work
Three older Commentaries are extant.
Thereto this exegesis I have tried
T' indite, the which, in that where'er 'twas fit
I strove to set the highest meaning forth.

These appended lines he gives in several of the Commentaries bearing his name. He appears to have lived now in S.E. India, now in Ceylon, but it is not clear whether he, too, was a translator. But this is clear: whereas it was the natural method of the Indian teacher in the long past to utter or repeat a Mantra and then expound it, much as is done for us in text and sermon, he had a relatively free hand in the exposition, and hence the current forms and values in the exposition, when the growing use and worth in writing were calling for exposition to be written as well as text, will have become very different from the more ancient versions, both in form and in emphasis. Yet much of the older matter may have filtered down. And it is thus a very interesting mixture that we get in these Commentaries.

There is as yet only one complete translation of one of them, and that is *The Expositor,* Commentary on the Dhammasangani, first book of the Third Piṭaka, by P. Maung Tin of Burma (Pali Text Society ed.). If it comes into your hands you will see that at the end it is ascribed to Buddhaghosa. But at the beginning it appears as if he had asked another, it may be a pupil, to do the task. The translator of the English version hastens to insert "Not the author of this work." But this is at once a traditional guess (for no one knows), and, as I said above, it is giving the ancient editor credit for too much. See how it goes on about the original Commentary :—

Mahinda brought it to the peerless isle,
Ceylon, and in their tongue they wrote the book.
Rejecting from that ancient scroll the speech
Of Tambapaṇṇi, I shall here inscribe
On the palmyra-leaf the faultless tongue.

In other words, he translates from Sinhalese into Pali, or, as they called it, Magadhese, a language which he as firmly held to be earth's original speech as, in Christian Europe, Hebrew was once held to be.

Even in the modified, if very arduous and worthy rôle of editor-translator, Buddhaghosa is accredited with works which we cannot reasonably ascribe to him, much as was Omar Khayyam with many verses by other men. The Commentary on the Dhammapada, for instance, is evidently by a man holding very different religious values, a man whose name has not lived, at least on earth, "for evermore." But the rule has been, in Buddhist tradition, to father all Commentaries on Buddhaghosa, save the six claimed for Dhammapāla.

Of the latter's work you will find excerpts in the *Psalms of the Early Buddhists*, giving a short account of the composers of these poems, men and women. But it will probably be some years yet before more Commentaries are translated in their entirety.

Between the writing down of the Piṭakas and that of the Commentaries—an interval of about four centuries—out of perhaps many other works in Pali only a very few have as yet reached us. One of these, translated by Rhys Davids in the S.B.E. as *The Questions of King Milinda* (2 vols.), is of intense interest, and for three reasons. It is an historical epitome itself, for in it we see, *first*, oral conversations later written down, as in the Piṭakas, *then* fictitious conversations written as compositions, probably from notes, *then* more fictitious conversations which were *probably composed when written*. Next, one of the protagonists is a historical character—the king—and hence we get some precision in the date. Then we note a certain divergence in religious values from those in the Piṭakas. These points are dealt with in my *The Milinda Questions*, which is not, of course, another translation, but a study on the book.

Another briefer and less readable book is the Netti-pakaraṇa, or *Book of Guidance*, said to have been the work of a school founded by one of the first disciples, Kacchāna or Kacchāyana, who left the little community to live in quasi-retreat at a hilly place called Avanti. But this work is in Pali only. So too as yet is the Peṭakopadesa, or *Piṭaka-References* of this school; this is now being edited, but is not translated.

A much more noted work is the treatise Visuddhi-magga, or *Path of Purity*, which may or may not be rightly held as based on an earlier work, Vimutti-magga, but which tradition unanimously assigns in its present form to

Buddhaghosa. This might also have been called a work of Piṭaka-references. In it we see for the first time an author, plagiarist or not, composing a book with all the written scriptures at hand, quoting from them right and left. This was a great advance from the preceding epoch of oral tradition, when each group of repeaters knew only its own section of the sayings and was ignorant of the corpus of teaching as a whole. Nevertheless, the emphasis, the outlook, the mode of exposition are not those of the Piṭakas, but have changed in many ways. Do not take my word for this. The whole work is now well translated by P. Maung Tin (Pali Text Society ed., 3 vols.), and is worth consulting after you have well soaked yourself in the spirit of the "Āgamas," and such a work as the Dhammapada.

On this work one Dhammapāla wrote a Sub-commentary, or "Ṭīkā," but it is not certain whether this was the commentator. On this and on Buddhaghosa, you can consult the *E.R.E.* under each name, articles by Rhys Davids. There are many Sub-commentaries, re-commenting each on a Commentary, but none is as yet edited. A few other mediæval works there are, not forgetting the two Ceylon so-called epics, the *Great Chronicle* and its sequel, both in Pali Text Society translations, by W. Geiger, assisted by Mabel H. Bode and by Mabel Rickmers, awaiting you, should you seek to know to some extent this literature.

You may now be asking whether any works on the story of Buddhism in other languages than Pali are accessible to English readers?

There are, in the first place, certain translations from Sanskrit Sūtras, such as the seven collected in the last volume of *Sacred Books of the East*, No. XLIX., entitled Buddhist Mahāyāna Sūtras. It will there be noted that these seven are all admittedly compositions of our era, and clearly such as had not been oral sayings in their present form. The style, as I have said, betrays this.

To the translation of the Jātakamāla (S.B.B.) I have already referred, and to that of the Lalita-Vistara, but the translation of this is in French, as is that of the Saddharmapuṇḍarīkā, a MS. among those brought over by Hodgson. We still await a translator of two notable works from what is termed Sanskrit Buddhism: the Mahāvastu and the Divyāvadāna, edited by Senart and Cowell, respectively, but a good notion of the former can be obtained from the digest of it recently published by B. C. Law. D. T. Suzuki has recently published an English translation of the Lankâvatāra Sūtra, another of Hodgson's contributions to Europe. It is chiefly on this Sūtra that what is known as Zen Buddhism is based.

Then in "Trübner's Oriental Series" you can read W. W. Rockhill's *Life of the Buddha*, from the Tibetan scriptures quoted above, and in the *India Historical Quarterly* for March 1931 a Tibetan history of Buddhism in India, re-translated from Schiefner's German translation, can be sampled. Rockhill has also, in the Trübner Series, a translation of the Tibetan version of the Dhammapada, to which the name of another Buddhist work (Udānavarga) has somehow come to be given.

Finally, in the same series is Bigandet's *Life of Gaudama Buddha from Burmese Sources*, and in his *Manual of Budhism*, Spence Hardy, writing about 1860, drew from sources he found in Ceylon, and from Beale's *Chinese Records of the Western World* (Trübner) and T. W. Watters's *On Yuan Chwang* (R. Asiatic Society), not omitting J. Legge's *Fa-Hien* (Clarendon Press), a good idea may be obtained of the Chinese pilgrims' journeys to India.[1]

[1] I have here neither space nor desire to discuss the (?) 11th century, still popular manual *Compendium of Philosophy*, translated (P.T.S. ed.) by S. Z. Aung and myself, nor Buddhadatta's works of the 5th century (P.T.S. ed.).

CHAPTER III

THE "BUDDHA"

A. *Who Was He?*

For that matter, was he ever real? Did he ever live? In the more sophisticated idiom: Is he a historical person? Has he historicity?

Curiously enough, this question is still occasionally asked, as I know, just as we find it asked round about the end of the era B.C., in the book *Questions of King Milinda.* I say "curiously," because at this time of day educated men—and such still ask it—should word the question more intelligently. They would concede that there must have been founders of Buddhism; for them the question is: Was there *a* founder?

With the question as raised in that book I have dealt in my study on it.[1] When it is raised the second time, by the unknown author himself, not by the teacher whose sayings he had edited, his argument would not satisfy those who would say "founders" for "founder." This is, that a given city, a model city, must have had an architect, a planner. The further query that there may have been more than one planner is not raised. Nor is it asked: Could there not have been more than one at successive epochs, whereby the original creation had become built over, or otherwise altered and enlarged? There is for us a somewhat childlike simplicity about that ancient settling of doubts.

But for all that the contention "founders," not founder, is not rendered valid. If a certain name had survived as that of the arch-founder of that city, and not more names

[1] *The Milinda Questions*, pp. 96, 129.

than just one, the sceptic has still not got round the fact that the one name has survived and not those of the others. Why, we can ask, should one name only have survived, and not two or more as first architects? Why, on the other hand, have two names, and not one, survived as the first founders of Rome—Romulus and Remus? Or, in the lesser case, Hengist and Horsa as Jutish conquerors of Kent, and not one of these only? In neither case do the two names stand for some dual idea or myth requiring two names. It is asking so much more of credence to say in these two cases: "Here will have been really only one conqueror, only one founder." Still more is it straining credence to say: "There will have been no conqueror, no founder." For why should the initiative of the individual, an initiative we still see at work in every land, at every kind of enterprise be held as unreal, if only the enterprise be of the long ago? Centuries hence there will always have been a Martin Luther to account for the Lutheran Church, a John Wesley to account for the Wesleyans.

But whereas I believe that a new enterprise will always have needed a man to will its actual beginning, it is not inevitable that that man's name will survive. Perhaps the most striking case in point is the man who, in India, began the teaching of immanent Deity, which we find accepted and urged by the Upanishad teachers. It may have been Yājñavalkya, but he in no wise stands out as personality and as surviving name, as is the case with the scripturally acknowledged founders of religions. There needs to be both the striking attractive man-as-seen, and also—and this is the more essential—the bringing his enterprise *before the many*. That "Yājñavalkya" will not have been the one or done the other. Socrates was not the one, but emphatically he did the other, and in spite of his looks, even among Greeks, his name has lived.

Yes, you may say, he has lived "in" his own individual name, albeit, as to that, how much the teaching linked with his name was his and how much of it was Plato's, we can never exactly know. But here it is not altogether a question of an immortal personal name, like Socrates—it is an immortal *title*. The "Buddha," like "the Christ," is not a personal name. Was the idea which has come to be adored as "the Buddha"—that is, literally the Wake, but meaning from the first, when so applied, the Wise, the Enlightened—was this "idea" ever a concrete man?

Surely, I would say, for you cannot here get away from the man-in-the-title. We may in a way worship ideas—truth, goodness, beauty, light, and the like—but there has never for us been a man's name personalizing any of these. Ultimately the titles, Buddha, Christ, are *nothing without the man*. Now there must have been a cause why this is so. You may quote such a name as Odin or Wotan, and say: "Here is an admitted myth with a name, but without the man." Well, we have said that hitherto; but now not so readily. We now incline to think that, even as the Romans deified their emperors, so in the long past this and that pagan deity may once have been a man, who in one way or another imposed his will on men, by acts of power, by acts maybe beneficent to man. The ideas, the qualities which came to be built up in course of time around, upon, the title Buddha, have ultimately been found linked with a man—the man Siddhattha Gotama of the Sakyan clan (or, in the case of earlier "Buddhas," with a man of another personal name and clan). The ideas may be more or less mythical, may be the structure of a succession of worshippers, but the linking of them, in the "title," with a certain located man, and not with any other man, is a historic fact, historic as scripturally true, which has to be explained away. It is that foot of the vanished statue from which, as is said, we "explain Hercules." We cannot explain away that foot. We say: "'It' has stood here." Equally must we say: "Gotama lived there." Else we must say, "How came all that 'Buddha'-superstructure to be so based?"

It is this man, then, on the one hand, and this title, about which you who read these pages seek to learn what may be learnt. Who was "Gotama"? Who was, who is, "the Buddha"?

You may say: "Are not both one and the same, as George is the King?" No, they are not so nearly akin as these two words are for us now. This man is, through the modern Press, so much with us from day to day, that we forget what an ancient structure of ideas, tendencies and usage is built up about him in his office and its title. For the Eastern Buddhist, the Buddhist we now call a Mahāyānist, Siddhattha Gotama—in Sanskrit, Siddhartha Gautama—was a real man, but, as such, an emanation or *avatar* (a down-comer-over) of that Buddha-who-is-God, one such inspired man among other *avatars*, a man who is More come from the Man-who-is-Most. The South Indian Buddhist attempts much more; for in his belief, he includes the two in one, and sees, in Siddhattha Gotama, one who was so much a superman that he was beyond all those of the unseen whom the world reckons as Most. And more, that he as Gotama was not born as such, but attained this superdeity in what is called his *bôdhi* or *sambôdhi*, when he was about thirty-five years of age, as the outcome of an immeasurably long process of becoming-more in the past—the past, that is, of former lives.

Neither of these holds that which is for me the truth. But it is you who have here and now to decide between the three points of view. Let us inquire into the scriptural facts.

These are nowhere collected into a complete biography of the man Siddhattha Gotama. (Siddhattha means "one-who-has-his-aim-effected," or his welfare.) He is never referred to by this name; he is often called Gotama both by followers and by outsiders. This word means literally "kine-most-desired," or "best"; *-tama* is like *-est*, the superlative affix, and Gotama is a family name met with as borne by other men, both among disciples and by others. Buddhists, at least at present, avoid saying the name, presumably out of reverence, much as certain portions of the Christian world (and only these) prefer to say Christ, or our Lord, for Jesus. I am assuming that my readers are not Buddhist, and may agree with me, that Gotama and Jesus are quite as worthy to express associations of love and reverence as are the respective titles, and will, with me, prefer to read of them under the names we think of them as bearing while they worked on earth. As I was saying, in the biographical documents about both the one and the other there are long lacunæ, a deplorable loss to our knowledge. There are several accounts in this or that work, reckoned as relatively earlier or later, telling of his ancestry and birth, of his adolescence and of the beginning and success of his ministry as a religious teacher. Of his last days we have only one account: this is a collection of what may well be very ancient memories, but it is wrought up into a veritable patchwork quilt of discourses, many of which occur elsewhere, on dissimilar occasions, in the Sutta Collections. And there are the brief introductory sentences in very many Suttas, showing him as touring here or there, and so teaching. All through the Vinaya collection, again, we find him referred to as *bhagavā*,[1] sanctioning or prohibiting this or that, in the establishing of some rule for the monks. Thus, at the request of a lay-patron, that he might bestow on the Order (at Rājagaha) better "robes" (*i.e.* lengths of cloth) than cast-off rags, such as many wore, the sanction is given: "I agree to the layman's suit (of cloth). He who wants to, let him be a rag-cloth-wearer; he who wants to, let him accept the layman's suit. With the one and the other I commend contentment."[2] Here is a very possible decision, such as a man with a spirit above

[1] The most usual appellative in the scriptures, meaning literally, Possessor or Sharer, secondarily Adorable, Blessed, Exalted.
[2] *Vinaya Texts*, II. (VIII. i. 35).

stereotyped routine might have given as his "vote." I would scarcely say as much of the scores of petty "agreeings" in minutiæ about food, dress, buildings, etc., which are all said to have been referred to him. The text of the rule, however it was at first registered, orally or in writing, will have had the same opening formula, "I agree," in the drawing up by some chapter of the Order, giving it the one permanent sanction of the Bhagavā's consent, long after he had passed away.

The life on tour which seems to have occupied some three-fourths or at least two-thirds of each year, save the latter years of his long ministry, was suspended in the spring months—that is, during the rainy season, when a sojourn was made at some "settlement" (*āvāsa*), or group of huts near some village, whence the daily alms might be procured. There is one Commentary, and, so far as we yet know, one only, which names the settlements where he spent the first twenty years of his ministry. There it leaves us. The Commentary is as yet not edited in book form. I have placed this task with a former pupil, and thus hope soon to know it for myself. The given reference I owe to Dr. E. J. Thomas, viz. to his *The Life of Buddha as Legend,* etc. Both he and Rhys Davids give details from it.

Dr. Thomas's remaining remarks in this connection are so sagacious that I am fain to quote from them for those who cannot read them in his book. On these biographical survivals he says: "It is impossible to draw a strict line between the legends in the Canon and those in the Commentaries . . . all belong to a period far removed from the stage which might be considered to be the record, or based upon the record of an eye-witness. Everything . . . has passed through several stages of transmission. . . . Some of the scriptural legends, such as . . . the miracles of the birth and death, are just those which show most clearly the growth of apocryphal additions, as well as the development of a dogmatic system of belief about the person and functions of a Buddha. . . . The only firm ground from which we can start is, not history, but the fact that a legend in a definite form existed in the first and second centuries after Buddha's death. Evidently if this is to be judged from the point of view of its historical value, it must be taken as a whole, the most incredible and fantastic, as well as the most seemingly veracious portions. We may reject unpalatable parts, but cannot ignore them without suppressing valuable evidence as to the character of our witnesses.

"One element which is usually found unpalatable to modern thought is the miraculous; and one way of dealing with it has been simply to suppress the miraculous features. The presence of miracle does not of itself invalidate a legend. The story that a certain arahat attended an assembly may be true, even if we are told that he passed through the air on his way thither. . . . When, however, we are told that the Buddha paid three visits to Ceylon, we get no nearer to historical fact by suppressing the circumstance that he went through the air. The presence of miracle has, in fact, little to do with the question whether some historical basis underlies a legend. Normal circumstances are quite as likely to be invented as miracles. A much more important means of testing a legend is to compare the different forms in which it appears. It may have been elaborated, or an elaborate legend may have been rationalized. Additional incidents may be inserted in awkward places, or quite contradictory accounts of the same circumstance may be recorded." (p. 1 f.)

There is more in this line of ripe historic judgment, and the reader should lose no opportunity of profiting by it. Here I am much less concerned with a legendary "Buddha," or, for that matter, even with a man as presumably of North India, as being of a clan called Sakka or Sakya, and named Siddhattha Gotama. My chief concern is with the movement in religion linked with his name; and only with (*a*) the man, who was an instrument in the bringing to man a New Word in religion, (*b*) with that section of mankind where and when he brought it, as there and then ready for it—as ready, that is, as man ever is to hear and accept a fraction of the absolutely true.

Let us take the last first: the "where" and the "when."

As to the "when": the date, let us say, when Gotama was born. About this, whereas much has recently been written, there remains no decision of any value that may not be at any time upset. There is no one year agreed upon in China, Japan, or Tibet. And Southern Buddhists believe the birth to have been in the year 626 B.C.; or at least that year 544 B.C. was the date of his death. This was when he was either eighty, or, more correctly, in the eighties.[1] Recent European research has fixed on the latter event as more correctly to be placed in 483 B.C. This is mainly based on the Ceylon Buddhists dating the accession of King Asoka as taking place 218 years after the death of the Buddha, the accession being placed in the year 272 or 273 B.C., the formal accession or "coronation" in 269 B.C. And it would date the birth somewhere about 563–567 B.C., *i.e.* not much before the South Buddhist date of the death.

I have said "may be upset" because, whereas the opening decade of this century found scholars of Europe settling finally on 483 B.C. for the death, and "somewhere about the middle of the sixth century B.C." for the birth, the second decade brought reminders that, if an inscription in a certain cave in Orissa, E. India, long known to epigraphists, were more carefully studied, it might necessitate putting back the dates of two kings, men admitted to have been contemporaries of Gotama, to the *earlier half* of that century, in the *middle* of which his birth had been placed. This putting back might seem to date Asoka's accession immediately after the collapse of Alexander the Great's conquests in India (326 B.C.), which will not hold water. Actually all it does upset is *those 218 years;* it becomes

[1] He is recorded as speaking of himself as *asītiko:* "eighty-ish," "in the eighties."

impossible that the Southern Buddhists can be right in *both* date of birth and this interval. I incline to think it is the "218 years" we can consider as very inexact. And when we note that the source of it—a succession of reigns of Kings of Magadha—is derived from works (Purāṇas, Jain documents and Ceylon poems) which are all either from oral traditions or were written long afterwards, we are not fortified in preferring this shorter period to the perhaps greater veracity of the older birth-date with a longer interval. In any case, the truth that we seek in this book does not depend on an event being brought down to a precise year or even decade.

The "where," again, is still a subject of conjecture, and likely to remain so. The oldest scriptural reference we yet have is, I believe, in the Vinaya Piṭaka. Here we find Gotama coming on tour to Kapilavatthu, where his father dwelt, and again later on tour when, after his father's death, his mother's sister comes to him. The unwavering tradition (unwavering save among Tibetan Buddhists) is, that here was his birthplace. But the exact whereabouts of Kapilavatthu we do not know. That it was about the south-east of what is now Nepal, and approximately 150 miles (?) north of Benares, a hoary city both then and now, is perhaps sufficiently informative for our present purpose.

Here will have been no great "kingdom," nor home circumstances of pomp and luxury, but a relatively simple society busy with tillage, with trade, with arts and crafts, where the leading tillers were all "rajas" with an elective head or maharaja. It is only the much later cult of the superman in this man Gotama which led, in the legends, to his father becoming a powerful monarch of widespread dominions, and his modest dwelling a palace, or, for that matter, three of them. Nor are these traditions about the man in his home the only misleading pictures as to the "where" of his life. There are modern Western misconceptions, pretending to be based mainly on Rhys Davids's writings, but derived in fact from that "little learning" which has been called "a dangerous thing." These are scattered about Part IX. of H. G. Wells's *Outlines of History*, and depict the "where" as a land where cold was not and house and gear little needed, where food was easily got, where meat-diet and alcohol were avoided "as destructive," where was no sea-life, and where the ruling class hunted, slaying tigers and chiefly "making love."

Now the many pictures we have, in the Pali Suttas, poems and stories, will doubtless not in every detail give life as it was in North India as far back as when Gotama lived. They may have been, as to these pictures, touched up by later culture, just as in the early Upanishads we have a few pictures of a slightly, not much earlier culture. Yet taking them for what they are chronologically worth, in neither the one nor the other have I found anything to justify any one of the foregoing descriptions. Life, save for such religieux as happened to be in popular favour, was a fairly strenuous process, and the man who shirked his work in sloth was strongly blamed. The nights could be very cold, and we hear much about the shelter of the well and tightly built house. Food was so far from being ever plentiful that scarcity is not infrequent. With tillage and dairy-farming in the fields, with weaver, smith, woodcraftsman and other artisans in the village, men are seen with their hands full. The beef-vendor's shop is a frequent parable, and the strong-drink bazaar is a Jātaka feature. Caravans of traders take long journeys, with star-pilots as guides, or the merchants are as often to be met with at sea, whither flows down great Ganges. Tiger-hunting finds no mention: the sport is in deer-hunting. And courtship, love, marriage, divorces are as much as, but no more, obtrusive than they are in our own literature. The raja is as often to be met with presiding as a judge, making "business" journeys, and collecting intestate property as he is found fighting, hunting, or taking his leisure. I should not have gone out of my way to make this protest, had not Rhys Davids been cited as in the background. And the description of economic and social conditions in the villages and towns of his *Buddhist India*, published several years before the work in question, does not warrant the statements to which I have made objection, any more than do his other works.

All that legends have built up about and around this man Gotama you will find indicated in *The Buddha as Legend and History*. That which, when stripped of the frills about ancestry, parents, upbringing, leaving home and why, we can accept as residual and reliable is given in my *Gotama the Man*. It is true that, in the latter work, are given views ascribed to him about women and working classes which are not to be cited in so many words from any scriptures, and for this I have been taken to task. Now herein I have not imputed to him any views whatever save *such as he must have held*, to have acted in the way he is generally believed to have acted. This brings me to the very way by which he eventually became, not merely a laird's son on a "grand tour" to see the world before settling down in his own little world, but a world-helper of men. And that is a tremendously different matter.

He became impressed, we read, with things that made men—that is, men and women—unhappy. He is repeatedly shown as expressing this in the terms "Alas! the world has fallen upon trouble!" (or we might render it as "has come into a grievous pass"). Now any man who is acutely concerned with this, especially if he is wielding authority and likely to wield more of it, will include under world-woes any drawbacks of a general nature besetting any class of his fellow-men. The drawbacks in woman's life were coming even then *to find expression*. The reverence for the mother in the Indian is well known—that is, if she be the mother of sons. But it is curious that in the unique collection of poems, ascribed some of them to contemporaries of Gotama, called Therīgāthā, there is much expression of woman's woes, but no reference to this saving feature except once, and that is a protest that the father of the son is disregarding such reverence!

> *And this child-blossom, O my husband, see*
> *Thy gift to me—now surely thou wilt not*
> *Forsake her who hath borne a son to thee?* [1]

The poems reveal woman as realizing that she merited more of the race than to be treated as plaything, or as drudge, or as "kittle cattle" not to be trusted. She was feeling after her potencies as Man, whereby she could take her stand beside her male counterpart.

But if she felt this, how would not *he* feel it who was fit to be a helper not of males only, but of Man! If we use our imagination at all, we can see he must have felt it, even if monastic chroniclers have kept alive no clear record of it, for whom, as in Europe, woman was just *dulce monstrum*.

Similarly in the case of social inferiority. Caste barriers of to-day were yet to be born; nevertheless, that the slave, the manual worker, the trader was, as man, considered inferior to kshatriya and brahman is betrayed in early literature, even though no articulate protestants had arisen, as was the case among women. But here again the man of vision who was pondering how to help would see injustice and a better social ideal. He could not be what he showed himself as being, had he not seen.

It is true that that cry of sympathy for the world goes on to show him bewailing for it one series of woes, and one only, thus: "There is getting born and growing old and dying and falling and being reborn. And from this suffering an escape is not known, even from old age and death. O when shall escape be revealed?" And you may say: "Here have we not a truly religious preoccupation, which is not concerned with the way of the world as to treatment of women and of workers?"

This objection has a plausible appearance. It is possible for a reformer to be mainly concerned with one way of

[1] *Pss. of the Sisters*, p. 133 (ver. 300).

human ills, so that there arises no call to foist all human ills on his active sympathy. But we are dealing, remember, with a world-helper, with the founder of a world-religion, not with a specialist in reform, like a Luther or a John Howard. And such a man will take Man to his bosom. And more: such a man in his vision will see life as, in this way and that, a possible More for man, not a Less; he will see Man as potentially a More in his nature, his destiny, his life. On this possible More, and not Less, in the matter of such Helpers I take my stand. And it is to do what I can to redeem the fair fame of the most maligned of such Helpers that I bring you yet this one more book. What, then, is it I would have you see in the words concentrating on old age, illness and death, which we find this man made to say?

What he is said to have said comes after a series of experiences which are recorded in many works, both earlier and later. The young kumāra, who had been married, is said to have, on three occasions, met on a drive an old man, a diseased man, a corpse—one on each occasion. He is made out as being reared in such seclusion from and ignorance of life, that he has to be told on each occasion what is the matter with the unpleasant object. This feature alone is sufficiently ridiculous to render us suspicious that we have here an invented fable. In other legends his prowess as an athlete, his sharing in his father's judicial experience are in sharp contrast to it. In the Suttas claiming to relate talks by him when a revered teacher, he does place these three impressive but very familiar features in an ideal, if simpler framework, such as the prose ballad—its very style is of the ballad—gives here. He is speaking of judgment after death, and of how those three objects were messengers from the men of the next world, each conveying a lesson to men if they would but be heedful and not waste time. This talk, which, in its proper place, I find Buddhists ignoring, has got transferred to the legend of the founder before he left home.

And there are other features. In another Sutta-talk there are *five* messengers, the two added being a new-born babe and an earthly tribunal. In the three "messengers" legend we do not find these, but there is added a monk, or *pabbajita* (a world-forsaker), or, if you will, a friar or *religieux*—we have no fit word. "Why in the world the baby?" you say. Ask the monk. He will tell you. The babe means Man reborn to undergo once more all the ills of illness, old age and dying, to say no more. The other case—the culprit at the bar—is apparently an apt reminder, a deterrent. Yet is it not really fit, for human laws are fallible, and at another period the culprit might, by these, not be held to have offended. In religion we are dealing with what is right, or not right, for all time and for every land.

The monk, added in the legend, is referred to in these words: "And he saw, as he was driving . . . a shaven-headed man, one-who-had-gone-forth, yellow robed." Asking his driver who this was and what going forth meant, he was told: "It means: fine is his conduct in dharma, fine in evenness, fine his action in goodness, fine his action in meritoriousness, fine his harmlessness, fine his compassion for creatures." He stops the chariot, accosts the man, puts to him the same question and gets the same answer. He then and there dismisses the chariot and also becomes one who has gone forth. In other legends the breaking off of ties is not so summarily carried out. It is here of little consequence, save that it is a fairly obvious and irrational interpolation. It *robs Gotama of any motive* in leaving home to study and learn, for several years, how to find a solution for those ills of man's life. He is shown as saying on his deathbed:

But twenty-nine was I when I renounced
The world, Subhadda, seeking what is't that's good.
Years fifty, yea and more it is since I
Have been a pilgrim visiting the lands
In quest of dharma and a mandate true.

This makes it clear that he did not hold he had found these at home by any ready-made solution, such as imitating a world-forsaker.

Do you *now* see why Gotama is made to bewail the world-ill in terms of just those three ills: old age, illness, dying? The man who as *religieux* offered the solution should have been, not a particular *class* of good man, but just the good Everyman, earnest in his brief earth-life, the lot of all, to lose no time to live at his best. We should then, at all events, however illogical were the man coming in just here, when the search had not yet begun, be at the start of a gospel for every man and woman, and not for a religious Order of persons holding aloof from the world of their fellows as a solution for certain ills. These persons of such an Order had given up life in the world as unfit for pursuing the quest of salvation. And they had to justify their act to men, who were to maintain them, as beggars, in life's necessaries. Their argument was, that life itself —birth, work, love, old age, dying—was woeful, and that what they sought was, in the first place, not holiness, nor to help, but "a way-out" (*nissaraṇaṃ*), an escape. It is true, of course, that illness and old age are ills befalling the body, and often the mind too. But there are other ills, to the eye of a seer equally patent. And these he will have seen in the unsatisfactory status of woman and manual worker. These he will have included in the ills of the world.

Do you say, "No, let us keep to the records, nor put in what is not there. Let us not make this seer too much one of our own day. Let us leave it at this—that it was this particular aspect of life's ills that he concentrated on; it was this for which he sought a 'way out'"? I think that with a little more weighing of the what, the when, the where, and the how, we can here find ourselves at one about this.

First, then, we are dealing with no ordinary man. This

no one is likely to dispute. But few, whether they be Buddhists or not, recognize what is herein involved. The Founder has, in idea, been magnified to any degree of superman, yet that he had at heart all that in his day was hindering the upward growth of this man, this woman, is lost sight of, and only this threefold "ill" is put into words.

If you insist, ignore the social ills that I brought to view. I would not have done so had the scriptures not revealed it as felt in that day, surging up now and then as in all literatures it has surged up. But I hold to my contention, that it has befallen this man, more perhaps than it has befallen any other founder of a world-religion, to be, in fact, *belittled* by his after-votaries, even if, of all, he seem the hyper-exalted. He, who was to bring a gospel of the More in man to his world, cannot himself have been a man of shrivelled outlook on the humanity of his place and time. He may not—nay, he did not—when he was in worry over the world's ills, have made such mention of that twofold ill that we find it in things recorded. But aware of it he very certainly will have been. And it is of him as aware of it that I have written what I have written.

Secondly, as Founder of a world-religion, it was his to bring a message to his fellows of a More in man's nature, life, destiny; it was not his to come charged with a gospel that in any way contracted man's outlook on these. And this is, as yet, not more generally conceded than my first point. Adherents of this world-religion, of this branch and of that, will certainly admit that he brought "light" in his teaching. Europeans may grant him the title Light of Asia, Splendour of Asia; but the adherents will say "Light of the World." Yet in the same breath they will speak of him as made to see the woes of the worlds tied up in the fact of birth, illness and dying. In other words, it is life itself, as they see it here, or—for this came to be included—as they believe it to be in other worlds, that is the great Ill; life itself, therefore, that must be somehow stopped, if Ill is to stop.

You will not find this worded just like that. But this was only an accident of *not having the fit word.* "No word for life?" you say incredulously. Not quite that. There was the expressive word *jīva*, and *jīvita*. But neither word was ever used for *life as a whole,* as we use our word. Nor could the words be acceptable in the plural: "lives." *Jīva* we find as limited to that invisible *sine quâ non*, more or less identical with breath, without which the visible man cannot live; how far it was the same as, or different from the body was a common point of debate. *Jīvita* was the fact and procedure of this in the body. Thus to murder or to reprieve is "deprive of" or "give *jīvita*." In Europe, Greek thought for centuries was evolving a wider, deeper conception of life, as something belonging not to the body only, but to the "soul," to the very man. So that when the Jesus message came, with its emphasis on fullness of life, the fit word was ready to hand.

This is a strange thing to find, for we should have looked to find the fit word much more in a culture, where a man's life—notice I do not say "the life of *men*," but an individual man's life—was conceived as so much longer in duration than just this little ordeal of one earth-life. The Greek played, we may say, with the alluring idea of former and future lives, but for the Indian in Gotama's day it had come to stay. None the less is it true that, for life as a whole, no matter how many the "rebirths" (a word that is quite European), there was no fit word. And the word that grew up was just *saṃsāra*—that is, faring on—and, though less favoured, *sandhāvana*—that is, running on.

To return: Not only does their scripture make him see but three ills in man's "faring on," it also makes him bring to man a message incredibly limiting, nay, wilting man's idea as to what he is. Not only was he, as being tied, body and mind, to the world of life, "ill" (*dukkha*), not only was he, as being so tied, transient, impermanent (*a-nitya*), just as life is—he was also, as being so tied, "not-of-the self" (*an-attā*). More of these last two later. I would here only stress at the start, as I would stress at the end, that world-religions, which are the world's most wonderful phenomena, do not at their birth bring to man such words in the Less of him as are these three imputations. They are found in scriptures, perhaps; here they certainly are. But they are of the decay of a world-religion, not of its birth, its first youth.

And just here is my Thirdly:—it is only the narrow-minded, denominationally minded Buddhist who will refuse to admit it:—There is no thoughtful-minded writer but will admit that, in these Pali scriptures, oldest available though they be, we have no reliable records of things as they happened, of words as they were first spoken. To this, too, we shall come later. (And note, that Buddhists make no claim to have scriptures divinely inspired by the Holy Spirit, as is claimed by all Christian bodies.) But let this illustrate what I mean:—

Picture a minister of to-day in some Christian ritual about to read from "the Word." Suppose that, in place of a Bible, he has before him a little thin metal plate, on which are inscribed a heading, a single text, a couplet in verse. He has this, because he has nothing more that could be called "bible," book. He proceeds to give, not a portion, a chapter, a "lesson," a reading; he may read his "text," but then he may, he must go on in his own words and expound that text as in our "sermons," or in the old English homily from which I quoted above. Here we have the procedure of a Buddhist teacher long after the Head had passed away. Here, however orthodox he were, his own leanings would play a part. He would tend, on life's ills, say, to place his own personal, or his own professional view before us.

Is it not likely that with a text on that little plate, which in India preceded the bark or palm-leaf manuscript, say, with the words: "The Blessed One reflected: *Kiccham vat' âyam loko āpanno!*" ("On evil, alas, this world has-fallen!"), he should go on to give his congregation the monks' view of what that meant? Gone for *him*, home-forsaker, were home-troubles, market-worries and the like. There remained these bodily ills—old age, disease, death. And on these he would harp. The more, because it was for him of great importance that his hearers should see in him a convinced pessimist as to life in the world, and continue to respect and support him, thus uncompromising, as a holy man, from whose nearness they would in death's hour derive merit.

But some monks might discourse differently. A mixed tradition would arise, revealed, perhaps only when occasion arose, of revising the versions of these living bibles. A more standardized version would then be adopted as alone orthodox. Then one day the new way of recording swept along: of recording not by mere memoranda, but by the full manuscript, and the finally chosen standardized version was at long last written down. After that, the need for revision would be concentrated on scribes' errors. We ourselves know how many these can be, have been—we, who not three centuries ago had a Bible (*printed* edition) with *Thou shalt commit adultery!* in it. But on the written editions of the Buddhist scriptures the imprint of the monks' ideals, the monks' outlook, was come to stay.

Thus, granted that we have in a world-religion (1) a man of more than ordinary vision, inspired, (2) a new word brought by him of a More in life to set before every man (not just "men"), (3) the long, growing imprint on the records about (1) and (2) made by the Vehicle through which these have come down to us, can we not agree to see in (3) the monastic scriptures, a version of ancient things which must ever be read with full heed to the channel (3) along which they have flowed—a channel, that is, of repeaters, expounders, livers, who have taken to their heart a way and a teaching *of the Less* in and for each man—namely, that life's main ills are old age, illness, death, birth, and that each man is *not* a self (or what we often call a soul or spirit)?

That it was in consequence of an ardent will to bring light to his kith and kin on the things that most mattered that Gotama left his home, we need not doubt. It will have been a very unusual expedient for a kshatriya to take, and this, perhaps, coupled of course with what he found and did, is why so much has been made of it in legends. I can think of only one other Odyssey of an indefinite antiquity among Indian rajas' sons, and that is the charming narrative of the Kusa Jātaka (in the hero of which orthodox Hīnayāna book the Blessed One himself in a former life is to be seen). This young man of infinite will, grit and parts went forth on the quest of re-winning his wife, a woman worthy of such a man. I have limited Gotama's will to help as including only his own folk of the Sakkas or Sakyas; we have no warrant for assuming he was at this time aware of a call to a wider mission. He may have been; it is more likely that he was not. "The world" will not have meant for him what it means for us. It is more likely that he saw himself in hope returning with the light of new knowledge, gathered from teachers in cities of which he had heard, wherewith to brighten the outlook of his people. I do not know at what later period the term Mahā-nishkramaṇa ("great renunciation") came in. We do not find it in the Pali scriptures. He was taking for that day, for one of his class, a big step out of the groove, with all that this meant in resolve, breaking, deprivation and adventure. We cannot be sure there was more.

In the Pali records we have, (*a*) on the one hand, an account of his upbringing, dilemma and leaving home, in which I see a kernel of historical truth with some only of the legends incorporated; (*b*) on the other hand, in two or three Suttas, reflections imputed to Gotama as told to his disciples about that upbringing, worry and departure. Such are, for instance, those in the translations, *Gradual Sayings*, Vol. I., pp. 148 ff., and in *Further Dialogues*, Vol. I., pp. 115 f. Now if these reflections were genuine repetitions of what he was heard to say, they would be of utmost value to us in getting at the motives of his quest. Unfortunately, they are part and parcel of a constant feature in the monastic commentarial style. This is for the narrator to put into the mouth of his subject the thoughts which he supposes that subject will have been thinking. Here, it is true, we have text, not commentary, but remember that the Sutta grew up out of just the, at first, freely worded expositions round about a "text," using that word here as we do in sermons. Thus there is no hard and fast division between the Pali scripture narrative and the commentarial narrative. And in these reflections, wherever they occur, we cannot but see the mind of the chronicler imputing to his great man the things *he would himself, in his place, have thought.* Thus it is here, not two alternatives that we have, as has been suggested, but a *triple* feature of ancient records—that is, we have not to choose between (1) the reflections as historically true and hatching a brood of legends, (2) the legends as partly true and being mused on in the reflections. We have rather to assume (or infer), (1) a kernel of historic truth, (2) hatching a brood of legends, (3) being reflected upon by monastic expounders reading themselves and their monk-ideals into the will of the historic founder.

Your acceptance or rejection of my solution will much depend upon the kind of ideal you judge likely, even possible, to have been cherished by the founder of a world-religion. Is he, namely, one who, as he appears in these reflections, will have been "troubled, shamed, disgusted"—(better is "wanting to shun") by the fact that he would get old, ill, and die? Would such a man, I ask you, who could stoop to thoughts of this kind, concerning body and mind only, who could be obsessed with them, ever have been fit to bring new light to man? Can we not rather mate such a man with poor King Richard II. "on the Coast of Wales," saying:

> *Let's talk of graves, of worms, and epitaphs;*
> *Make dust our paper, and with rainy eyes*
> *Write sorrow* (dukkha) *on the bosom of the earth . . . ?*

Do you say: "Will there not be all sorts in the noble army of world-helpers—they who have dwelt on the tragedy of life as well as they who see the promise in it? And did not this man also see promise?"

Yes, of a "way out," so those chroniclers have written. I say again, I am writing not of Helpers in general, but of the very limited class—the founders of world-religions, so far as we can know of such through scriptures. These few men have in every case brought the light of a More into man's life and vision; their eyes were on the morning, on the wonder in life, if life be rightly viewed, as not of mind and body alone. And once we concede this, the transience of body in old age, etc., becomes of very little account for the greater, the longer view, the More-thing that is inspiring them. On the other hand, into the outlook of the world-forsaker, the recluse, the monk, those reflections fit very well.

I would not here be misunderstood. I do not see in any founder of a great religion a man who would not heed the fact of death. For me the main concern of religion, as distinct from morals, ethics, is the linking of earth-life *across death* with the greater life, the "beyond," the "unseen"; and the main object of religion is for me the living, *even now,* in more worlds than one. The next step is before each of us. But not on the stepping over do I see religious *founders* concentrating. And I would suggest that we distinguish, in the Pali scriptures between this monkish preoccupation with old age and death, and that which I deem to have been the stand about it taken by the founder. This is that death as a stoppage of activities here was very near, and that a man had little time to accomplish such of his life-task as lay here and now. Here, for instance, is what Gotama is recorded to have told the King of Kosala.[1] Note in it the vivid earnestness: "Well, sire, whence come you?" The king expatiates on his pleasant leisure from wars (*e.g.* with his neighbour of Magadha and, according to the Commentary, from a bandit-raid). Gotama puts to him the case of a messenger coming to warn him of a mighty landslide approaching, involving him and his city in appalling mortality. What would he do? "Live righteously," is the answer, nothing else would remain. Then breaks in this rejoinder: "I tell you, sire! I make known to you, sire! old age and death are rolling in upon you! what is here that you can do?" The reply is the same. Earthly politics and pleasures suddenly appear as relatively unimportant.

Here is death put into its proper place, and old age too. It is the word of Jesus: "I must do the work of him that sent me while it is day. The night (of the body) cometh when no man may work." It is, too, the warning conveyed by the parable of those three Messengers of the devas, that man be not careless to live righteously while yet this stage lasts. There is no preoccupation with something shameful and tragic in the natural process of this body wearing out. This might weigh with the Greek, but not with the Indian, save only so far as the Indian had got sidetracked by a morbid growth such as was that of monastic pessimism. And our business is to draw out and redeem the Sakyan and his mandate from that morbid overgrowth, and to show him teaching a More-in-life in will, in work, in joy, to win at length that ineffable goal *which had already been held up* to men in his own land of India.

[1] *Kindred Sayings*, I., p. 125, § 5.

B. *The Adventure*

About the wife of Gotama, who, doubtless a historical person, is in the Piṭaka account cited above called only Rāhula's mother, but who in other records is named Yasôdharā, Gopā, Yasôvatī, Bhaddā Kacchānā: he is free from blame for the leaving of her, if we see—as it is reasonable to see—in his departure an absence intended to be temporary. There has been in later legends and modern poems some attempt to be sentimental over his leaving her and his child, as well as over her reaction on his visit to his home as a teacher. On both of these the Vinaya account is as good as silent, save only that she bids her young son follow his father, just as she herself many years after, in the Apadāna—a Piṭakan book of *Acta Sanctorum*—is shown as having done. This is in three variant versions, when, as an aged lady leading her disciples, she pays him homage with a proud, independent dignity. She may before that have become widowed a second time, as I have elsewhere suggested, the unmarriageable widow and suttee being unknown in Pali records.

As to Gotama's objective on leaving home, here the legends are less geographically vague than the Piṭakas. The latter leave us with a very scanty fare wherewith to fill six wander-years of a pupilage somewhere, under at least two teachers, a visit home, and a period somewhere of sampling *tapas* or physical austerities, with the object of winning spiritual vision through mortification of the body. Topes or cairns, named after some act linked with his riding forth, with a favourite horse and a sympathetic master of his stables, which are prominent legendary features, are alluded to in late records. But we know not where these were seen as surviving, nor do their names show any but monkish appreciation of his venture. The *Buddhacharita*, a frothy, wordy, sentimental poem, ascribed to one Ashvaghosa of a date half a millennium later than

Gotama's, gives a long night ride to a woodland hermitage, where a seer gives advice, then the court of Rājagaha, capital of Magadha, then the near hermitage of the teacher Ārāda, then the teaching of Udrāka and then six years of *tapas* at Gaya. The *Lalita Vistără*, date and author unknown, gives a more detailed itinerary, mentioning Vesālī (Sanskrit, Vaishālī) as one of his halting places.

There is a possibly historical truth in this. The new Jain church had its headquarters close to the city of Vesālī; you can read of this in Jacobi's *Jaina Sutras* (S.B.E. Vols. XXII. and XLV.).[1] And the practice of *tapas* was a prominent feature in their teaching. Its main object was, by reducing the physical life, to set free an expansion of spiritual power—namely, of abnormal vision. To live on next to nothing, to be materially equipped with next to nothing: this has been the object of austerities, of "penance" in both East and West. And the East, with an eye on earth-lives past and future, had the further object of cancelling pleasant but evil times in the past by an equating with painful not-evil periods in the present, the while refraining from making growth of fresh debit in the present. This manipulating of acts and their results, which together came to be referred to as karma (*i.e.* action), comes up in Pali records wherever is contact between Sakyan and Jain (called there only Nigaṇṭha, or Not-tied). But for Gotama it was the obtaining, in this way or in that, of new spiritual light. That he did try the effect of ascetic severities is generally attested in records earlier and later. And that this was at—*i.e.* near—Vesālī I see good reason to believe. His associations with this town, both in his first ventures, during his ministry and at his life's close, were many and strong. It is the one place he is recorded as having, when he last left it, turned round to look at in farewell. I shall come back to it.

[1] Also, but in Pali only, in the *Majjhima Commentary*, II., pp. 268 f.

Where the two teachers lived with whom he studied is uncertain. Late tradition sees them near Rājagaha. As to what they each taught, I disregard wholly the very sophisticated, psychological metaphysic put into the mouth of the former, who in the Suttas is called Āḷāra, by the *Buddhacharita*. Not because it is psychological, for the mind, as distinct from body and also from the "man," was, it a new, yet a growing subject of study. But because the brief account in the Suttas points to something very different, but which belonged to a yet older line of thinking, in which Gotama appears to have been deeply interested. This was called Dhyāna (Pali: Jhāna); it means the man with mind alert, but in a way vacant—that is, not considering, measuring, reasoning, but brooding or musing. And it is the attitude in which the man, coupling with it reduced function of body, might, it was held, gain the deeper vision he sought. The actual record is in *Further Dialogues*, Vol. I., pp. 116 f. Both teachers followed practically the same course. Both are said to have so greatly estimated Gotama's proficiency that each invited him to partnership in tuition. There was a certain difference in the system of Uddaka, son of Rāma, the other teacher; but the terms in which you will find this expressed are obviously not the recording of a real memory, but are supplied later from the stages in a formula of Jhāna-curriculum, and need not be taken seriously and literally.

Gotama declined both offers. His reasons are stated in the Sutta account with some fullness, but as a clue to the mentality of such a man as he already was, as he was going on to be, they are no true guide. Read the passage in the *Further Dialogues* (Vol. I., p. 116), or as cited by Dr. Thomas (*op. cit.*, pp. 62 f.), and judge for yourself, *when* you have considered both what he was seeking and what he taught. He had found "the world is out of joint!" He did not respond with Hamlet's, "O cursèd spite, that ever I was born to set it right!" That Hamlet hesitated and cursed was the curse that hindered Hamlet. Gotama's response was to set out upon a quest to right, at least, his own little world. To do this, it would be necessary for him, as leader in that world, to make for an ideal suitable, not for a limited set in that world, but for every honest seeker, man or woman, rich or poor, manual worker or mental worker. This would of necessity lie, not in pondering certain ideas about things, no matter with what intensity, *but in living itself.* Life must be shown as bringing a More in it, which would so minimize the handicap of old age, illness and dying, that these would shrink into their proper magnitude and be shown as incidents in something greater, wider, filled with highest promise of a More to be done here, a More to be entered upon after the next stepping over, a yet More after more progress elsewhere and otherwise. Now all this we can trace him—it is not, alas ! more than "trace"—teaching in the Suttas. But there is no word of it in what Āḷāra and Rāma are shown revealing to him. There is no word of it in the reasons imputed to Gotama for turning away from them. The record shows him as seeking after a Less for himself, and with himself, for man : aversion,[1] passionlessness, ending,[2] rest,[3] higher knowledge, nirvana. These terms, ever to the front in the monastic discourse of the Suttas, suggest the secluded life of world-renunciation, the contracted vision of a brief life of introspective intensity. They do not suggest a way of the better life, the bigger life for missioner, *or for mission-field.*

In rejecting these reasons as a true record, I do not claim for Gotama that he yet saw clearly. Not even the votary claims that. I reject them as not valid even for him then, as valid only for a man who was out to "find an escape," and I hold that we must bring him clear of the monk's

[1] *Nibbidā* (not "renunciation").
[2] *Nirodha,* a causative form, not "cessation." Stopping is a good alternative.
[3] The rest that follows toil (*upasama*).

brush both in this imputed quest as well as in the alleged reasons in favour of it. There is much in making plain the way he trod that we have to do, and it needs watchfulness at every step. Too long has it been accepted uncritically.

With regard to the *tapas* or austerities which Gotama is said to have experimented in, there is agreement in essentials to be found in Sutta and elsewhere, but with an important difference. You will see this if, after reading of it in the Jātaka Introduction, you will turn, in *Further Dialogues*, to the Sutta *Noble Quest* (No. XXVI.), and compare. Both show an attempt to live through extremely severe fasting; the latter adds an attempt, practice in which we hear of even to-day, to suspend respiration. The elaborate account of this suggests a later interpolation. There are two or three references in the Suttas to such discipline in breathing as any physical-culture teacher would teach to-day, but not a word about this more drastic form of Yoga. Indeed, all such references lack the appearance of being integral to the teaching. And more: in the Sutta there is a refrain, six times repeated, showing that what the experimenter sought was not vision of new light, but a point of psychological interest. Namely, none of the desperate efforts he makes is said to result in suffering "obsessing the mind." The man, or self, or "I" here is watching introspectively the effect of feeling on thinking. And this new interest in the self as aware of mind, the study of Sānkhyā, was growing apace during those centuries after Gotama's day, and fits in rightly if we see here a later editing. Still later, in fact, the *Buddhacharita* poem makes Ārāda (Āḷāra) talk in terms of Sānkhya (S.B.E., Vol. XLIX., pp. 124 f.), but that he really taught it, there is no other evidence.

The real feature of interest for our insight into Gotama's life here betrayed is the reference in both Sutta and Jātaka passages to an opening given him of just the new light he had been seeking. Fainting from hunger, he is said to have seen and heard men of another world (*deva's*) anxious about the saving of his life, and wishful to inject nectar into his veins. There may or may not be some truth here in the record. That in such a pathological condition he may have heard and seen "psychically" is, as we know, very possible. In any case, he could only himself have told of it afterwards. And he is frequently shown as telling of other such experiences. Modern writers do not hold it worth while to discuss them seriously; either they are Buddhists, and follow the tradition, which tends to slur over the Great Man receiving any light or aid from any world, or they are men of our modern way, who wave aside everything, not yet charted in our science, as mythical. But to get a consistent living picture of this great Helper, if we ignore the fact that for him life meant living in more worlds than one, is for me, I confess, a hopeless task. Founders of world-religions are not men for whom life was of earth only, nor only real when so considered.

But what of watchers and friends on this side? Gotama's quest is at this stage closely linked with the apparently similar quest of five other men. The Jātaka chronicle says they were connected with eight named brahman augurs, whom raja Suddhôdănă invited to make augury about his son as a babe. The youngest of these, Aññyā Kondañya, when Gotama left home, induced four of the seven sons of the other seven brahmans to join Gotama with him. Brahmans, as we shall see, formed the majority of his first disciples and co-workers; but the story is too shadowy to warrant us in believing that all his first converts were brahmans. Aññyā and one other of the five, Vappa, are said in the *Theragâthā* to have been brahmans, but neither is this echo evidential. In the Suttas they appear quite abruptly, with no reference to those augural antecedents. We read only: "With me at the time were present [the word may mean "on me were attending"] five bhikshus [almsmen or monks]." The Jātaka first refers to them as *pabbajitā* ("world-forsakers"). One legend makes them only become such (and that magically) on their conversion! Since at the time all were seeking tuition, it is probably correct to infer that they were not ordained in any Order, but were lay-students in their "wander-years," such as Europe knew in the Middle Ages, and who were in Pali called *paribbājakas* ("touring-round-about-ers"), or, to use Rhys Davids's term, Wanderers.

As co-seekers after "the good, a mandate, dharma," they will not have been ordinary men, any more than were the first men chosen as helpers by Jesus. It is true that the missioner-call does not come out clearly here, as it does in the "Follow me and I will make you fishers of men" of the Jesus-call. Equally none the less was Gotama out to cast his net (as the Commentaries at times express it) to "save" men; equally did he look for co-workers herein; equally therefore must we assume that it was with this first object that men first threw in their lot with him. This is too much forgotten.

And yet we look in vain in the scriptures for memories of mission-work by these five. It were too much to say that in them he drew a blank. Doubtless they will have been among the first missioners he is recorded as sending forth, it may be at first for day-tours only. The fact remains, that of the three who alone have sayings ascribed to them—Aññyā, Vappa and Assaji—each appears as entirely absorbed in his own progress in salvation, entirely unaware that there is anyone else for him to help save. Aññyā ends the verses said to be his with

The good for which I bade the world farewell,
And left the home to lead the homeless life,
That highest good have I accomplishèd,
What need have I as cenobite to dwell? [1]

Not even his fellow-monks does he deem as needing him.

[1] *Psalms of the Brethren*, CCXLVI.

Vappa merely judges men's want of vision to know a great man.[1] Assaji appears as a mere formula-repeater.

We shall probably err if we think meanly of these men. Gotama was not the man to will to be the one-eyed king of the blind. His own generous tribute to them, in two canonical records, is: "They helped me much." This is all that the Jātaka, held to be a later work, makes him say. The Sutta, held to be an earlier compilation, adds this: "who were with me (when I had) the effort-establishing." (The compound here is an effort to express, not what he did, so much as what he was trying to do; as we might put it, trying to find himself.[2])

In the Commentaries, when they are just chronicle and not exegesis, we have matter in possibly very old values. Bearing this in mind, I incline to see in the Commentary on this Sutta passage a piece of later exegesis. "Were with me" in the Commentary is explained as having waited on him as so many valets, or as novice-monks would on their seniors. This is a childish device, appealing to monk-hearers, and in tune with the cult of the Superman, which had become dominant when the Commentaries were written. But Gotama was seeking, not hearers who would listen with folded hands, but able helpers. It is far more likely that the "helped me much" referred to a spiritual sympathy and comradeship, of which these men had shown themselves capable while they were students together, discussing ideals of life and work.

[1] *Psalms of the Brethren*, Vol. LXI. Cf. *Grad. Sayings*, II., "Vappa," Here we find one Vappa, spoken of as a 'Sakyan,' and as an adherent of the Niganṭhas, that is, the almost equally new Order of Jains. He is shown discussing a point of monkish culture with the Sakyan disciple Moggallāna, and then as addressed by the Bhagavā. The Sutta is evidently an "antique restored" by much editing. It may possibly be a fragment of a long orally transmitted memory of the Vappa who was of the first five. It is not impossible, that he may have left the new Sakya-sons band of missioners, and joined the slightly older Order of the Jains. For other treatment of the first men, see *Gotama the Man*, and *Sakya*.

[2] *Vin. Texts*, I., p. 147 (I. 23, 10).

At the same time, we have to take this and these men, as it were, on faith. On the one hand, they were, to judge from the meagre record, all the friends and comrades he then had. He wished to enlist, we read, his two former teachers, but found—it is said through an other-world communication—that they had recently died: this was when he had received his inspired mandate. And it seemed to him the next best thing to enlist those friends, and get them to adjust their ideals of teaching to that since given to him.

On the other hand, in reading further, we witness the coming in (through Assaji, one of these five) of two men, distinguished young brahmans of culture, who so impressed the infant movement with their personalities and gifts that they have remained for all time remembered as his chief apostles, and were called the Lucky Pair (*bhadda-yuga*). These men are patent in the Suttas as able to discourse and as discoursing. One of them is equally notable as having supernormal powers. I am referring to Sāriputta and Moggallāna. Why has their fame survived and that of the five died out?

Here is a problem, solved hitherto by seeing in the five not able co-operators, but docile sheep following a super-shepherd. To come to grips with it, we need to collect everything that is recorded of the five, and more especially of the two, in word and in deed. Space will not allow me to do that here.[1] But let two things be noted. That great pair both *died before their leader*. We have witness to this in Suttas and in the Commentary. And it was probably before the leader was aged. We do not find them associated with his sayings when he was old, as, for instance, was the disciple Kassapa.[2] The latest dated reference we have to them is twenty-five years before his death, when both volunteered to fill the post of body-attendant, and when

[1] This wants doing, and I am taking steps to get it done.
[2] See *K.S.*, II., "Kassapa-Saṃyutta." Cf. below, p. 261.

Ānanda, his cousin, was chosen. The other point is this: Gotama's original gospel, which we shall proceed to consider, will have been taught in its pristine force as long as he retained physical and mental vigour. When in his last decade he had become feeble of body—he pathetically testifies to this;[1] he was no wonder-man in body, even if he was in will—we should think of him as being left behind by the younger stalwarts of his Order; not, indeed, in outward reverence to him, but in the putting forward of newer tendencies in thought, and among these, especially such as were ever more in divergence from the religious standpoints governing his start. We shall soon see this.

Now let us put two and two together. In a system of oral teaching it was inevitable, in India, too, that changing values should more quickly permeate the teaching than if it had been at once, or even within a century or two, recorded in writing. And we read that from time to time the Order (*a*) found that its sayings had been tampered with, (*b*) revised its teaching. Revising it, men would inevitably retain versions of sayings of the newer values, rather than such as gave values *then held to be corrupt*. Why? Mainly because the latter were no longer in sympathy with the newer wordings. Well, then, those two disciples did not live long enough either to become infected with the newer notions or, as uninfected, to be shown resisting them. Had the latter happened, one of two things might also have happened: (*a*) they would have succeeded in turning the new divergence back to the older mandate; or (*b*) they would have fallen into relative obloquy. But they went from earth, and neither of these things happened. But what if the five, living on, did incur this obloquy, so that records of their sayings were let die? One such case is recorded, and this teacher's very name was covered up by calling him

[1] *Dialogues*, II., p. 107:—"just as a worn-out cart can be kept going only with the aid of thongs, so this body can only be kept going by bandaging it up."

just "the man of old," Purāṇa. (*Vin. Texts*, III., p. 380.) It reminds us of our term "Die-hard!"

There is one more possible conclusion: the five, in some way, may have left the company. One certainly did—Assaji—for we find that he also predeceased the leader. Another probably did—Aññyā Kondañya. Tradition makes him already old when he joined Gotama, and it is possible that he was soon incapable of mission-work. But there was also the evergreen tradition that he was first to give in his adhesion, and was welcomed by his new leader. This you can read in the *Vinaya*, and in *Kindred Sayings*, Vol. V., p. 360. You can also read in this work (Vol. I., p. 246) how, "after a very long interval, he came to Rājagaha, to see" his dear Leader, and fell down, kissing and stroking his feet, murmuring in the usual way his own name in greeting. Nothing, alas! remains to us of what was said by the two men. To fill in the all but blank record, we get verses about Aññyā, as uttered by the improvising poet-disciple Vangīsa. But we get this, that Aññyā is said, after strenuous work, to be living in happy ease, and to be the "Buddha-heir."[1] It is thus possible that Aññyā, after faithfully handing on the message he had at first agreed to teach, ceased, from old age, to be active, and passed away many years before the venerable leader. So that of the very man from whom we should chiefly have looked in the records for echoes of the gospel, not one discourse or even text is preserved.

But let us, before we come back to the leader himself, cast one more look at the poetic relicta for which these two first disciples, Aññyā and Vappa, have the credit. Many lines in verses over the former's name are also ascribed to other bards of the Order. These we will discount, but leave him (*a*) those ascribed to Vangīsa, (*b*) the rebuke to a colleague, (*c*) the last four lines. (*b*) shows

[1] *Buddha-dāyādo*: one version has only *-sāvako*—hearer, *i.e.* disciple.

him as teacher; (*a*) and (*b*) show him as having won through, at the end of the day's work, to a vantage-point in progress, in what I may call the way of becoming. This it is that makes him a happy old man. Vappa's lines also, in a distinctive way, show him as aware of the acquisition of vision. Wiser himself than formerly, he knows both who has wisdom and who has it not. We cannot now know how far either is truly accredited. But there is something in both poems, so far as quoted, that we shall find again presently.

I have brought those "devas" and these few names—they are now little more to us—in here to help form, more fitly than has yet been the case, the foreground in our picture of the birth that was at hand—the birth of a message that in the records is insistently said to be "for the welfare, the happiness of *both devas and men*." Linked with those names but very few words survive; it does not follow that their influence on their world was as naught. A tradition comes down in the Suttas that both the Leader and his men were silent men, lovers of silence, men of few words. This is fitting, for their gospel was largely, that it is the life, more than the word as such, which is all-important for man's salvation. And it is not true of Sakya only, nor of the first Sakyans only, that of most of them few or no words survive. Of most Christian missions, from that first one to Glastonbury to the Franciscan brothers at Canterbury, we have no record of "sermons." It will have been the communal living of the missioners, radiant with faith, hope and joy in a More in life, coupled with indifference to what does not matter, and with fellowship unmarred by bickering that made the living presence of them better than all the spoken words. This is not to say that they had no words for their life; but it is the words that will have endorsed the life, more than the life that will have endorsed the words. We have to make shift with such words as survive, and weigh these critically, but the wondrous first growth of a new world-religion will never have been a work solely of the spoken word.

What had been happening, that Gotama came to have to seek these men, who had been with him for part or all of his six years of quest?

We have seen that he is recorded as practising *jhāna* under two teachers, and then severe *tapas*. We may read that he was dissatisfied, not with *jhāna*, but with somewhat in the teachers' ideals or emphasis; dissatisfied, too, with the fasting as sterile of leading to the growth he sought, and that he reverted to normal nourishment. There is, further, the tradition that disagreement as to that fasting arose between him and the friends, who were also practising *tapas*. They are recorded as accusing him (among themselves) of *bāhulla*—literally, of "muchness"[1]—*i.e.* of forsaking the "simple life," they still believing in abnormal spiritual results as attending the abnormal physical life. It is reasonable to think that, as they ceased now to "help him much," he left them for a space, to take stock, it may be, of what six years of quest had brought, or failed to bring, him alone. We are not warranted in imputing ulterior motive. Nevertheless, that, at the back of his mind, there was faith in light as possibly coming by *jhāna* appears from the Sutta referred to, where he is said to have remembered certain happy experiences that had come to him at home, as a result of the sort of *jhāna*, or musing he then indulged in, when there was no question of *tapas*. In the Jātaka this has been elaborated into a pretty legend of him as a baby, with nurses, and a miracle, in the unshifting shade of the *jambu* tree, while his father, like other rajas, was busy with the ploughing of his fields. The Sutta version is more sanely sober over this, yet it is none the less crude in setting a later formu-

[1] "Surfeit," used in one translation, is too strong a term.

lated, much-contracted *jhāna* over against the stages in *tapas*, stage for stage.

More about musing later on; here this much only. When we read in the scriptures the repeated phrase, that in *jhāna* a man seeks "to make a way for access to other worlds," when, again, we read of Gotama much given to it, when we read of him, in such access, conversing with persons unseen by others, and referred to as *devas*, when we remember how dark for us is the occasion—if it be any one occasion—when a world-helper gets his inspiration, or his mandate, or however we like to put it, we may deem that we are here brought as near as may be to a signpost to the solution of our perplexity. I have not seen so far that votaries of Buddhism look upon this allusion as such a guide. By them the founder is believed, when in prolonged meditation, to have had "come to him" what is termed *sambōdhi*—literally, thorough understanding, but more often rendered as "enlightenment." The Suttas word it in this fashion: After this and that had "occurred to him" (lit. became for him), the summing up also "became" as "a vision into things not before called to mind: knowledge (*ñāṇaṃ*) arose, wisdom (*paññā*) arose, experience (*vijjā*) arose, light (*āloko*) arose." And all is said to have been round the two ideas *Samudaya* (lit. continuous up-going), arising, and *Nirōdha* (lit. down-obstructing), stopping or ending. How—I will not say these ideas; they savour too much of monastic atmosphere, but—his real inspiration, how *that* "came to him" is left implicit, as the inevitable culminating experience of an indefinite previous evolution in his humanity becoming more and more into a Most. No external agency is recognized. Almost inevitably it follows that in the records there is nothing to warrant us in heeding too much that informative access.

At the same time, that which in the records is said to be the expression of what did come, or had come to him is too unlike what he forthwith went forth to teach, is too much presented as a set piece of put-up construction, to be accepted as the climax of self-mandating in such a man. Moreover, the Piṭaka versions differ as to what that climax was. The Vinaya states it as *vimutti* (emancipation, or release, deliverance, liberty; there is virtually only one word in Indian tongues [1]). The Suttas state it as coming after he has put to himself that problem which we saw him worried over before he left home, and as answered, not in terms of "release," but in a formula showing insight gained into the fact of a man's birth being conditioned, being caused by certain agencies: becoming, grasping, craving, feeling, contact, the senses, name-and-shape, and *viññāṇa* (a term which could mean both the man-as-surviving and just his consciousness), each one of these considered as, in a series, both a cause and an effect. The notion of release occurs only at the end of the section, in a fairly obvious gloss, claiming to give a later experience in attainment.

Now the first words he is reported on three occasions to have uttered in a public way are *quite different from these.* Moreover, as formulas, they fail to bring conviction that we have here the pondering and the solution going on in a critical hour of such a man's life. We may possibly get nearer to him if we try to trace the problem from within, keeping in view what it is recorded he did actually teach at the start. We shall be better able to attempt this when we have considered him, not as an unconnected appearance in the Indian humanity of his day, but as the child of its religious evolution.[2] For the present chapter I will only suggest one or two things to be kept in mind without our needing to call in that further consideration.

Namely, we must think of him as out to solve a difficulty

[1] Variants of the root *muc*, to let go, or loose: *mōksha*, *mukti*, *vi-mutti*.

[2] See next Chapter.

for himself and his fellows by a new way, a new word, which would open up *something more* in the meaning of life. We have to assume this as the cause of his strenuous quest. Next, he will have had his task present to him as involving, not only his own will, but also that of each man. He could not impose what he willed on men, as a dictator. It was to be a new way lying within the *choice of each man*. Moreover, his way was to be a message *in words* to each man. He had more than the will of a brahman teacher with a little world of pupils. He was out, as we say, to broadcast. No academic subtleties were here possible. Again, his task was not limited to making a man think in a certain way only—it was a matter of *how to live, what to do*. This was bound up with his new way of thinking. Lastly, his new way in word must point to an end, the putting a stop, at some time, to "ill" (*dukkha*). Nothing less than that was to suffice. Positively worded, the goal was that man become utterly well.

All the time it is Very Man concerned to bring a New Word of the true to Very Man that we have here before us. We have to avoid seeing in that new word any exalting of *an Idea* to which men were to cling. For this is just what the records are ever tending to do. It will seem to certain persons presumptuous to have let those records make way for these suggestions on what the crisis will have meant for him. And had the records not shown what he will *not* have been up against, I would gladly have let them tell their tale. The effect of them upon the scholar of to-day is to make him say, We cannot, in face of these records, know any thing positive whatever that he thought and said, and to leave it at that. I do not leave it at that. I believe that, holding fast to the very man—I mean, the spirit in man, the man of will, the man of the search for the Best—we can so study the records of such a man's day, compared with records about him made up in a later day, that we can bring out something of him and his quest that is true and worth saying.

C. *Problem and Hesitation*

A word only on legends connected with this moment of his life, which you will find fully dealt with in *The Life of the Buddha as Legend*, etc. What of the tree, and what of Māra's attack or temptation?

I am not writing this book to try to make historical facts out of these two legends. I would see no historical truth in either. I am not basing this entirely on the fact that the Suttas all but ignore both. Their reference amounts to just this: that in the "Great Legend" Sutta of the Dīgha-Nikāya each of seven Buddhas is said, Gotama, the seventh, being the narrator, to have been "thoroughly awakened (or enlightened, *abhi-sambuddho*) at the foot of a different tree: an aspen (*assattha*), or (going backwards) a banyan (*nigrôdha*), a fig-tree (*udumbără*), an acacia (*sirīsa*), a sāl tree (shorea), a lotus (*puṇḍarīka*, this presents something of a difficulty), and a trumpet-flower tree (*pāṭali*). There is this bare enumeration, nothing more. The more famous name, Bo tree, *i.e.* bôdhi-tree, occurs twice in the Vinaya-piṭaka, Mahāvagga I., 1; 6,[1] where we read that the "buddha bhagavā stayed at the foot of the Bodhi-tree (at Uruvelā, on the Nerañjarā) after he had been enlightened . . . crosslegged for seven days." And in the third Nikāya is a Sutta, prose and verse, about Māra's three daughters, Rati, which we might render "will-to-pleasure," Arati, or "Repining," and Taṇhā, or "Craving," trying to tempt Gotama, despite the father's warning of its being useless. Of the dread onset upon him of which the ballads tell with much gusto I find no word, save here and there a phrase, such as Māra's army, assembly, mount or steed (*i.e.* elephant), which imply that the legend was known, when the books were edited into their present form, and, further, a passage in the Dīgha (Vol. I., p. 112) recording the aged Teacher

[1] *Vinaya Texts*, I., pp. 1, 90.

as referring to Māra coming to him just after his enlightenment, and urging him to pass away then without delay.

Here is, after all, enough to make it possible that there may have been a residuum of fact in connecting him with a tree, and with a person or persons urging him to fall back or be foolish. But the main concern of the Suttas is with a religion and with a notable man believed to be the source of it. The poetic, the constructive imagination is, in them, not dominant; their business is the handing on of certain traditional sayings in a way which the editors find morally and spiritually impressive. For them it is first and last the religious mandate and the man who delivers it that is the theme.

But with the *growth in time* of the man to a purely ideal figure, and therewith the fading out of earlier environment and pristine associations, the work of that poetic constructive imagination comes evermore into power, and surrounds the Man with symbol and sentiment. The tree under which some one may have found him while he beat out his problem alone becomes that world-tree, connected in folk-lore the world over with a man or a woman [1] pondering and uttering decisions, or with world-protection, or with sources of fertility. Again, the inner world, with all its impulses, hindrances and crises in the matter of choice, coupled with the dire experiences awaiting wrong choice, is sometimes prompted by human agency, and this makes it but a short step for the poetic constructive imagination to see, in the whole of this, death (*māra*) or sin personified. And the more momentous the Man's decision is believed to have been, the more will the ballad's dramatic fitness need the attack on it to be pictured as desperate.

Temptation of a sort there may well have been, but it came *after* all the Māra-flummery, and it is this that the

[1] I have Deborah judging in mind. Judges iv. 4, 5: "Deborah, a prophetess, the wife of Lapidoth, she judged Israel at that time. And she dwelt under the palm-tree of Deborah."

Suttas bring out with fit impressiveness. For an intelligent Buddhist it should now be absurd to hold that an elect man, on the eve of maturing in sanctity, should be even assailable, much less assailed, by mental and emotional attacks, known only to a lesser man. His will, tuned to the best and highest, makes no such response possible, and hence robs the attacks of all point. His difficulties will be otherwise. What, namely, will he meet with in the will of the fellow-men whom he seeks to help? Will his mission be of any use? Here it is, apart from tree-allusions, apart from any Māra-allusions, that we find him susceptible to, assailed by worry, disposed to give up. Here we have temptation, but it springs, not from any ready-made bogy, but from the anguish of a noble man, awake to the magnitude of a noble task, and cherishing no illusions as to his own powers, or as to abnormal readiness for the New in other men.

As to what it was, in a new value, a new outlook, a new word, that he had beaten out in solitude, the scriptures are not silent. But I would ask you, Can you accept the record of it as a true confession of that which he alone can have told? What do we find? Take first the Jātaka Introduction [1]: it has features not found elsewhere. This, for instance: "The Bodhisat (seated) with his back to the tree facing the east, becoming strong-in-mind (thought): Let skin, sinew and bone dry down, let flesh-blood in the body dry up, but I will not break up this crosslegged-seat or ever I have attained right enlightenment!" Then follow cosmic excitement and the Māra assault. Night draws on, and in the first watch the Bodhisat reached over to knowledge of former lives (lit. residings), in the mid-watch to deva-sight (clairvoyance), in the last watch to knowledge in causal uprising. "Then to him turning and returning the twelve-linked mode-of-conditions, pondering backwards and forwards many times, the ten-thousand-

[1] *Buddhist Birth Stories*, new ed., pp. 190–8.

fold system of worlds making (their) limit in water quaked twelve times." Daybreak now comes and cosmic rejoicings. He, "having penetrated to omniscience, uttered the utterance not omitted by any Buddha: Through many births faring on, running on, not finding, seeking the housemaker: woeful is birth again, again! Housemaker, thou art seen! again thou'lt not make house! For thee all rafters are broken, house-ridgepole is destroyed. Mind has come to plan no more; attainer I of waning out of cravings."

These lines, here for the first time quite literally rendered, are met with elsewhere in Pali and also other Buddhist literature, with but slight verbal differences. Oddly enough, in the Elders' Anthology they are assigned to a brahman convert, Sivaka, and with silence in the Commentary (if I rightly remember) on other contexts.

If we now compare the accounts in Vinaya, Dīgha and Majjhima,[1] we can dismiss the last book, in which two brief and quite differing summaries are given. We find the Vinaya giving a narrative of Gotama's pondering as a finished thing, put into the flowing terms of a set formula, while in the Dīgha the compilers have tried to present the same formula as the work in detail of a conscious intellectual process: "then for him through thorough work of mind became by wisdom comprehension," that, *e.g.* "where birth is, there is old age and dying. . . ." The Vinaya also has allusion to a back and forth, but given *after* a solemn verse: "When verily things are manifest to the ardent musing brahman, then for him all doubts are dispelled, in that he understands thing-with-cause." So much for the first watch. In the mid-watch, after the back and forth, he is made to repeat the solemn verse, but with the ending, "in that he understands the waning out of causes." In the last watch more back and forth, and the verse, but with this ending: "he stands blowing away Māra's army like the sun lighting up the sky."

[1] *Dialogues*, II., Sta. XIV.; *Further Dialogues*, I., Sta. 26.

The Dīgha pursues throughout its compiler's wish to give us conscious mind-process; working first, as we saw, back from effects to causes, they present a tradition of ten such steps, not twelve, as in the Vinaya tradition, and, stopping at the *viññāṇa* (or man as surviving), they sum up the series in the generalization: *Samudāyă!* "coming to be!" So far, in other words, for *cause as producing effect.* Then, taking the series again from old age-dying as so many *causes which may be eliminated,* they sum up once more in the generalization: *Nirŏdha!* "stopping, or ending." Then, in prose only, comes the triumph: "Attained now for me is this way of insight for enlightenment, in that from the stopping of name and shape is stopping of *viññāṇa,* etc. . . . thus is the stopping of this entire body of ill."

Now let us glance at this causal series.

The burden of the formula is, that if we take those ills, old age and death, and inquire into their causes, we come upon (*a*) the fact of birth. This for European thought is a short cut, unless we go on to heredity, and heredity, which even for us is new, was then and there not taken into account. India was concerned not with men, but with the man. And what a man is, is the result of what *he,* in past lives, has been, not his forbears. Hence possibly it comes that in getting at the back of the latest birth, we find (*b*) "becoming" (*bhava*) assigned as the cause of birth. This is like replacing a particular cause by a more general statement of the cause. But the word, when the formula was made, had to come to mean the place or circumstances of the new birth. Next (*c*) grasping, or laying hold of, is then put as the cause of *bhava;* the word means also fuel, as when materials for a fire are supplied, and we cannot therefore adequately reproduce this word. Preceding this serially are (*d*) craving, or strong desire (for life), (*e*) feeling, (*f*) contact, (*g*) senses (*h*) name-and-shape, a very old term, once meaning the inner man or spirit and the outer visible man, and (*i*) the *viññāṇa*. The two other terms omitted in some versions are (*j*) *sankhārā*, whence *viññāṇa*, and (*k*) *avijjā*. The former means movements, whether material or immaterial, such as have gone to produce the survival of the man in a new birth. Literally, it means complexes, compounding, and it has, as term, a curious history, too long to go into here. *Avijjā* is literally "ignorance," "nescience," and served well as a limit-point to human investigation. Even the omniscience imputed to a Buddha is not credited with getting past it. He is made frankly to say that, as a general truth, origins are past finding out.[1] Nor do the stories he is recorded as telling on phases of evolution exempt him from inclusion under that truth.

Cause and effect find expression in the Suttas in series differing much from this, the most emphasized of all. Nor are all these variants made with one and the same object, viz. to show emergence of ill and its ending. You will find some account of these in my little work, *Buddhism*, in the Home University Library. And in one context—and one only—there is a series giving suffering emerging through faith into joy and insight. This is, I believe, unique, and remained in oblivion for writers on Buddhism, East and West, till the Pali Text Society published my translation of it fifteen years ago. How, as I then said, might it not have altered the whole face of Buddhism to the West if that sequence had been made the *typical illustration* of the causal law! Thus: "Conditioned by ill comes faith, conditioned by faith joy, by joy rapture, by rapture serenity, by serenity happiness, by happiness concentration, by concentration knowledge and insight into things as they have become."

How is this no less true than the type-series! Yet how is it hidden away! How have not Buddhists of East and West ignored it! And not wholly without reason.

[1] *Kindred Sayings*, II., p. 118 ff.

They go by what is everywhere repeated, but here we have, as it were, a freak passage, an exception. And yet surely a world-religion needs to give equal emphasis to the joy there is in life's opportunities, and the insight that comes, not in escaping from life, but in using those opportunities to grow into a More. Even here, too, this bright oasis is flanked on both sides by pessimistic extensions.

This is one reason why, for me, the application of a meditation on cause and effect, in itself worthy and significant, to emergence of ill alone, and the fact of causation as useful only to end ill, is a quite inadequate solution to rank as enlightenment won by a man capable of founding a world-religion. Smaller men and women have arisen and taught nostrums in the name of religion even down to our day, which have won followers and have petered out. But we are here at the birth of a message mightier than these, and one calling for a very elect man. In that man and his message we need find, if we rightly seek, the bringing of a More and not a Less into man's outlook on himself and into all of which he is by nature capable. We look to see him symbolized, as this very Sutta goes on to show, in the hill-stream expanding into the river, and this finally merging into the ocean in very perfected being, in very perfected becoming. But of this there is, in the record of inspiration won, not a syllable. It is a wilted, truncated outlook.

And then there is this other reason—namely, that in the ensuing record his first utterances as teacher *bear no resemblance* to the way of inspired meditation along which, it is claimed, omniscient insight came to him. I am not urging that the immense significance of what we have come to call natural causation was not present to him. I can even believe he felt drawn to make it his gospel, as no one before him had done. It is fairly plain that it was engrossing attention among the young intelligentsia of Vesālī and elsewhere. Not that *y* as normally following *x*, in what any man did and saw happening, was not one of the hoariest things in man's knowledge. But causation had not before this been applied as normal and inevitable *in the world of things unseen and immaterial.* Divine providences were arbitrary, chance had its realm, the study of mental laws was a very new matter. *Here* it was that "natural" cause and effect were beginning to impress man, just as in a preceding generation they had been voiced in the Brahmanic teaching of and to a select few.[1]

But if he weighed causation as an instrument by which to help man—that is, Everyman—to a wider religious outlook, I also believe he rejected it. It would not stir the pulses of Everyman. We actually see him later trying it on a man of culture and utterly failing to make an impression with it.[2] How that formula of a causal series came to be thrust into the silence brooding over that retreat we cannot now know. We will follow him in the next step, and return to this matter of causation later.

The story of the hesitation, not as to what he should teach, but as to whether he should teach at all, is found in three accounts, in what are reckoned as comparatively old records—Vinaya, Dīgha, Saṃyutta. They agree in this very closely, and can all be read in translations. The Vinaya account alone gives him a restful period of happy experience (*paṭisaṃvedī*; the rendering "meditation" is not accurate) of four weeks, one week under each of four different trees, such as the Goatherd's Banyan, the Kingstead tree, such names implying the shelter of an adjacent hut-settlement of sorts.[3] All accounts agree that there came over him a faltering of what *we* should call the will to teach. I am not agreeing that the somewhat sophisticated phraseology about this is a faithful record of what he felt, or confessed, probably to one or more of his first men.[4] It is so curious a mixture of a More and a Less in the message he

1 Cf. *Shvetâsvatara Upanishad*, I., pp. 1–3.
2 *Further Dialogues*, II., p. 17 (Sta. 78); below, p. 167, 195, 224.
3 Cf. *Dialogues*, II., p. 4 *n*.
4 Cf. the *opening* of Sutta, § 33, b, *Gradual Sayings*, I., p. 118.

claims to have thought out for men. It is claimed to be "Dhamma which is deep, hard to perceive, or understand, peaceful, and sublime, no mere dialectic, subtle, intelligible only to the wise . . . it is that all that happens is by way of cause." It is "tranquillizing all the *sankhāras* (movements), the renouncing all grounds of rebirth, the waning out of craving, passionlessness, ending, nirvana." Here is a message aiming at making man calm, refined and intellectual, but outwardly a Quietist, a practiser of what Carlyle called the everlasting Nay, one who gives up this, eliminates that, and sees a Goal in negation. Calm and refined thought is to culminate in the quiet thinker becoming a "Not."

Now here was no suitable word for Everyman. It is judged to be for him new, unwonted fare. Discounting causation as the intellectual aspect, the remainder states that *which was then the growing monastic ideal*, new at the time for India. And man, it is felt, as the creature of "habit" (*ālayo*: what is clung to [1]), would not be easily induced to cultivate the one or the other. "I might indeed teach this, but others might not accept (or acknowledge: *ājāneyyuṃ*) me. That would be for me weariness; that would be for me hurt."

The heed here for himself alone is noteworthy; later we find him fearing harm, in another matter, not for himself, but for the unbelievers. Shall we not say that this great man had not done growing?

Can we, then, make a sounder guess at what he then had in his hands to bring to man? We see in him the strong will to bring help by new "light" of some sort, daunted by the task of overcoming the beaten way of the old, the accustomed. What that new light was we must try to get at by considering Gotama as we have yet to do—that is in the religious environment of his own day. It is the only

[1] The associating of this state with lust is not a good rendering. Cf. the name "Him'âlaya"—"*abode* of snow," or of winter.

way left us of getting past the later, the *finally written* record about him, when man had come to see in him some one out of all proportion to his surroundings.

That this hesitation was very temporary, we can believe. That it was banished by a vision will be accepted as a sane conclusion by those who hold that other hesitations, such as that of St. Peter,[1] were similarly banished. It is but a childish impatience that dismisses these visions with the handy word "superstition." We can accept the story of it as one that must have been told by Gotama himself, famed in his tradition for truth-speaking, without seeing in the name imputed to the other-world visitor, of Brahmā-sahampătĭ, one that he will himself have used. The deva nowhere names himself. The substance of his petition to Gotama we will consider when we try to guess the real burden of the New Word. We will then also consider his own response, as throwing more light on his first utterance than all that is alleged as having preoccupied him.

But from that hour the strength of will to bring a More to men never faltered, and the faith and gratitude and love of his church thereat found voice in the verses by some poet of a forgotten name, which have been placed in this moving scene:

As on a crag on crest of mountain standing
A man might watch the people far below,
E'en so do thou, O Wisdom fair, ascending,
O Seer of all, the terraced heights of truth,
Look down, from grief released, upon the nations
Sunken in grief, oppressed with birth and age,
Arise, thou hero! Conqueror in the battle!
Thou freed from debt! Man of the caravan!
Walk the world over, let the Blessed One
Teach Dharma. They who learn will grow.

To this scene I must ask you to come back presently. Here we leave him passing out to find men who will be capable of receiving the New, and of helping him to teach

[1] *Acts of the Apostles, x.*, verses 9 ff.

it. To the man he meets—Upăkă—we shall also return. But the traditional reception of him by his five friends, who had, it is recorded, gone away to Benares, has for me a later flavour, born of the Buddha-cult that grew up *much later*[1] about his person and powers. Both in his reply to Upăkă and in his greeting of the five we come upon that overweening sense of his own majesty which our young people call "swank." Great man, he was too great to have called himself great. It is a repellent feature, albeit it has made strong appeal to his later votaries, when recited by reverent monks, who saw not that he had no need of such self-mouthed apologetics.

[1] Cf. below, pp. 106–9.

CHAPTER IV

THE NEW WORD: (A) WHENCE IT CAME

WE shall never rightly understand what it was that Gotama Śakyamuni, as founder of "Buddhism," taught unless we place him in his true frame: the religious teaching of the India of his day. We might as well try to understand Jesus' teaching aloof from all reference to the religious teaching in Palestine at the beginning of our era, or John Wesley's teaching apart from the Christianity in eighteenth-century England. Great teachers have their setting in the historical tradition of their own countries; if they are founders of world-religions they have a further setting—namely, in the history of the world as in process of religious becoming. Our business here and now is with the former setting. And as we read in the Vinaya the episodes we have been following, we come up against it.

We read that, in the second week after Gotama is said to have been "enlightened" (lit. to be thoroughly awakened), and was at the Goatherd's Banyan, he is accosted by a brahman, belonging to a school or clan, of which the name has been oddly corrupted—the Huhunka-jāti.[1] After courteous greetings on both sides, the brahman asked these questions: "To what extent, master Gotama,[2] is one genuinely 'brahman,' and what are the things that make a 'brahman'?" The reply is much to the point, but it has been

[1] There are many readings of this word. I hold it was probably Su-sukkajāti. We know how *h* and *s* have interchanged among Indo-Aryans. We thus get "Very-bright-clan," an idea we can parallel in Teutonic names. (*Huhuṃ* is "humph!")

[2] The word *bho* is not easy to reproduce. We can hardly say Mister or Sir Gotama. I use the archaic "Master" as a compromise only. "Brahma-faith," again, below is equally to be rendered by -cult, or -teaching; *-vāda* is literally "speech."

edited in verse, which bears the mark of a stock scriptural saying, that is also used elsewhere.[1] It is not the reply we can hear one earnest inquirer stopping in his walk to make to another earnest inquirer.

A brahman who has barred out evil things, is not
A man of humph and pshaw, whose is no stain,
Who has the self controlled, in Vedas versed,
Who lives the Brahma-life, 'tis he may say
His is the Brahma-faith, for whom there are
No false excrescences in all the world.

Each speaker apparently goes his own way. Almost the little fragmentary episode was lost. For us it is of value. We can hear the corresponding modern question: What man do you, Mr. So-and-so, judge to be a Christian indeed? Not just one who has been baptized, or who is an ordained priest. Or the exclamation about Nathaniel: "Behold an Israelite indeed in whom is no guile!" The brahman, as such, was much like the Levite to other Israelites: one in whom, in virtue of his birth, religious duties were vested. His, and his alone, it was to recite the Veda hymns, learnt and borne in memory; his it was, and his alone, to celebrate the ritual; his it was, chiefly, to be teacher of the sons of those who could afford to pay him, giving them many years of what we should now call a University education. He was honoured for this, and for this he honoured himself. He was in that day the "churchman" in a very full sense. As teacher, he had not full monopoly, for *kshatriyas* (nobles, even rajas) could be teachers, as we find in the Upanishads. In these and the brahmans we see the world of culture of that day. It is not the world of "the Many," but it was a world of attention to the things most worth while. And we see Gotama, by this time well known (the commentator reminds us of this) as a persistent, earnest student, with brahmans and other nobles, of such things, consulted as one in sympathy with their inquiries.

[1] *E.g.* cf. *Sutta-vipāta*, verse 783; *Udāna*, I., p. 4.

The question indicates, too, that within as well as without this church-cultural world, among brahmans, as well as among Jains, for instance, there was going on an active religious interest, a quest for the real, the sincere, as more worth while than a world of codes and rites and habits, or "formal" religion; a feeling after the better as a something New, as a something More than established religion was giving them.

As these inquiries gained force, shortcomings in the established church, especially, as it happened, in the North-east of India, would tend to be shown up. We find many strictures on brahmans emerging in later Piṭaka books. Look, for instance, at the Jātaka, No. 495 (Dasa-brāhmaṇa). And this tendency is visible here, as we see it in the finally edited version of the Mahā-vagga of the Vinaya. It is, in fact, in the telling, made so absurd, so unlikely in its absurdity, that it is easy to read between the lines, and there see the serious, lofty inquiry, meet to be met by a serious, lofty and *courteous* response. It gives us a fleeting glimpse of what was afoot at the time, and is akin to much else that emerges in Upanishad and Piṭaka: an interest both in practical religion and in things of the unseen, both during and after earth life, in what I have called musing, in the working of incorporeal causation, in the new analysis of mind.

I do not think we may look to find any world-religion launched without a preparatory responsiveness of this kind being astir among men, just before, just where, the birth of it takes place. Its world is getting ready for it. It is not easy for us, to whose world no recent gospel-mandate of any proven power to grow, to sway men, and to persist has come, and who have very fragmentary records of the days when such a mandate was come, to put ourselves in such a world as that. Even were there no such fragments, some explanation of the phenomenon of that response would be needed. As it is, we seem to see this: the message made a singular appeal, a strong appeal, the appeal of a supply to a demand, the response to something waited for.[1]

It will not be one way only in which the New Word will be felt as wanted. There is, for instance, this way, one that we have read of in this and that religious reform within a faith, and not as belonging to the birth of a new faith alone. This is the felt need of a more vital and sincere *living* the faith professed. It is the appeal for "works" to make real the faith, since a man only really believes what he will live for, and, if need be, die for. This is what we saw in the brahman's question. This is what we feel is not stressed in the Upanishads.

Another way will be the need of something more in the faith itself. This will probably prove to have been preoccupying the cultured few, and to be emerging as a felt want by the Many. And it may be that while it is emerging for them, it will meanwhile have been falling away among the few. This may be, because the right or die-hard wing of the established religion has suppressed the more progressive movement in its fold. Or it may be owing to a faltering in that movement itself: some ardent teacher has aged or has died, some ardent but perverse junior has diverted the movement, brought in a way of the worse. But that progressive movement will have been taught to many young men, and so filters out to find Everyman to some extent ready for it. But Everyman is a practical fellow, and will need something he can grip. The movement may need expanding, clarifying for him. But above all, it may need to be made practical, a part of his life.

This is how I see the progressive movement among the brahmans, as followed up by that which I see as its expansion in the first Sakyan mandate. It is shown, for me, in the increasing way in which the man was being regarded less as a static being, more as a being in process of becoming other, different, changed. I could more easily show you what I

[1] This is more fully treated in my *Sakya*, pp. 15–52.

mean if translators of the Upanishads had not so often, with one exception, slurred over this striking feature. But much depends on your considering this carefully, if what I have to say about the message of the Sakyamuni is to have due weight.

Translators and readers, whether of text or translation, have overlooked this new feature, mainly on one of three grounds. First, they, we, are the children of the Darwinian epoch. Consciously or unconsciously, we look at things from the standpoint of evolution to a degree unknown before. Not because we see man as changing only—there was nothing new in that—but the way in which we envisage change in man has become less of a mechanical, arithmetical change, more of a biological, more of a psychological change. We are more concerned with change as a matter not of quantities, but of values, of quality. There is nothing new about this standpoint in the scope of our religions. Its newness lies in its present all-inclusiveness in our culture. Hence for an old-world literature to be putting this standpoint to the front may escape the notice of the modern translator, just because he sees nothing strange in it.

But that alone would not suffice. It may be that *grammatically* the translator does not see, in the way of expressing this "process of becoming other," as much as I see in it. And here, as unversed in Vedic—that is, in old Sanskrit idiom—I am at a disadvantage. For him this verbal root *bhū* ("become"), with its derivatives, may be merely a help to the other verbal root *as* ("to be") the future form of *bhavishyati* being the same for both. We see this, as you doubtless know, in German also, in *sein* ("to be") *werden* ("to become") where *wird* can mean either "becomes," or just "will be." Hence he may find it equally right to translate, say, *bhavati* by "is," *or* "becomes."

Thirdly, the translator may not be *disinterested* about this matter. He may see unwisdom in rendering *bhū*-forms by "become," because he both knows, that the cultural movement, favouring man being considered as essentially (*i.e.* as very man, not in body and mind only) in process of change, was eventually quashed, and holds it was well that it was quashed. Hence he will *tend* to render *bhū*-forms by many makeshift terms.

Whatever the reason, it is certain that (*a*) a greatly increased use of *bhū*-forms over the use of them in preceding literature can be statistically shown (roughly I make it about six to one), (*b*) this increase must be seen in the text, not the translations, to be realized. The one quasi-exception is Dr. R. E. Hume's *Thirteen Principal Upanishads*,[1] where you can make the comparison yourself by noting his "becomes," etc., with the "is," or other word, in other translations.[2] Even he at times evades the "become," not always with sufficient reason.

I would not be unreasonable here, who am off my special range, by claiming that the *bhū*-contexts *always* indicate the full force of "becoming," as more or other than "being." Obviously where the future tense is used, the meaning may be either "will become" in the way of growth, or just "will happen"—for instance, as you might say in German *es wurde Nacht*, for "night fell," or "came on." Or, as in the Upanishad passage, "the wood of the figtree *bhavati* fourfold," for "is split into four." Here is happening apart from a matter of becoming more or growing or expanding, and I would not force the meaning.

Such a case has seemed to be the oft repeated *tad api eso śloko bhavati*, which is usually rendered: "As to that there is this verse . . ." and the speaker is inferred to have been quoting or repeating. But I would suggest, as more likely, that we have here the teacher feeling the need of making an impressive point in his lesson. It comes over him either to improvise a verse, or to cite, as our own orators would do, some one else's impressive mantra, and he says, "There

[1] Now in second edition, 1931.
[2] Notably in Max Müller's *S.B.E.*, I. and XV.

becomes (*i.e.* arises) in me these lines." Such is the meaning in the Pali books, where the past tense is always used: *evam assa ahosi*, "thus it became to (*i.e.* in) him."

In any case, even if we deduct all cases of mere statement of a happening, more than enough are left to show a new feature in Indian literature. There will have been a reason for it *just then and there*, and it should be accounted for, as having stood for something new, something calling for expression, which had not been there before as so calling. If the word needed for that self-expression is there, it will be used; if it is not, makeshifts will be used. And because these will not be adequate, the ideas expressed by them will tend to get overlooked or misunderstood. Now the word needed was there, a much better word than what we now have left ourselves, we, who in our old literature could speak of *wairthan* and *weorthan*. Thus in our East Midland dialect:

> *Falleð in ðat welle-grund,*
> *ðer he wurdeð heil and sund,*
> *and cumeð ut al newe.*[1]

I would not belittle unnecessarily our "became"; it is we who have suffered it to become ambiguous, at a period when we were not enough *needing* expression of growth. In India the word, I say, was there, and in taking to use it more than before, some new need of it was being felt.

Let us take an instance. In the old Taittirīya Upanishad is a little homily to the student: *mātṛdevo bhava, pitṛdevo bhava*, etc. (Vol. I., p. 11). Here it is possible to translate: "Be one to whom mother is as a god . . . father is as a god," and so for teacher and for guest. Dr. Hume is here content with "be." But surely the teacher is seeking to make his pupil a better man, a more than he is; surely here is where "become (a mother-god-man)" is a truer

[1] *A Bestiary*, early thirteenth century; "The Eagle." "Fell into that well-bottom, there he became whole and sound, and came out all new." Morris's *Specimens of Early English*, I., p. 136.

expression of what he is trying to bring about. Here the two verbs were there, "be" and "become," *edhi*, *bhava*, but *only the latter is chosen.* Here, again, just previously, it is the teacher asking for himself: *amṛtasya deva dhāranī bhūyāsam*, may I, O god, become bearer of the immortal! This time it is Deussen, who as a German had a word at least as strong as the Indian, and yet who renders: "may I be" (*möge ich sein*)! Surely he would have admitted that prayer is a reaching out to the divine will willing to *become a more than one is?* What a waste of a good word ready to hand! Or take this well-known passage on the dissolution at death of the bodily and mental complex: *kvâyaṃ tadā puruṣo bhavati?* [1] "Where, then, comes the man (the soul) to be?" In other words, "Where thereafter does the becoming (the very life of the soul) go on?" Deussen makes the feeble rendering: "*Wo bleibt dann der Mensch?*" (Where then remains the man?), losing all the force in the question. But here was the case of a man who wished, in the interest, as he saw it, of Indian religion, to evade the use of *werden*. One more instance: in the Brihadāranyaka Upanishad, a man in deep sleep, free, as himself, not body, to depart (in an invisible body) and enter other conditions, is thus described: "Then a father becomes not father, mother not mother," and so on for a number of earthly relations, which for the brief interval become invalid. Here one would again think that a *bhū*-form is fitter than an *as*- (or a "be"-) form. Yet Max Müller's rendering is, not "become," but "is"!

The latent significance in *bhū*-forms becomes most impressive when we meet with what grammarians call the causative form. We have not, alas! this useful inflection. When, *e.g.*, we express "to make stand," we have to say "place"; in Indian tongues we just alter the inflection of the verb *stha* (to stand). Here our own substitute is neat enough; it is less so when we have to say, not "do,"

[1] *Brihadāranyaka Upanishad*, 3, 2, 13.

but "cause to be done"; in Pali we have but to say *kāreti* (or *karāyati*) for *karoti*. Now the causative of *bhū—bhāveti, bhavāyati*—is found, though rarely, in the Upanishads, and so impressive has it seemed to translators that, not content with the literal "make become" or even "make be," they have brought in such terms as "nourish," and again "comfort." Thus, in Aitareyya Upanishad, the pregnant mother, being she-who-makes-become, becomes (herself) one who is to be made to become: *sā bhavayitrī bhavāyitavya bhavati*—as if the poet-teacher were revelling in the quasi-punning force of the *bhū*-forms. Again, in the Bhagavad-Gītā (Vol. III., p. ii.): "Let him make the devas become, and they make him to become"; this is translated by Dr. Barnett as "Comfort ye the gods and let the gods comfort you."

Against this, the choice of a very learned and poetically feeling master, it may be an inaccurate forcing the literal meaning to place the former rendering, and it certainly sounds less edifying, at first. I say, at first, perhaps not so much, later. For consider, we have to picture *here* a background, not of Vedic, Olympian almighty ones, but of brave and pious gentlemen who have passed, as "devas," to the next world, only to come back one day as men. We see them as such warding man and also being spiritually warded by elect men, in a mutual furthering of progress in the long, long way of becoming. If only we could express "become" causatively with æsthetic effect, as could the Indian, *we should not need to* go afield for such a word as "comfort." The mutual "making to become" is far truer, is more direct, is more impressive.

We cannot all of us check our translators, and if we can, we cannot all of us, any more than can I, presume to say we differ decidedly. But it is hardly to be wondered at that we outside readers have failed to see as yet, in the increased use of *bhū*-forms, something that was pressing for utterance, or may have been pressing for utterance, pressing, if it was so, between the years 600–500 B.C.

Can we now light upon something which was felt as needing expression in the world of religious ideas and aspirations? I surely think we can, thus: We are not merely concerned, in this new preference for one word rather than another, with a social, political, ethical, or even philosophical change in North India. We are up against a religious change, and one of the deepest significance. In the early Upanishads we find ourselves in a world of teachers who are profoundly convinced of the truth in a new mandate, not put forward by them, but which they are developing, amplifying, vindicating, exercising imagination about. This will have been introduced by some helper of men a little before their time, but of whose very name we are not certain. This new mandate was, that man has it in his nature, by becoming more, to become ultimately That Supreme Godhead Who he "potentially" is. (If he and they had had such a word—a word which we virtually owe to Aristotle—it would have been used.) To express this potential being, they were compelled to fall back on such words as they had. Now there was the word *vardh*—meaning quantitative increase as growth, and this was clearly not good enough. It is only later, in the Pali scriptures, that we meet it, as itself a "grown" word, applied to spiritual growth, and other words too: *vepulla*, *virūḷhi*, for growth, derived from the plant world.[1] So new may have been this idea of the very man, the soul or self (which is the true subject of religion), as a something that grows as surely as, in its own way, a plant grows, that teachers were in straits for a good word, or would have been had they not had this great-little word *bhū-*, or *bhava*. This, as indicating movement-in-being, was the very word their new mandate needed.

If we ignore their preoccupation with this word as expressing what they were trying to teach, we are forced to see in that teaching something quite irrational. That is, we

[1] E.g. *Majjhima-Nikāya*, I., p. 117, etc., etc.; "growth, increase, multiplying."

seem to see a logical absurdity in the oft-repeated telling man that he had, as it were dwelling " within " him, that supreme Being Who was one with himself, a world-self or God-self, one with the self who was the very man. We seem, it is true, to approach this in Christian teaching in the words of John the Elder : " Dearest ! now are we the sons of God . . .," but there is here no such identity as in the Indian teaching, and the sonship, too, is taught as being an act of " adoption " : " that we might receive the adoption of sons (υἱοθεσίαν) " namely, " by grace."[1] On the one hand, we have the Highest, the most perfect Man or Being as yet conceivable by man ; on the other, we have man the conceiver actually and consciously not-the-Highest, far from perfect. Can these two ever be one ?

It may be said : Was not then and there the idea of the Highest, the Perfect so far lower, more crude than it became later, that identity was more plausible than it would now be ? I reply : in the Upanishads those lower, cruder conceptions of Deity, such as we find, not in a primitive degree, but to a relatively unmoral degree, in the Vedas, have been discarded. Previous to our date, Zarathustra (or Zoroaster) had lived and taught in Persia, taught a morally lofty conception of Deity as the Good, Word, Good Deed, Good Thought, and by ways of which we have no surviving record, this new word had infected Indian thought, leaving both a general uplift and other traces in Upanishadic and Pali teaching. In the former teaching, God, *i.e.* Brahman, was conceived as eternal wisdom, truth, dearness, happiness, steadfastness—terms in which an approximately perfect man of that day would be described. In the latter, man's conduct is often worded as " deed, word, and mind," good and bad.

No, it is not, I think, by narrowing the gap between the highest self and the actual self that we shall rightly value the Upanishad teaching. The fact that the gap remained,

[1] Gal. iv. 5.

and that to bridge it remained as a terrific " task as well as a fact "[1]—this it is we must keep in view. Teachers told their hearers: Thou art That (*tat tvam asi*), meaning, that ultimately man's nature is God-nature. How man was to make the potential actual was variously taught, but the one way its exponents have stressed is that a man should " know " God. The knowing meant a realizing that, in every way of life, the divine self was active as the human self. This should not be understood as an undue exalting of the man; it was rather a realizing of the tremendous possibility and responsibility latent in his nature. But neither of these terms was then in Indian tongues.

But if we supplement exponents, and if we supplement this " knowing " with the insistence on " becoming " which is also there, we shall then divine how teachers were feeling after the importance of *living an idea*, as being not less than that of having the idea. The notion of knowing something, however, had always a great start over all we connect with *will* in Indian culture. This was an old culture, and it is the way with such to express the coming to know—namely, to " see," to be impressed—*before* there is expression of purpose, of will, of reacting to impression. And so, whereas in the Upanishads the vital importance of knowing, of coming to know, man's oneness with the Highest finds full and varied expression, indeed conveys a will-power foreign to our thought, the yet more vital importance of so living that he is ever becoming a less glaring inconsistency with himself-as-what-he-may-be is far less clearly worded, and is only, as I have said, felt after in this: " that he is " not so much as " that he becomes."

But that this " feeling after " was no mere after-thought you can see, if you ponder the passages where it attains the deepest significance. This is where becoming is seen as an attribute of Deity Itself-in-action, in creation. Here

[1] S. Radhakrishnan, *Indian Philosophy*, I., p. 209.

we find not just the fiat uttered: "Let there be," or "become" . . . We find the divine Artist Himself *as becoming*. Oneness is felt as unsufficing: "Let me bring forth myself." It sought from being One to become many; till this was accomplished It did not "become-this-and-that"; here we get *bhū* as compound with the disintegrating prefix, *vi*: *na vyabhavat*:[1] 'It, or He, did not "develop."' Becoming is here no longer a state of progress from a more imperfect to a less imperfect; it is raised to the higher level which we tend to see in the work of such a man as we call a genius. Becoming is in such to be rather described as a becoming-other, a becoming a new manifold, as it were a divine play. And this, at a later date, was the very way in which the Indian thinkers regarded divine operations, as when Rāmānuja dedicates his commentary to that "highest Brahman . . . who in play (*līlā*) produces, sustains and reabsorbs the entire universe."[2]

At that later date, the earlier Upanishadic idea of Deity Itself "becoming" over Its creating had been repudiated. But in those early days it had been a bold word, in which man was seeing, in the Highest as then conceived, the best and noblest that he saw in himself, as something of which he was, at least ultimately, capable and heir. And more: not only would he as essentially one with Deity become, as was That, immortal; his becoming would not stop there and then.

I mention the word immortal because we see the teaching in the Upanishads struggling to make it man's birthright, but hindered by the older tradition which taught, that man must win that right by sacrifice while on earth and by vicarious sacrifice after he had left earth. No phrase is more frequent in these books than "the mortal becoming immortal." Here at least our translators can do no other

[1] *Brihad. Up.*, Vol. IV., p. 11 f. Max Müller renders: "was not strong enough!"

[2] S.B.E., LVIII., p. 3.

than render the *bhū*-form by "become." Bold here, too, was the teaching, undermining one great claim made by celebrant brahmans for the ritual. Yet was the teaching consistent if we concede that the force there will have been in the word "become." Where the teacher might have said: "Man, mortal as to his body, *is, as very man, immortal*," he said, "Man *becomes* immortal," because in him being is becoming. Had he used the future tense (*bhavishyati*), we might have hesitated, and seen only a statement of future happening. But it is the present that is used, and our English translators should rightly have availed themselves of the superiority here of English and said, "The immortal *is becoming* immortal."

Here again, however, I do not wish to stress unduly. There may have been a concession to tradition in the "become," as a state conditional on sacrifice. Yet I am convinced we have, in these great books, strata of teaching revealing at once the priest and the prophet distinct, much as in Israel they were distinct. Word of prophet was suffered (more or less perhaps) to survive, but the mantra of priest remained also. It was as "Thou art That," not as "Thou art becoming That," that the mantra prevailed and survived. And the reaction against Becoming we can see creeping up in the middle Upanishads; and then we see it worded as a contention that had come and is now past.

Thus in the Maitri Upanishad we find a hedging on the idea of creation. The Creator here (*a*) "broods upon himself," (*b*) "thinks, Let Me enter . . .," (*c*) "utters. . . ." Yet the way of becoming lingers in the words: "This One became threefold, eightfold, etc." And it is in the same book that, in a list of epithets of Deity, *Bhava*, Becoming, is one.

In the probably just preceding Shvetâsvatara Upanishad, creation is not touched upon, but still we read that the man, when he "sees the very Âtman (God), becomes unitary, end-won, griefless." And it is here, too, that we find the line: "Who is to be seen as beyond the three times (become, becoming, will become) . . . who is to be praised in becoming what has become."[1] It is of interest that in one context in it, the third "time": "what will be," is called "what the Vedas tell"; but possibly metre was here the rudder that guided the ship.[2]

When we turn to the Īshā and Māṇḍūkya Upanishads, which are probably later than either[3] of these two, we see as implicit that this matter of "being" versus "becoming" had been a battle-cry in religious debate, "becoming" being now termed *sambhūti*, a word not found before. Becoming is now reduced to mean, not exercise of an ever new Manifold in that which is, but as an originating from that which was not. This is not the same thing, and may involve a complement of decay and ending, as in all material becoming, or physical growth. And in the Commentary of Gaudapāda (which Deussen's biased zeal forces upon readers of his translation) we are landed in a view, which sees, in the becoming manifold, "illusion"; which sees that what is real cannot become, becoming being only in what is already there.

In the Īshā text itself, the dying faith in becoming is virtually contradicted by the surviving faith, that man, in becoming, wins the goal. But in the Māṇḍūkya the halting logic of the Īshā is purged, at the fearful cost of "becoming" in the very man being voted to be an illusion. And this conviction, that becoming must have a complemental decay, is the weapon we find used, round about 250 B.C., by the newer as against the older teaching in Buddhism.

I have shown for a moment the Commentator, steering the conclusions to be drawn by the hearer or reader of the

[1] *Shv.* 6, 5.

[2] Butler's Hudibras:—

> But rhymes, like rudders, are the verses
> By which, like ships, they steer their courses

[3] It is an Appendix of Maitri that quotes Īśā.

text by the changed values of his own day. Here we have a fourth reason which I would add to the first three above which have mightily influenced the *learnèd* translator. Commentaries have even yet their uses. Historically useful, as revealing these altered values, they are arch-will-o'-the-wisps in diverting us from the values that were original. For they—that is, the age in which they were recompiled in writing—have no longer understood the real message round which the Sayings on which they comment were uttered.

To come back: the bogy of decay as involved in becoming somehow intruded, not without cause, and I suggest it was from a double cause. I seem to see in the middle Upanishads a new interest in the structure and functions of the body, which came to be so marked a feature in early Buddhism. We find this in the Katha, Shvetâsvatara and Maitri Upanishads. And I venture to see herein a cultural evolution which is the reverse of our own. With us it was physiology that stimulated, indeed almost gave birth to, our new psychology. Our first psychologists were mainly doctors. But in India it may well have been the new interest in the processes of mind, viewed as distinct from the "self" or man, started by one Kapila, which gave rise to analysis of body, as important, not for physicians only, but also for religion.[1] And this contemplation of bodily parts and processes would tend to preoccupy men with decay as inevitably supervening on growth,—that is, one variety of becoming.

Moreover, it may have been the very fertility of the idea of becoming that led to the same result. Indian teaching is steeped in parable and simile. And you cannot get far in the idea of becoming without hitching the notion to physical, organic becoming, *i.e.* "growth." We see this,

[1] We may compare with this Bergson's suggestive remark: "What would have happened if modern science . . . instead of converging on the study of matter, had started by a study of the immaterial (*de l'esprit*)." *P. Soc. for Psychical Research*, 1913.

in Buddhism, in the *bhū*-forms being equated by *vuḍḍhi* (Sanskrit, *vṛdh-*), and in the constant use of "fruit" (*phala*) for result or effect. And as the identity of Holy Spirit with human spirit died out in Buddhism, the spiritual significance of man's becoming would become worsened too; the term is seen inseparably bound up with decay.

Thus it is in a world where the idea of man's bridging the gulf between Deity and man by the notion of Becoming was faltering—a world, that is, of the cultured few rather than of the Many—that the Founder of what came to be known as Buddhism gave his message. That message was to the Many, and *there* the idea of man as becoming a wonderful More would be only just emerging, as fruit of much teaching to the Few. We see an analogous happening when Jesus brought the fine teaching of human fraternity known to the Stoic Few out to the Many, together with its ground-motive in the Fatherhood of Deity. A new way of bridging the gap had meanwhile been springing up among the few in India. This is known as the dual method of Sānkhya and Yoga. Into these terms I cannot go here, but you would not be far wrong if you understood them roughly to mean intellectual knowing and volitional effort. You will find them first emerging in the Shvetâsvatara Upanishad: "Him . . . attainable by Sānkhya-Yoga, by knowing the Deva. . . ."

It was especially the latter method as an exercise, a willed process, meaning literally "uniting," "joining," which had as its avowed object a bringing the human self nearer to its divine ideal and counterpart: "my Kinsman, won to evenness and unity with whom become I really he who I am." [1] Literally a mechanical idea as compared with the essentially biological idea of Becoming, its stress for the Indian mind lay more in the effort, the toil that being yoked suggests, and the concentration therein, than in any

[1] *Mahābhārata*, "Mōksha," on Yoga.

external bringing together. And Yoga did good service in Indian religion.

We shall find it emerging in early Buddhism with a distinctive use it did not have in Brahman teaching. This is because the former teaching was, as the latter was not so much, in labour-pains over the fellow-man. This must never be forgotten in any study of the birth of Buddhism. It was a mighty complication in the religious problem. Man was giving birth to the vision of religion as meaning, *for each*, not only a realizing God more intensively, but also as bringing in a realizing more intensively *who* the other man is. But just as in the Stoic ideal and the Jesus-gospel the ethical idea was a corollary, following from the ideal of God, so should you be prepared to see that the expanded values about the fellow-man in early Buddhism are a corollary following from the expanded teaching of Becoming which its birth signified.

I would go yet farther, this time in surmise only, and leave our contemplation of the background of our picture with a suggestion, how it may have influenced the meditations of Gotama of the New Word for the Many. It will possibly have influenced him—this need of a linking up of two tremendous issues: Deity as apart, external, terrifically personal and omnipotent, and Deity as not apart, not externally personal, as the innermost Inner of man's being—to this extent, that he framed a message as one of the man choosing between two alternatives to win an uttermost Good. *We* can see the two in perspective as his age could not; his age was up against the latter alternative, but with the former alternative still mighty for the Many. As a gospel it would not have been practicable—or was it this about which he hesitated? . . .

The foregoing may have left you impatient to get back to our subject-title. But my long labours in this have convinced me—and I am not alone here—that to understand the history of Buddhism we must wash off the complexion given it by alien skies, we must get under the lines ploughed in it by the growth of the two great ploughs monasticism and early Sānkhya, and see it as the child and heir of the India of its birthday.

CHAPTER V

THE NEW WORD: (B) WHAT IT WAS

MAN values ever and much the old, the wonted, the accustomed. None the less does he value the new. He is curious, inquisitive. "We all are seekers still," in Matthew Arnold's words. The Quest is that which has ever attracted him; a getting away from the accustomed has lured him, now more, now less. It is a holding the New in worth that leads him far and high and deep; it is the not yet experienced, the unknown, that draws him on. For him is true the law of the centripetal, the centrifugal, no less than for the physical world. We need to value both tendencies in him when we read any chapter in his history: his adherence to what is arranged, ordered, established; his quest for the fresh, the unsettling, the not yet ordered, as leading to a More, more in what he has, in what he may be. Both are necessary to him as man. Were he animal only, clinging to the wonted, the habitual would preponderate. If he sought change, it would be because he was driven to it. He will have been pushed to go forth ; to return again, or not to return. He would not have sought the new from an inner, a spiritual impulse or urge.

We see him acting in response to this impulse even when his environment is not making such a change necessary, or to the majority even advisable. He is seeking something new in the spiritual world because of something which has come to seem lacking in the settled spiritual environment. The Old no longer gives him all he has come to need. It does not follow that he wants to destroy the Old. He is coming to see it in a new light. He is coming to see a More in it which was not made articulate. He wants to expand the Old, to make clear in it some worth not clearly seen.

But he may find himself in some way brought into conflict with the Old. This will not have been of his first seeking. It may come from resistance offered to his seeking by men who are not yet sharing with him the need for the New. And this may lead to his eventually breaking away from the Old as he would not otherwise have done.

This seeking expansion and this eventual breaking away are what happened at the birth, and then in the childhood, respectively, of Sakya, by which I mean the period covering about the first two centuries of what we lump together as "Buddhism." This expansion, and then this breaking away I ask you to keep carefully in mind. Thus, in our Pali documents, we find a man coming forward to speak what is expressly called a new word, not spoken before. If what I have just said be true, if he was one to whom "religion" was of the highest moment, we shall find in his teaching this: it was not opposed to the most highly revered religion of his day; it was held by him to be an expansion of that religion; it was intended by him to make good something lacking, needed in that religion.

What is this, then, that we find him made to say?

It was the placing certain matters of great moment before his hearers under the aspect of "two ends" and "a middle way," or course (or course by the middle), as confronting the man, here called wayfarer. The ends, or rather side-issues, are: (*a*) the natural desire of man to seek happiness or pleasure (he had but one word here to use), on the one hand, and on the other, (*b*) the natural desire of man to curb, restrict, repress his desires by rule, by code, by pruning. Neither side-issue alone leads to supreme welfare. The method which does so lead is a way that is of both of these, in that it is the midway, the Mean. The wayfarer should refrain from the excess incurred by following either side-issue exclusively; he should "well understand" the middle way.

This, and no more than this, is for me the very Mantra or mandate. Called in every book a "sermon," it is in that word miscalled. It is really better termed the "text" only. From it any number of sermons could be elaborated in exposition. As text or mantra it is longer than that of Jesus: "Repent, for the kingdom of heaven is at hand," or: "for the kingdom of heaven is within you." But I believe that the original mantra was only the first part of the "sermon" we have. Like the Gospel-mantra it could be, and was, expanded in many ways. But both bear equally the stamp of the New Gospel of a world religion: both are concerned with a New for man that is a More he is to enter upon in his heritage as man. In such mandates it is not a less that is pointed out to him; it is not a bidding that he maintain what he knows that he has. "Come," it says to man, "I will put a new song into your mouth . . . behold! new things do I declare . . . behold! I will do a new thing, I will make a way. . . ." Here we have, in words on which so many English readers have been suckled,[1] the vital thing at a religion's birth. What, then, of the portion that follows?

You will by now be asking me to give you the "sermon" as the scripture gives it, for translations may not be within reach. But bear with me a little longer. The utterance, said to have been given to the five friends, is famed in tradition as the Dhamma-cakka-pavattănă-Sutta,[2] or Discourse of Turning the Dharma-wheel. Yet it does not find mention among the Suttas of the two first collections in the Sutta-Piṭaka, and we have to go nearly to the end of the third collection, the Saṃyutta, before we find it. Properly it should have been placed in the first group of the section where we find it. That section is the "Great Section"

[1] Cf. Psalm xl. 5; Isaiah xlii. 9; xliii. 19.
[2] Pronounce the *cakka* as *chakka*.

(*mahā-vagga*), and the first group is on "the way." This was its true place: *at the commencement of that group*. But we find it only in Nikāya III.; nor is it then placed at the head, but in a very late division only. What a story it would tell us to account for this strange procedure, could it only speak!

But we also find it in the Vinaya, and there its place is so far fitting that the record, as you have seen, shows the Founder, his pondering, hesitation and inspiration over, coming to find helpers in his new mission. It is true that, for the editors of the Vinaya, its chief importance will have been the inauguration of the Sangha or monastic Order, rather than the New Word of a Gospel; nevertheless the telling is made with a fit sense of the more than earthly worth of the message.[1]

The Mantra itself is led up to with utmost solemnity of preparation in a few, but often reiterated words. These show the Founder taking up a position of authority over against his friends, claiming to be *arahā, tathāgato, sammā-sambuddho*, no more to be addressed by them as their friend and comrade. Those words mean literally "worthy-one, thus-going, rightly awakened." The first was used at the time for what our old literature would have called a "holy man." The second came to be used for any worthy disciple as well as for the Founder. The third will only have come into use long after this date as his exclusive title. In the presence of such scanty records as we have, this may seem a bold conclusion. But I think we may find support in the Vinaya accounts of the first two "Councils," recorded as held after his death and, again, a century later. Here would have been a certain reference to him by the most honorific titles, had they then been used for him. But at the first he is invariably referred to as Bhagavā, and *as that only*. At the second he is called both that and also Teacher, in the compound *Satthu-sāsana*: "the Teacher's teaching."

[1] *Vin. Texts*, I., 97 *f*. I return to this in Chapter VII.

In one passage all such teachers are spoken of as "Buddhas." Such is what we find in a record which will have taken its present shape, as written, very much later. In verses suggesting interpolation is the phrase "spoken by Buddha, kin of the sun." It is only in this incidental fashion that we find this further title; of those first three we find no mention. That he is made to claim those titles as his own at his first utterance indicates, therefore, that in the record of this we have something which has undergone editing, *much subsequent* to any touching up of the Council-records.

It is important to keep this in view just here and now, for the first utterance bears many marks of such editing. The editing has been worked under the influence of a change in values which had come up. Thus: Gotama will have spoken surcharged with the will to help his world by an inspired new word concerning the religious teaching of his day. It will not have been his to be possessed with the idea of his own infallible superiority. That he was infallibly superior will have been the tenet in the cult about his person, which was full-grown when the books came to be written down. No man who had been just torn by doubt, as was he, could have made such a claim. He is shown not only as making this claim for himself: he is also shown as making a very high claim for the religious efficacy in the *amata*, the *dhamma* (literally, the ambrosia, *i.e.* the undying, the "ought," *i.e.* ideal) which he is about to teach. Namely, "you, thus progressing as has been taught, will before long abide in (or live), having each thoroughly known, realized, attained, that uttermost goal of the Brahma-life even in the present, for the search of which men of good family rightly go forth from the home into the homeless."

Here is the loftiest aim very fitly described in terms of a culmination of personal will and effort required in each seeker. And it is one that comes fitly from a religious helper of that day in India, to whom the word *Brahma-chariya* would bear its original meaning of, as Christian tradition would say, "walking in God," and not the later depreciated meaning of a vague "best" living, or that of "celibacy," which through monastic influence it has come to bear, and still bears. Obviously it did not mean that here. I should see in the phrase *anuttaraṃ Brahmachariya-pariyosānaṃ* a genuine word of the beginning.

But not so two other phrases. *Kula-puttā*, "men of good family,"[1] has stuck in the throat of many a well-wisher to Buddhism. Does a world-gospel make its appeal chiefly to the well-born, the highly respectable as to social status? What of its drawing power for "publican and sinner"? What of Sunīta, dead-flower-sweeper, but an honoured convert? Or Chandā, poor widow, and others you will find in the Anthologies I have called *Psalms of the Early Buddhists?* And then the other phrase: "rightly go forth from home into the homeless." This has not stuck as has the other, yet should it stick no less. For it makes the gospel of the Śakyamuni a message addressed directly and chiefly to recluses or monks, to *religieux*. And so far as it is that, it is no longer a message to Everyman, the more in that it speaks here of attaining a supreme salvation "in the present"—*diṭṭh' eva dhamme*, literally, "in the very seen conditions," a common idiom for this earth-life. Now this involves the later teaching in what I will just here call the theory of the *arahan*. This is at present accepted as original teaching, just as the monastic status is at present believed to have been enshrouding the very birth of Sakya. For me neither such theory nor such status dates from this first Mantra.

The passage making this claim for the teaching belongs to a formula, of which it lacks only the first five words: "alone, withdrawn, zealous, ardent, with the self established," one of the four alternative formulas used in the Suttas to describe attainment of the status of *arahan*. The fine old terms have

[1] I have sought, in translations, to evade this literal meaning by the term "clansmen," in a quasi-Scottish sense.

become interred in estimates of monastic values. That the formula is found here is but a part of the editing which stamps the whole.

This double claim, put into the mouth of the Founder, is followed by a protest from the five friends, that he, who could win no super-insight by *tapas*, should claim to have won it without, living in "the manifold." The Founder is made to repudiate such living, or any wavering in effort, and then to repeat his summons that they attend to his claims. Repudiation and claim are made to alternate back and forth with protest three times, the former being then made for a fourth and last time. They thereupon give in and listen.

I now give a translation of the first utterance closer to the original Pali than that which is in the translations entitled *Vinaya Texts* (S.B.E., Vol. XIII., p. 94) or in *Buddhist Suttas* (S.B.E., Vol. XI., p. 146). You will find it crude, but I seek to give you the old-world wording of old-world ideas. Gotama speaks:

"These two ends, almsmen,[1] by one-who-has-left-the-world are not to be followed. Which two? That which is clinging addiction to the will-to-welfare,[2] low, pagan, of the average man, ignoble, not belonging to the Good (*attha*), and that which is addiction to the tormenting of the self, ill, ignoble, not belonging to the Good. Now by the Wayfarer not having gone up to either of these ends, a middle course has been thoroughly understood, making vision, making knowledge, which conduces to calm-after-toil, to thorough-knowledge, to understanding, to waning-out (*nirvāna*). And what is that middle course (etc.) . . .?

[1] A literal rendering of bhikkhu (Sanskrit *bhikshu*). Buddhists somewhat resent this rendering, claiming that the word has for them a spiritual meaning of, not "broken (*bhik-*) meats," but snapping of bonds. But it did mean "men of alms" at first, and we are concerned here with the "first." (Dotted lines are repetitions.)

[2] *Kāma-sukha-*. *Kāma*, desire, in earlier Indian thought nearly equalled our "will." It was growing worse, meaning merely "sense-desire." *Sukha* is happiness, pleasure, well-being.

Just this noble eightfold way—namely, right view, right purpose, right speech, right action, right livelihood, right endeavour, right mindfulness, right concentration. This is that middle course. . . . But this now, almsmen, is the Ill-noble-truth: both birth (is) ill, and old-age (is) ill, and disease (is) ill, and dying (is) ill, yoking with things not dear is ill, disyoking from (things) dear (is) ill and that he gets not what he is wanting, that too is ill, in a word, the grasping of the five groups is ill. But this now, almsmen, is the origin of ill-noble-truth: that which is craving re-becoming-ish, accompanied by pleasure & passion, finding delight here & there, namely, craving for will-to-sensuous-welfare, craving for becoming, craving for prosperity.[1] But this now, almsmen, is the ending-of-ill-noble-truth: the fading out and ending of just that craving, giving up, surrender, release, not-using. But now this, almsmen, is the going-to-ending-of-ill-course-noble-truth, just this noble eightfold way, namely, right view, right purpose, right speech, right action, right livelihood, right endeavour, right mindfulness, right concentration. At 'this Ill-noble-truth,' vision arose in me of things not heard before, knowledge arose, wisdom arose, Veda-wit[2] arose, light arose. But that now: 'this ill-noble-truth must be completely known' being completely known by me, vision arose in me . . . light arose. At 'this origin-of-ill-noble-truth' vision arose in me of things not heard before . . . light arose. But that now: 'this origin-of-ill-noble-truth must be got rid of' being got rid of by me, vision arose in me . . . light arose. At 'this ending-of-ill-noble-truth'

[1] *Vibhava.* This word, meaning "prosperity," at the time when Gotama lived, *came to mean* the opposite of becoming, *i.e.* the ending of further coming to be at death. *Vi* can mean expansion, and also disintegration. In the anthology called *Iti-vuttaka* (§ 49), a later very monastic work, the later meaning is clearly seen, and was enough to make Oldenberg hold that "prosperity" was incorrect. He did not allow for changing values *in* the Piṭakas, nor did he recognize that at first Buddhism was greater than a monk-gospel.

[2] *Vijjā*, Sansk. *vidyā*, a comprehensive term for knowledge, learning, "lore," especially Veda-lore, magical as well as religious.

vision arose in me of things not heard before . . . light arose. But that now: 'this ending of ill-noble-truth must be realized' being realized by me, vision arose in me . . . light arose. At 'this course going to ending of ill-noble-truth vision arose in me of things not heard before . . . light arose. But that now: 'this course-going-to-ending of ill-noble-truth must be made to become' being by me made to become, vision arose in me . . . light arose. Now so long, almsmen, as for me concerning these four noble truths knowledge-and-insight as-it-really-had-come-to-be, thus thrice rehearsed, twelvefold schemed, was not made clear, so long I admitted was I not thoroughly awakened to supreme understanding as to the world with devas, with demons, with brahma-(devas), as to (this) generation of recluses and brahmans, with devas and men. But when once that knowledge and insight had become clear in the way aforesaid, then I admitted I was thoroughly awakened to supreme understanding concerning the world . . . concerning (this) generation of recluses and brahmans with devas and men. But then knowledge in me and vision arose thus: unshakeable (is) for me release of purpose; this (is) the last birth; there is now no rebecoming.

"This the Bhagavā said; elated the five almsmen delighted in the utterance of the Bhagavā. But, the declaration being uttered, for the venerable Kondañya *dharma*-vision, dustless, stainless, arose, that whatsoever is an originating-thing all that is ending-thing."

I would give much to learn of the impression made on you, thoughtful and critical reader, by the first reading of this, made, not by the inevitable clumsiness of the literal English, but by the composite meaning that seeks to reach you through it. Do you see it as "composite"—that is, as trying to express more than one set of values in religious things? This is how I have come to see it. For unless we come to see it as composite in that way we shall find it baffling, shifting its ground like a quicksand; we shall see its opening clarity of issue merged in a maze of formulated refrain; we shall see it laid bare as unworthy of its sublime motive of being a call to Everyman, so to live as to be in the better way to compass in the long run his eternal salvation.

In this way the ground is shifted—you will surely see this:—"two ends" are not to be followed as not belonging to *Attha*. *Attha*, the *summum bonum*, is thus what is to be sought. But the Middle Way, which obviously is that which does belong to *Attha*, is said to lead, not to *Attha*, but to four other things. These prove to be, not so much final attainment, as preparations for it; even Nirvana was, in the Suttas, clearly defined as a getting rid of, a wasting away (*khaya*), of the springs of evil: lust, hate and stupidity (*rāga, dosa, moha*). And at the end of the discourse *another summum bonum* is substituted, to wit, "thorough awakening to supreme understanding as to the world."

Emphasis again is altered in this, that whereas at first the Middle Way is the great, the chief feature culminating in an implicit *Attha*, it is then abruptly shifted to the fourth place in a fourfold formula, in which the *chief* theme is plainly not Way, not *Attha*, but Ill. That formula has been, in a late commentary (not Buddhist), compared to a doctor's way of diagnosis; and defenders of it have found it fitly chosen by a Great Physician of mankind. But it is not a wise doctor's way *thus* to take his sick man by the hand in a diagnosis made by a hale helper. For the patient the Coué principle is best: to dwell in hope and faith—in a word, with "will"[1]—*not on the ill* and its beastly causes, but on the becoming well. Here is for the spiritually sick man the first emphasis and the last; here is the real, the best ejector of spiritual ill. If it be said: But was he not

[1] Had Coué and Auto-suggestionists been better psychologists, they would not have so attempted to oust "will" from imagination. Cf. my *Will to Peace*, 1923, pp. 41 f.

speaking to those he hoped to make his fellow-doctors, and was it not therefore a wise word to predispose them to the way of diagnosis? There would be some force in this, had he been made to approach those five men in this attitude. But he is expressly made to approach *them*, too, as a doctor to sick men, *first for their own healing*, and the argument falls.

Lastly, the sick man to be healed is reduced to one class of men, the "one who has gone forth." Here we see the worst shifting of all, the changed value. We have to turn from Everyman, seeking free play so far as may be in living as a natural, a whole man, who is admonished to bring that free play into accord with rule and order, to the world-forsaker who *has already forsworn* a life of that free play to live a semi-natural, not-whole life, for whom it only remains that he be admonished not to press that discipline too far.

But once we read the whole utterance as having been at first remembered, then the remembered words as put into a fixed wording, then as revised from a number of versions (all brought in by living manuscripts, by repeaters) into a standard oral version, then again revised, again a standard version selected or even in part re-composed, the changing values being brought to bear all the time and every time, then at length being written down, perhaps in the foreign island—*then* we shall no more be surprised at its composite character; nay, we should expect to find it so.

Accepting it as such, we may well wish we could get at what that first Word meant for Gotama Śakyamuni. I have twice ventured to try to do this, without referring, in the second effort, to the first. This should not be to the Buddhist an irreverent thing. The commentators are much given to telling us how the great man will have thought, before he is made, on different occasions, either to speak, or to refuse to speak. And they write naïvely, not seeing themselves as in any way impudent or profane. I am not suggesting odious comparisons; but be it remembered that we of to-day can have a better conspectus of the whole of their scriptures than was possible to the first compilers of those Commentaries.[1] And this conspectus makes it possible, and also reasonable, for us to see the history that is betrayed by those scriptures, when the commentators could not see, nor, for that matter, wished to see. I quote here my second interpretation.

"I am telling you of the better way in which a man should walk in life. Most men choose to walk either in the way of self-indulgence and worldliness, or in the way of being the slaves of rules. I am willing you to take a different way. It lies between the two. It is like the former because it calls upon you to walk according to your will. It is like the latter because it calls upon you to have some principle according to which you will to walk. You have yourselves the knowledge that, when two ways lie before you, one is what you would call better than the other. That is, the one is the way which if followed will lead to your doing, and so becoming, better than if you follow the other. It is not always quite clear, but a man usually knows. Now if this better way be followed as long as you live on earth, the result will be better for you when you leave the earth. And this is true for the rest of your life. You will by such choosing come in the future to the very goal of life. You will then know what it is to be utterly well, even though now you have no clear idea how or what that will be. Now you are not often well. You are often unwell in body and in mind; you are unwell in your very self. You are very imperfect; you are truly as a babe. You suffer in many ways. You want not to suffer. Use that want to become better. Use your will to choose the way to become better. Let it be your firm

[1] Thus Buddhaghosa, in his own work *Visuddhi-Magga* (= *Path of Purity*) is copious in Piṭaka citations, but the commentaries very rarely discuss any parallels between Suttas in different Nikāyas.

belief that you can become better. Word the better to yourself. See yourself in a long, long way of life, long enough for you to grow to what you do not dream of. You see but a very little of the way. As you keep on choosing the better, you will be seeing ever more and more of it. You will be wayfaring in the way to the utterly well."[1]

Do not credit me with the fancy that I here give any correct record of the original, even were I to translate it into Pali or Prakrit. I claim only that it gives the spirit of the essential message in such a way that in it Everyman can see a message to himself, from Very Man to Very Man.

In my longer work, *Sakya*, I have raised many more points than is possible here, where I will touch on only two. (1) Why, you may ask, was it that whereas *attha* is begun with, in the compound (*attha-sahita*: 'belonging to *attha*'), it should have been replaced, without, or with the affix, by those four terms, apparently as equivalents? I believe the reason for the replacing to have been that, for the later editors, *attha* had come to take on a much more literary meaning—namely, in the pair of opposed terms: *attha* (spirit or meaning) and *vyañjana* (wording or letter). Hence a more unambiguous term was felt to be necessary. You will find the later pair of terms used by the editors in the Vinaya, on the conversion of Sāriputta.[2] There was one old compound which would have sufficed, but even that became ambiguous. This was *paramattha*: highest Good, as we see it used in the Sutta-Nipāta: "with energy stirred up to win the highest Good."[3] But here again the later meaning of "highest"—*i.e.* "ultimate"—sense or meaning had come, when final editing was carried out, to be an important term in theological debate. Added to which there was yet another usage of *attha*, to mean just "matter," "thing," "affair." Indeed, one commentator gives some

[1] *Sakya*, p. 62; cf. *Gotama the Man*, p. 42.
[2] *Vin. Texts*, I., p. 146 (*Mahāvagga* 1, 23–4); also p. 113.
[3] *Araddhaviriyo paramattha-pattiyā*, ver. 68.

seven meanings of the word.[1] Thus blurred, the word was naturally edited into other terms, which, for a later day, had come to possess powerful, but *specialized* religious significance.

(2) You may ask: In the literal rendering of the First Utterance you say "Wayfarer." Is this the Pali word *Tathāgata?* And is this not a term exclusively applied to the Sakyamuni himself? Is he not represented, in the original, as the model to be followed, because he has himself "thoroughly understood," and therefore directs? I answer: This term, meaning literally the thus come, or gone (*tathā āgato, tathā gato*), was non-existent when the Founder first spoke. When first used, it will have been a term for any disciple as "Wayman," owing to the prominence first given in the teaching to the Magga, or Way. And still in the Suttas it fairly obviously means sincere follower, or "Wayman." The past participle *gata* can also bear a present-participial meaning, "going," as it does in the parallel verb *paṭi-panno,* used often to describe the disciples as "walking" rightly. There is also another such term *su-gato,* "well-going"; this is also a Way-term which we find applied in Suttas to sincere disciples, and which may well be the older of the two compounds. Both terms came, in later days, to be reserved solely for the Founder, as Wayfarer *par excellence,* well-farer Way-teacher. India, however, used *Sugatas* as a name for Buddhists till modern times.[2] I would suggest that the following passage is contributory evidence to my opinion. We read in the Second Collection that Ānanda, after his great kinsman's death, was asked by a brahman of Rājagaha whether the Order reckoned they had any one equal to Gotama? Ānanda's reply, as yet overlooked by exponents, was, "There is none such. For he was maker-to-arise of a Way not arisen, maker-to-perceive of a Way not perceived,

[1] See *KS.*, I., pp. 108, 317.
[2] See *Sarva-darśana-sangrahac:* "Bauddhas or Saugatas."

declarer of a Way not declared, he was Wayknower, Waywitter, Waymaster!" Comparing this with the usual set-piece in the Suttas, where reference to the Founder's mission and work is formally made, and which always begins with ". . . a Tathāgata arises in the world, Worthy One, Rightly-well-enlightened," the *omissions* in Ānanda's fine testimony strike us as a ray of light. We judge we are listening to a revealing word which has fortunately survived, a word from which Tathāgata and the rest would certainly not have been omitted *had it been of a later editing*.

Both terms are occasionally used of Gotama in a refrain, giving sanction to a saying as spoken by "Tathāgata, Sugata, Satthar" (*i.e.* Teacher). Of these the last is probably the term his order used for him, as we saw surviving in the record of the Second Council. The first gained in editorial popularity precedence over the others, it may well be because of the, shall we say, Messianic ideas that grew up in the "Buddha"-tradition. Namely, that Gotama was but one in a Buddha-succession, which we find in the Four Collections, as sevenfold, but which in later poems and Commentaries has grown to twenty-four! In one or both he is come or goes thus, even as did they:

> "*The way by which Vipassin went . . . by that same road did Gotama come*"

runs a line in the Elders' Anthology. As you may already know, there is in the figure and work of Gotama-Buddha nothing unique for the believer. He is but one in a world-order of five orders, that called the Dhamma-order, the order of the Compassionate Ones. Nor is he the last. The Buddhist could cheerfully subscribe to all but the last clause in the great opening to the Epistle to the Hebrews: "God" (he would term That "Dhamma") "who at sundry times in divers manners hath spoken to us by . . . hath in these latter days spoken to us by . . ." So the term, once vivid with the tradition of Everyman's Way, came to be staked off for the Teacher-way of the one great man of one "dispensation," in the Pali term, "in this Buddha-uprising" (*imasmim buddhuppāde*).

But when, in the First Mantra, we see, in the editorially inserted word Tathāgata, the Teacher viewed as a foregoing model who is to be followed, then for me all the force, all the fire, all the originality of the New Word evaporate. I hope you will come to see with me that this is so.

Let us now come to the Wayfarer in the Mantra with Ends and Middle Way put before him. Do you say: Are not the "ends" usually translated "extremes"? They are, and I think wrongly so rendered. I wish I had seen this earlier myself. Oldenberg used "extremes" in his Vinaya translation, but he changed to "Enden" in his own work *Buddha*—at least, the latest edition has this. German idiom does not lend itself to using "extremes" here. But neither is "ends" the equivalent of the Pali *antā*. *Anta* is a word of large loose meaning, only partially covered by "end." Had the meaning been "extreme," we should have found *koṭi* or *agga*. *Anta* means only "end" in the sense of "the terminal of what lies next." Hence it may mean (and is also defined as) "what is near." Compare the phrases *jīvitam maranant-ikaṃ* (life has death as end, is death-endish) and *ekam antaṃ nisinno* (seated at one side), and you will see that we have no word to coincide. It is for this that I rendered *antā* just above by "side-issues." And it is because the two ends presented are not really wholly, essentially to be eschewed, but are, on the other hand, not to be solely pursued, that the Way which is better is called Middle, or way of the Mean, the *via media*; and be it here noted that we are anticipating Aristotle[1] by at least two centuries.

Do not fling at me that, in the wording of the "ends" as courses, they are strongly condemned. They are, but that is so much the worse for the editors. It was in the tradition of these, to see, in the life of the layman, a cultivation of the

[1] *Nicomachean Ethics*, 2, 9; 3, 9.

sensuous, the sensual, the manifold allures of a distracted attention, and in the practices of the fakir, which they enumerated in a long category, that which was in an opposite way also, but not more, harmful. They narrowed down life to a select way, narrower than that of the pious brahman, let alone that of other classes. Their object was to get rid of the Much and the Many, and to value only the "one" or "oneness" (*ekatta*), and this seemed to them not the Less that it was, but a very More.

But if we restore the Mantra of Benares to a new word for just Man, for Everyman, we shall no more find this *exclusion* of the Ends a fit teaching. Everyman seeks his welfare as something pleasanter, happier, and he needs to use his senses in the search, his will in the search for a worthy, as for an unworthy quest. For we esteem Everyman in his whole life. We esteem him, as Gœthe said, in so far as he seeks *im Ganzen, Guten, Schönen resolut zu leben*. And it is clear that to do so he needs to put forth activity—that is, will—in many ways. He must be engaged on a More. At the same time, he needs to regulate that will, and live to a great extent by rule, by principle, to check himself here, to refrain there. Thus we can see that, in a mandate for Everyman given by a man we call inspired, the Ends would mean ways among which he must so choose that he combines the best in each End, avoiding excessive pursuit of any one of them.

But the First Utterance is not the only Mantra where we meet with the man confronted by ends and having to choose a middle way. There are several such contexts in the Suttas, and it is important to compare them with it. It is but reasonable to think that the new teacher, when he had lit upon such a framework for his teaching, should apply it to many important religious subjects. And whereas we have no explicit statement in these that he had recently begun to teach, they have, with one exception, the look of old sayings. There the ends are not as such condemned; but in one context a reason is given for seeing either end as an inadequate way of considering things. It is only about the Middle Way that we can see the hand of the editor. Thus, in one context,[1] one end is that the man who does the deed is the same man when he experiences the results of it, say, in the after-life. The other end is that the doer is other, a different person. In another context[2] one end is that "everything (and hence that the man) *is*;" the other end is that "nothing (and hence the man) *is*."[3] The "is," "is not" meant, at that time in India, "has static, permanent reality," or "is only transient, ephemeral, unreal." There is here no later doctrine of illusion, or *māyā*. But there will have come up, with the growth of immanent Deity, a crumbling of older faith in the permanent reality of external existence, whether of gods or things. The critical comment given is, that you have but to look around to be convinced things, in a way, are; you have but to look, as *we* say, under a time-aspect, to see things, in a way, are not.

What, now, is the middle way for the choosing thinker, not in the first Mantra, but in these other two contexts?

In an identical wording to that given in the First Mantra it is said: "not having approached either end, a middle course has been thoroughly understood by the Man-of-the-way." This course is described in the formula, the fixed set of words, assigned to the Founder when pondering his message about the causal sequence of man's life, both inner and outer. If you will turn back to what I there said (p. 77), you will see that the one term which covers all the terms, *bhava*, becoming, can only be justified as to its place by the word having come to be given a more specialized meaning. It had shared the fate of that other term *attha*. It no longer, when the formula was compiled, meant "becoming in general," it had come to mean "any given

[1] See *K.S.*, II., p. 15 (cf. p. 17), 51.
[2] *Ibid.*, pp. 12 f., 53 f.
[3] The Pali idiom of the negative is here "Everything is not."

rebirth in any given world." Used in the Upanishads, in the day of the birth of Sakya, to mean a fundamental aspect of the whole of life, it came to be applied to any given stage of life. This will have come about the more easily from two verbal accidents, as they might be called—namely, we never find "life" or "world" used in the plural, "lives," "worlds." *Jīvita*, *loka*: never *jīvitāni*, never *lokā*, save in later Pali.[1] For instance, when the term "former lives" as recollected is the topic, the term always used is "recollection of former dwellings," not "lives." It is we who have, of our modern wealth in this word, inserted "lives" into the Buddhist idiom. Again, you will have seen, in the latter part of the First Utterance, how, for "worlds" we get "the world *with* deva, *with* Māras, etc.,"[2] with evasion of the plural. So that what were just *opportunities* for Becoming, in the long way wending towards perfection, *came themselves to be called "becomings."* This must be carefully kept in mind, if we would understand the evolution in Buddhist values of the word "becoming."

Thus, the monk, as monkdom grew, put it on record that "lives," "worlds" were so many channels of "Ill." To escape those channels here and now, he had left the "world," forsaking both its duties and its pleasures. But other "lives," other "worlds" meant other channels of Ill, *i.e.* being born and dying, with the enfeeblement of age: no monopoly, for him, of earth alone. And in speaking of lives and worlds as *bhavā* (becomings), he meant these rather than becoming-in-general. But he began also to depreciate not *bhavā* only, but also *bhava*. He never, to do him justice, depreciated the thing, only the name for it. His whole teaching was a setting forth of ways and means of spiritual progress, *i.e.* of becoming, or growth. But in his records all that he retained of *bhava*—with a few notable exceptions—as a term of appreciation, was the causative

[1] Cf. *e.g.* Dhammapada Commentary.
[2] *Loko sa-devako*, etc.

form: *bhāveti:* make-become, *bhāvanā:* making-become. This verb and this noun are commended in use in all the Pali scriptures, and to a large extent reveal to us what *bhū*-forms once meant for Sakya, and incidentally go some way to make good the lack of a good word for will. The man who makes-become is he who wills. Willer is chooser. The chooser is one with two or more ways before him. Thus closely is becoming wrapped up with this teaching of Ends and Middle Way.

But you will need to read the Suttas, many of them, to get a right idea of the degree to which the monk-recorders industriously stamped upon the word "*bhava.*" No abuse is too bad for it. No category of bad vicious things but includes it. Any of it is as bad as "the least smell of filth and ordure to the nose." And much more of that sort. The worthy, moral layman might go forward in his faring (*saṃsāra*) to find, in a longer, pleasanter, if also temporary "life" elsewhere, a minimizing, a postponement of the ills of earth. But for the monk, who deemed he saw further, the one solution that really availed was so to live, even in this short stage, as to cut short the "faring" once for all, ending the "lives," the "worlds" of *bhava.* This is what I have referred to as "the arahan theory."

Let us now come back to the day of the First Utterances, when no formulas had yet come upon the scene, when "becoming" will still have had the general meaning we find in the Upanishads; let us cut out the formula from the reply, in those two contexts used to describe the Middle Way. We shall see that *the one word needed* is just Becoming. Thus: the man who does the deed is the man who hereafter reaps the result, yet as reaper, he is no more identically, statically, the same as when he was doer. There has been in him a process of change going on, not in body only, but in the very man. Sorry will he have become, if the deed was bad, bringing to him ill, let alone to others; glad will he be in the will to do yet better, if the deed bear good fruit.

Not the same, nor yet another, *he is becoming*. And so for the other context: the mighty hold over India, old and new too, in "the myth of the Word," which we see in Being (*sat*), is here attacked. Things, man with them, are in a constant flux. Yet is this no mere succession of "other things." One thing is what it is because of what it has been.

Ay, was the much later Indian orthodox retort, you "Saugatas" (*i.e.* Buddhists) say something becomes out of nothing.[1]

Not at this stage. The mystery of the ultimate Source came to be worded as *Avijjā* (nescience). But in the day of those first utterances the answer would be, to refer it to That "who is to be praised for what has in becoming become": *bhava-bhūtam-iḍyam*."[2] And who, then or now, pretends to conceive, much less understand that Well-spring?

[1] *Sarva-darśana-sangraha* (Trübner, "Oriental Series"), p. 224.

[2] Shvetâsvatara Up. 6, 5.

CHAPTER VI

THE NEW WORD: (C) THE MIDDLE WAY

WE have seen that, in the two other contexts quoted, where there are two Ends, the Middle Way is one and the same. It will evidently have originally been "Becoming," but the word has been smothered, or, if you will, expanded, in a formula about Becoming: becoming, not of the man in his growth, but of a notion about his life: about Ill. Now does the Middle Way, in that First Mantra of Benares, differ from this word "Becoming," or from this formula about Becoming? And if so, why?

As we saw, the Middle Way in that utterance is entirely different. It is not one word; it is not the formula round about that one word. Formula it is, but of a different character. It is now not a consecutive series, causal or otherwise; it is a congeries, a collection of factors or parts: *anga's*, eight in number. Well, then, why should it be different? You will say: Because the object of the choosing is here different. It is no longer one of theory or of belief as to the nature and destiny of man; it is choice in conduct, in living. To a certain extent this is so, yet is there a link between the Way here and the Way in the first of those two contexts: that, too, was connected with the way in which he reaped what he had sown. But putting that aside, the object here, in the First Utterance, is the choice of such a course as will bring about the Best fate, the highest *Attha*.

About the presence of these Eight here and the why of it, I am going to ask you to consider the taking of a bold, not to say iconoclastic step. I speak thus, knowing well how that, for the Pali scriptures and for all Buddhists of any country who would be ranked as Hīnayāna, but who call themselves of the mother-stem, the term "eightfold" is inseparably linked with the Middle Way. In fact, for any one passage, for any one reference to the Way as "Middle," you would hear or read scores, hundreds, to the Way as Eightfold. "Path" is the usual term: an unfortunate one, without justification, but one that will before very long give way to Way. The step is, that you see in the eight factors *a substitute for an earlier description,* just as those four terms for the highest Good are a substitute for *Attha,* alluded to already in the description of the Ends.

Why, you may here say, do you wish to eject this time-honoured Eight? Not for a moment would I wish to, if, where they stand, they were the fit way-mandate just then and there. Very worthy in themselves, and, as far as they go, as a Way for the Many, I only condemn them as occupying that place. They are *keeping out something bigger, something better.*

What, then, is it that, I believe, did occupy that place as the Middle Way of the First Mantra? I believe that the Middle Way once stood there as name and as symbol for just what it does in those other contexts. Here, too, the formula must go. That other formula was compiled by the monastic editor to state, to account for, the "coming to pass of this entire mass of ill": a compilation fit only for the world-forsaker, the world-shirker, the monk. In the First Mantra the man is choosing his way to uttermost welfare. So the other formula could find no place here, partial, pessimistic application as it is of the causal law. But the general idea underlying that application, and including a very different application, holds good for the Way to *Attha* here, as it holds for the vision of the True there. And that is *Bhava:* Becoming; the *Bhava-Magga,* the Way of Becoming, the faring on, in becoming ever better, ever less imperfect, ever narrowing that gap between man as he is and Man-in-the-Highest. Desire to become, Will to become, using body, sense and mind in the quest, is necessary; necessary, too, the guiding rein, the curb, the whip of rule and discipline and training. Following neither "end" alone, nor to excess, by this Midway of becoming shall the pilgrim to the topmost height fare on.

As to evidence that the eight factors are a palimpsest only: direct crucial evidence there is none. Of contributory evidence there is not a little. I will place it before you as briefly as possible.

(1) If you have followed with any degree of assent what has been said on the development of a teaching of man-as-becoming in the Upanishads, you will admit here, that to see, in the Śakyamuni, a teacher who sought to bring his religious training with a new force to the help of the Many implies, that his teaching will fit into the frame of his day. Indian teaching had never showed man as being the more, the better for those eight as *sammā*—fit or right—but it *had* taught that man was the more, the better in becoming. That there is far less of a break-away between this teaching and the new mandate than most writers would lead you to suppose I will show, when we have looked at two other groups of contributory evidence.

(2) I have used, above, the phrase "inseparably linked" about the use of the terms Way (or Path) and Eightfold. Keeping this in mind, we ask: Do we ever find, in the Pali records, the one without the other? Even if we do, it will only "prove the rule," *i.e.* test it. Yet does such testing show a rule as by so much the weaker, the more circumscribed, while remaining a rule. Now we do meet the Way without the Eight, and the Eight without the Way; and the disjuncture occurs where we should have expected to find the conjuncture. You recall the glowing, loyal testimony (p. 116) made by Ānanda to his beloved and lost teacher as the *Man of the Way*, and of nothing else as deserving mention beside it: he does not call the Way eightfold or anything else; just Magga. Here is another

fervid ascription: A *deva* is recorded as telling to the Śakyamuni the tribute paid to his work by the ruler of the next world. Dwelling on this in general terms, he goes on: "Well revealed . . . by that Bhagavā is the Way leading to Nirvana; they run one into the other: Nirvana and Way, as Ganges and Jumna flow one into the other. Such a revealer . . . we find not . . . save only him."[1] Here again is no Eight. Nor is there mention of these, nor exploitation of them, such as might have been expected, in two precious passages, where the Founder is giving what we might call an object-lesson on man's life in terms of the Way. Way-features are mentioned, but none is likened to any of the Eight.[2]

Of passages where we find the Eight without the Way I know of only two contexts: in Dīgha-Nikāya III, where, in a catechism of categories, betraying a very old summarizing of teaching, the Eight come under the Eightfold list as just the wrong Eight and then the right Eight, literally the Wrongnesses and the Rightnesses:[3] and Anguttara-Nikāya V, where are groups of ten about the wrong practices and the right practices.[4] Merely contributory evidence, I repeat, having nothing but a little cumulative strength.

(3) I next take evidence showing the great prominence of the term *bhava* (and not in the causative form only) in the Suttas. I am not merely repeating what has been said[5] on the fierce condemnation of *bhava* everywhere met with, doubtless as having come to mean "lives" and "worlds." But on this I will add, that had the subject of *bhava*, however meant, not been a burning question in the teaching, no such zest would have come to be shown in stamping on it.

[1] Mahā-Govinda-Sutta: *Dialogues*, II., p. 261.

[2] " Tissa in *Kindred Sayings*, III., p. 90; *Majjhima*, Sutta 107, in *Further Dialogues*, II., pp. 157 f. See below, p. 205.

[3] *Dialogues*, III., Sangīti-Sutta, pp. 237 f.

[4] Vol. V., p. 240.

[5] P. 122. See *e.g. Grad. Sayings* I., p. 31.

You can see parallel cases in other great religions. I am going on to show you where, by some lucky contingency, *bhava* has got left in, without the cursing, and with a glint of its original virtue surviving. So surviving, it reminds us of some atrophied "rudimentary" organ to be found, as we know, in our bodies, perhaps only in the embryo, pointing to an earlier environment than that in which we now live. Here are some:

There is, in Indian tongues, a future participle meaning a state or act which means "is to be," "may be," "should or ought to be," "is bound to be." It ends in *-avya* or *-abba*. Such a form is *bhavya*, or *bhabba*, "bound to become." Now this was a term of high appreciation to give a man in the Suttas. "Let not the little hen," it was said, "worry about the issue of the eggs she is sitting tightly on and making become; they are *bound to become* hatched chicks. So are you disciples bound to become that which is at the goal, if you desire and strive and are heedful" (I render freely).[1] Clearly with the worsening of *bhava*, *bhabba* will also come to have had a specialized meaning, yet is it none the less significant in its possibilities.

For again, we find that for a teacher to make *bhavya* or *bhabba* his subject was commendable, and only to be checked, for the hearer, by the practical issues of what it was in which he taught becoming. That it was "suitable for becoming" was not in itself enough.[2]

Take now this valuable corroboration, that a teaching of *bhava* was, for the average worthy nobleman, if not for the brahman teacher, *something new*. We read of Ānanda, cousin to the Founder, asking him: "What is this that is said: *bhava, bhava?*"[3]—a sort of question often met with in the Suttas. The reply, if we read between the lines, which are edited so as to throw discredit on *bhava*, is that, "in

[1] *Further Dialogues*, I., p. 73 and 257 (*Majjhima, Suttas* XVI. and LIII.).

[2] *Gradual Sayings*, I., p. 203 (*Anguttara*, I., p. 223), wrongly rendered in other translations.

[3] *Ibid.*, p. 203.

becoming, a man is as a seed, planted now in this world, now in that, needing for his growth the watering of will" (lit. thirst, *i.e.* desire). "Man" in the text is *viññāṇa*, mind; but when, as I have said, life in other worlds is included, *viññāṇa* means man as spirit, soul. Remember this when you read "consciousness" in translations; and note here the worsening in the use of "craving" and the like. And note equally that Ānanda is not bidden to stamp on becoming, or spew it out, as is often the bidding. Now turn back, in the same Nikāya to I., 18, 12 (in the Pali Text Society's translation it is *Gradual Sayings*, Vol. I., p. 31) and read the last two sentences. Note the foul abuse of *bhava*, and note also how obviously the two *are a gloss*, of later insertion, differing in wording from the preceding portion! Here we have the later values.

Come now with me to the Piṭaka called Abhidhamma. The fifth book is traditionally said to have been compiled (not written) to be "recited" at the Third Council, the great congress in Asoka's reign, around 240 B.C. This is very possibly true, but true only of the first few Debates, of which the whole lengthy work is made up. A monk of the new orthodoxy is debating with now this, now that monk of the older or of other teachings, all such being lumped together as heresies. The first debate is the longest and much the most important. The attacking monk is maintaining that "the man (the person, the self) cannot be known in any true highest sense (*paramattha*), viz. as distinct from mental things called *dhamma*'s." In the debate, he of the older teaching (*I* call it so) holds that "the man persists (survives) in dependence upon becoming.", This the attacker rejects, *because becoming is necessarily followed by decay*. We have seen this affecting the Upanishad teaching centuries before. But here we have a testimony, to me of the first importance, as yet quite overlooked, by myself also when translating, that "becoming" was a very basic teaching in earliest "Buddhism."

And I venture to think it appears as actually accepted

and maintained by King Asoka in his rock-and-pillar Edicts at this very date. In six of these occur the terms *bhavaśudhi* and *bhāvaśudhi*, as a goal to righteous living here, and in this context only. We are never left long in the Edicts without reference to happiness as to be gained hereafter according to conduct here, and it is variously expressed. *Śud(d)hi*, literally "purity," is a venerable term for the spiritually desirable in Indian religion from early days, and was naturally taken over, but as it were with one hand only, into Sakya. *Bhāva*, with long vowel, more usually means, not "becoming," but "being" or "state." Yet the great Sanskrit dictionary[1] defines it as "Werden, Sein"—just like that. Translators of the Edicts have ignored the former term, just as, in the Upanishads, it has been hitherto ignored or slighted, and render by "purity of soul," or "of mind," entirely ignoring the *bhavaśud(d)hi's* with the short *a*. Well, I am familiar with compounds having *bhāva* as affix, but with none having it as prefix in the meaning of "state," much less in that of "soul" or "mind." And I find these renderings very strained. It is so much more in keeping with Asoka's injunctions to link *bhavaśudhi* with his *eighty* references to "growth," and see in it "purity (to be won) by becoming." It is true we do not find *bhava-magga* (way of becoming) in the Edicts; but, then, neither do we find the Way as eightfold. Way, advance, is *implicit* everywhere. But the three main ideas made *explicit* are Dhamma (the standard of right conduct), growth-and-becoming to be striven for, and ulterior happiness beyond this life. I would not have any reader suppose me to mean that *bhāva* may not be rendered by "being," as in the middle-Upanishadic antithesis (of the Shvetâsvatara, 5, 14): *bhāva-abhāva*. But I would say this much, that this compound could equally have been rendered by "becoming-non-becoming." It is clear that the European *Werden, Sein* and Becoming, Being lend themselves far less to the approxima-

[1] Böthlingk and Roth.

tion that is possible in *Bhava, Bhāva*. The fact remains, that Asoka uses both forms in the compound, but in his contexts, reiterating "growth," leaves it highly probable that he in both cases meant becoming.

(4) I come finally to a context which for me is also contributory evidence, albeit it has never as yet been held to point that way. I ask you to come back to the impressive scene where Gotama is seen wavering as to whether to seek the Many as a teacher. I left that scene promising to reconsider it when we were more ready to do so.

In the vision (which is also an audition) the *deva* implores him to teach, saying that unless he do, men will perish. The text, which is obscured by Oldenberg's over-free rendering (S.B.E., Vol. XIII., p. 86), but not by Neumann or Chalmers, runs literally thus: "There are beings who happen to have little dust in their eyes; from not hearing of *dhamma* they are perishing; *they will be* learners of *dhamma*." The last clause we translators have always rendered by "there will be they who understand (*dhamma*)." Yet the verb, which is "know" with the prefix "*ā*" [1]: gets the meaning rather of learning or coming-to-know,[2] as you may see in Fausböll's Sutta-Nipāta (S.B.E., Vol. X., p. 196, ver. 1063). But the more important change I would suggest is, that "they will be" can equally well mean "they will become," thus: "learners of *dhamma* are *men-who-will-become*."

You who follow the scene in the Pali may say: Surely in prose we should have had the verb put last, not first in the clause. Well, look a little further, where the *deva's* urging is repeated in verse. Here the *bhavissanti is* put at the end (its more natural place, if the meaning was not, as it were, to balance the preceding "there are": *santi*, as we have it in the prose only). And, in this long-unwritten, much-edited scripture, be it remembered, a version

[1] *Aññātāro*, from *ā-jān*.

[2] As in *connaître*, *erkennen*.

in metre is credited with being older than the corresponding passage in prose, if only because the saying was put into metre to be the more easily memorized, and that, once metricized and *chanted*, change was harder than in the more freely *talked* prose.

If my suggestion is ruled out, it may be because our word "become" is too weak to pass here as the synonym, which it is often granted to be, for "growing, developing." But when we pass in review that much exploiting of the word we found, as a new growth, in the Upanishads, and see the *bhū*-forms implying that potency of growth which our "become" implies but feebly, we may concede a significance in this passage not seen before.

Anyway, we next read of the Founder, thus appealed to, considering his fellow-men in their different stages of growth or becoming as being more or less able, ready, to "see," to learn, to receive. Then comes the simile of "lotuses or water-lilies" growing: *saṃvaḍḍhāni* (the *saṃ* indicates process, continuity) in a pool, some yet submerged, some up to the surface, some upraised, with unwetted blossoms. It is a parable that may possibly have been so linked with his teaching that iconography came to present him seated on a lotus-flower.

A couplet follows in which he says, he had refrained from speech, "aware of hurt"; "Open to them who hear are the gates of the immortal; let them send out faith!" But these lines are surely the ardent response of a poetic recorder! I do not hear a man like Gotama giving this version of any reply he may have made. Rather do I see him, like Job when he said: "Behold! what shall I answer thee? . . . I will lay my hand upon my mouth!" It had been a tremendous moment of crisis, and there will have been flowing in upon him mightily the surge of will—will that was growth in the very man of him, will for the message that was now made plain. Will and speech were now utterly pre-empted. And he went forth to teach his Way of growth, of becoming.

But before he has gone all the way to find his audience, on whom he could begin, he is said to have met one man, who accosted him, it is said, "between Gaya and the Bodhi-tree."

It is worth while to repeat here, that Gotama, wishing at first to find co-workers, bethought him of his former teachers, Āḷāra and Uddaka. They, he thought, "will quickly learn it." (Note that here again translators have "understand it" (*ājānissati*).) In either case "an invisible deity" (*i.e.* deva) is recorded to have told him that those two had died a week and a day ago respectively. With the curious inconsistency you may find in the Piṭakas about the nature and attribute of omniscience ascribed to (and claimed by) the Founder, the editors have left in this implicit confession that he did not, after the enlightenment, know everything; *that there were beings who knew what he did not!* [1]

But this is by the way. I mention it here, in repeating, it was not just converts he sought at first, but comrades in his mission. The reason he is said to have given, so far as it is not the way of the recorder—it often is—to put reasons for the Founder's acts, is that those two teachers were "clever, wise, learned, with vision hardly dusty." Now a Teacher who wills to help Everyman will not seek out just this sort of man to "convert" him. To us who have Christian Gospels before us, the quest will seem natural to seek co-workers first. But such has been the power of the Buddha-cult in Buddhist lands, that all men are made to appear as dwarfed beside "the Buddha," and fellow-workers as so many sheep to be herded by him.

The man he met was one Upaka, called an *Ājīvika*, a mendicant "friar," who is met with again later in the scriptures. Some radiance and ardour in the man of the New Will must have been manifest, and, though it is in a

[1] In the Majjhima Commentary the deva's news is held to be insufficient, and omniscience is given as the reason for Gotama's knowing.

stock form of words, Upaka asks, if he have found an inspiring teacher? The reply is recorded in bombastic terms of no teacher being henceforth needed. Upaka replies: You claim by your words to be infinitely victorious? Gotama is made to qualify his claim as one of spiritual conquest only. Upaka, "with head-shaking,"[1] responds with the one word *hupeyya* (in the Vinaya, *huveyya*). This is, we learn, a dialectical form of *bhaveyya, bhuveyya*. Translators render it: "It may be!" But if we discard that exegetical head-shaking, it may possibly have been the exclamation: (Then) one may become! Or, (Man) may become! Or, discounting a little more editing of long ago, and substituting a new editing, it may have been originally handed down as *Bhavya!* "one" (or, man) is to become!"

Surely, you may say, the fact that the dialectical (or patois) form has persisted these many centuries militates against such an alteration being possible. And indeed I do not press the point, as contributory evidence. But we need to put ourselves, much more than we do, in the place of those Buddhist editors. Consider! In the first place, they had to make standardized versions out of the repeatings of *bhāṇakas* come up for the revision from scattered *āvāsā*—early settlements—where different dialects were spoken. Save for the relatively late introduction of writing in India, there was nothing unique about this. Our monastic editors had the same trouble to standardize English MSS. and the three groups of dialects: Northern, Midland and Southern, or Northumbrian, Mercian and West Saxon. In the next place, those Buddhist editors belonged to a time of changed values. Their main concern was not to get at historic truth at any cost to their beliefs, but to check the persistence and propagation of terms still used by some repeaters, which *they*, the "Church," had come to hold erroneous. How much better, in such

[1] Neumann has "bowing his head," but the word is "shaking."

a case, would a dialectical term like *hupeyya*, used at some "provincial" settlement of the Order, hide the term *bhavya* used by other repeaters, a term which they deprecated and wished to do away with. I say not that this did happen. I say only that I can see it may have happened. I do not know of any parallel to this odd word *Hupeyya*. There was a strong reason for cutting it out and replacing it by proper Pali diction, if there had not been some stronger motive in retaining it. For those editors *this motive was there!*

(5) I come lastly to a very different sort of evidence. In certain Suttas placed in one little group we find the Middle Way once more separated from the Eight factors, but this time it is not in any quite general reference, such as might naturally exclude any encumbrance of attributes. At the end of the "Threes" in the Anguttara-Nikāya [1] we come upon the Middle Way described, in succession, not as "eightfold," much less as "of Becoming," but as made up of certain other categories, fourfold, fivefold and sevenfold. These lists are held in highest worth in the Suttas, and are said to have been commended to the Order to be, when learnt, practised, "made-to-become" and expanded for the welfare of devas and men, in one of the final utterances to the Order by the Founder. Taken together with the "eightfold" way, they came, at a later date, to be called just "things belonging to Bôdhi," and then, "the thirty-seven things belonging to Bôdhi." You will find them treated in detail and in an interesting order in the Great Vagga of the Saṃyutta-Nikāya (*Kindred Sayings*, Book V.). Those Anguttara Suttas referred to set forth the Two Ends and the Middle Way *as Triads:* (1) the sensuous man, (2) the fakir ascetic, (3) the middle way. And each set of Bôdhi-things (*dhamma's*) is, as it were, tried in turn, as if any one of them *would do equally well* to describe the Way.

[1] *Gradual Sayings*, I., pp. 273 f.

Here again there is nothing we can call evidential. But I suggest that, when the Order had decided that Becoming must by no repeaters be suffered to remain in the First Mantra, and some revered term or set of terms was felt needed to fill the gap, *each of these lists was tried*, and taught, in an interim lasting possibly for a considerable interval. For monks are very human, nor are they the only organizers who have experimented with now this, now that.

These five groups of contributory evidence, not one of which goes very far when taken in isolation, do present cumulatively a ground of some firmness for the belief that the eight "parts," now so tightly bound up with the Way, were not in the original mandate.

Why, then, we may ask, and it remains a duty for me to ask, was it finally decided to select the Eight Fitnesses, and not one of those other "Bôdhi" categories? Let us again get back to the revising Sangha editors and their day, this being most likely the time of the great Patna revision. They had come to dislike the term Bhava very strongly, as then meaning "lives" and "worlds" (*bhavā*). But some teachers clung to the word and taught it as in the First Utterance. (Remember: all was spoken; there were no books.) It was decided that the word and the teachers had to go. Repeaters were charged to make the Middle way one of the lists called "of Bôdhi." But it was a clumsy business; *all* were by tradition equal in worth; none was best; to repeat all was too long.

Now there was the ancient threefold category of man's activities, common to Aryan peoples, often in Sakyan teaching, of "deed and word and thought." And there was one formula, or rather a dual one, the eight wrongnesses, the eight rightnesses, which included these. Here, it was held, was a short but comprehensive description of a way to be followed; and not by the monk only. Right speech, action and livelihood appealed to all men; so did right effort, mindfulness and views and purpose. And if *samādhi* (concentration) implied in India a more than moral, wise living, an interest in spiritual things, here was no more unreasonable appeal for the layman than is the Eucharist for the Christian layman. And so the change was made, and "becoming" remained alive only in the causative form, to mean what we might call developing, cultivating, but with its intensive force as man's essential nature drained away, and also its extensive force, its implying namely both the necessity and good fortune of carrying on the Becoming in progress through other lives, other worlds.

One more alternative as possible in the original wording of the way in the First Mantra may be considered. There is an ancient view, in the Suttas, of the Way as a gradual course by "Four Ways and Four Fruits." The first Magga is called "Winning of the Stream"—that is, virtually a "launching on the stream" of career bound for ultimate *Attha* (*sōt'apatti*). This might be equated with the Christian "conversion." The moment of realizing this was called its Fruit (*phala*). And this was when there had been elimination of any very immoral habits. The next stage was the "(Only) Once coming back" (*sakad-āgāmin*), namely from another world to earth, implying in its fruit the elimination of all but a residual trace of evil tendencies. The third stage was "Not Coming back" (*an-āgāmin*), implying a yet cleaner elimination. The fourth and culminating stage was the consummate "worthiness" called *arahatta*, which was virtually identical with *nirvana*, to become *parinirvana* at the next, the final dying of the body.

In the formula of the Way so detailed, whereas Becoming is inherent in the wayfarer, the objectionable word *bhava* does not occur, and the implication of "making the way to become" (*maggaṃ bhāveti*), a phrase we saw in the First Utterance, is made all but explicit. Here, too, we have the ancient value in the way as involving life in many worlds. I may add, that this formula is always kept separate from the Way phrased as eightfold, so much so, that survival of two Ways, or a dual teaching of the Way, suggests itself to the reader of the Piṭakas, who is baffled at the apparent mutual independence of the two.

The truth about the two is, that we have here a case of a "rudimentary" organ becoming atrophied almost under our eyes. In it we see Becoming, as a way of life as being a very long journey for each man, being slowly squeezed down to our own modern cry of "one life only," under the growing influence of the monk vogue. We may see this, both in the terms that came to be chosen and also in the lack of fit terms. Thus: so much is the will to no more "lives" (*bhavā*) becoming the ideal, rather than perfection *as requiring the opportunity of lives*, that man's career is measured off in terms of Less remaining, not of More achieved, or of a "Nearer-to-Thee": *e.g.* in the terms: a "once back," a "not back," viz. to birth and dying. It is as if Xenophon's demobilized soldiers were wayfaring in terms solely of parasangs done, and not of growing nearness to that view when they shouted "The sea! The sea!" and the homeland. Again, if you will consult *Points of Controversy*, Vol. I., p. 4, on "Putting away corruptions piecemeal," you will see how a contemptibly sophistical argument is maintained by the apparent lack of a term for qualitative becoming, the debate turning on the word *odhiso* as implying quantitative, or atomistic increase. Nor do we find any word for "stages" in the Way. Each stage is spoken of as a Magga. We cannot tell when the names for the stages came in. But it is noteworthy that there is no mention of them *where we should have looked for them*, viz. in an early attempt at a psychology of them in the first book of the Abhidhamma Piṭaka (*Buddhist Psychological Ethics*, §§ 362–4).

In the *Points* debate, we can see the Way of the stages

moribund. Preserved out of respect for the tradition, they are too gradual for the short-cut theory of the monk. For him slow growth was not the one and only way, but salvation was to be won at a bound here and now—was to be "leapt forward into," as you will see in the later book *Milinda Questions* (S.B.E., Vol. XXXVI., p. 200).

That the Way stood, in the First Mantra, as just Middle, without further description, is, I hold, equally untenable. As a Mantra about Ends and Middle Way it is already a very slenderly worded framework on which to hang so vital a message. If we take out the eight "angas," judging that they did not originally describe the Way, and do not insert the vital thing meant by the Way, we shall be left with an adage of worldly wisdom and prudence only, no loftier than the Greek "Nothing too much," or Aristotle's "The middle character is in all cases to be praised," without even his tilting us towards an occasional more or less, the better to "hit the mean."[1] As a pupil commented to me, "If you take out what the Way to be chosen stands for, the Mantra loses the right to figure as a world-gospel. It's not enough; means too little." Its Centre is the man choosing. Or in yet more general terms, it is the man exercising will—the willer. But the man wills *because he is man-in-becoming*, not just man-in-being.

One of the first abiding impressions made upon me now nearly forty years ago by the study of "Buddhism" was to see in it a gospel and discipline of will without a fit word for it. Great stress was laid on words for effort, endeavour, *i.e.* ways of putting forth will. Desire-words were there but depreciated. Will was smothered in "mind." Much later came the conviction that will without "becoming" was as the hand without the arm; was like a squirrel turning a wheel in a cage. Cluttered up with a

[1] *Nicomachean Ethics*, 2, 9, 9 . . . "but we ought to incline sometimes towards excess, sometimes towards deficiency."

consideration of eight ways of thought, word and deed, the main framework of Man choosing the best road to that Best Which or Who he, by his very nature, is becoming, is "bound-to-become," is obscured, is lost to view. But without the eight details, ill fitting in a general Mantra, and with that key-word which the eight do but try to body out, and inadequately at that, we get a really great gospel for Everyman, a great one and a new one. No one so much as the man of India has been, by priestly biddings, hectored and doctored, reined and prodded as to what he is to say, think and do on this occasion and on that. You must read to realize. Here, in this Mantra, he becomes "captain," not "of his soul"—that is absurd—but captain because he *is* "soul."[1] *He* is to steer his ship. And he can, for his compass stands not on a teacher's deck, but within himself. To this we shall return.

Very near at moments did Rhys Davids and Oldenberg come to see the presence of this Becoming in the very man. But they were here, if only here perhaps, as butterflies, alighting and flitting off again.[2] You cannot do that with a mighty concept like Becoming. Either it means, in the very man, nothing, or *it means everything*. Realization of this would have involved a recasting of their points of view. For in the fact and working of it lies man's very guarantee of ultimate salvation. And this, I believe, is what Gotama's first utterance meant for him.

[1] "I am the captain of my soul," Henley.
[2] Cf. *e.g. American Lectures*, p. 122; *Buddha* (6th ed.), pp. 143, 289.

CHAPTER VII

THE WAYFARER

When we ask ourselves: Who am I? this may be answered in terms of the way in which we may be known by other men. We are then describing "the man" as "known to men." But we may reply differently; we may reply to ourselves only. We shall then say: I am that-who-experiences, that-who-knows, who wills, feels, is happy, sorry and so on. In text-book language: That who is the subject of all that happens to "me." Here we shall need to name no name, no class nor calling, no nation nor race, no period of time, no reference to this or that group of relations. We are just "I" in an innermost way, and are not fixing ourselves in any way outside that Inner. As we might say, we are at the very heart of the man, "inside" all relations to this and that. Discounting all these, we are valuing a residuum, left over, as the very inexpugnable "Me."

We may ask further: Can we, outside those relations, say anything more that is true about this Me? Well, there is still the time-relation: I was yesterday, I am to-day, I shall be to-morrow. This relation embraces, in a way, those others. But if some one say: What if to-morrow you die? we are then up against this: In that case either I shall be, or I shall not be. I know this much for certain—my body will not be, that is, be mine in the sense in which it is to-day. We call it dead. Nor will my mind be, in the sense in which it is to-day, since I shall not have the body, with brain, nerve, muscle, to show the working of mind. I shall therefore, in a way, be without mind. What will be left of it, or of all that inner world, which I tell myself is "I"?

Here is a very important question, because by our answer we shall be saying how far we judge whether we, as described in that "inner way," are just body and mind, or are something more. And because, by our answer, we shall be confessing to a conviction about our very self. As that "I" we admit we are something that does not seem to be covered by mind, let alone body. For if that "I" were covered by mind, then the mind, in losing its vehicle, the body, in death, will be to that extent crippled, impaired; and so, as being still "I," after body goes, we shall be a lesser "I" than we were. We should not say a musical composer was not equally, much less more as composer, if he were bereft of any instrument by which to express himself, including means of writing what he composed. We should say he was to that extent the less as composer. His work, "head"-composed only, would not come into any being deserving the name. As musician he would be sterile. We see by this what body means for us. It is a means of giving "more-being" to what we judge we really are.

This important matter comes into our subject from the very beginning. In India's religious teaching it was never doubted that the body never meant the whole man. There was visible man (*rūpa*), but there was something more. That "more" we in our day tend to value as mainly, or even wholly mind. But that was not how men thought in India 600 B.C. There was body, but there was also the man himself.[1] But he was not then considered as being mind in any way. Mind was a collective way of wording man's inner activities, such as knowing, purpose, speech, feeling, becoming and the like. He could thus be appraised in many ways. He was he, but his *karman*, or action was manifold, both inward and outward.

[1] *Nāma* as contrasted with *rūpa*, otherwise *puruṣa*, Pali, *purisa*.

But just at this time there was beginning to be a newer value of that inner manifold action. There had lived and taught and passed a man, of whom nothing beyond this fact and his name has survived: Kapilă. Associated with this name is his teaching, in which he attempted to show, in those inner activities, something as being different from "the man," and yet as systematic in its ways, as is the body. This was not to see in either or both active systems, the whole man. On the contrary, so far as we can gather as to what was his original teaching—for it came to be much elaborated later—he sought, by disentangling the very man from mind, as well as from body, to establish a sep arate being for the very man even more clearly than before.

When the Sakyan movement began, this teaching was beginning to attract many. It was what we should now call the beginning of a psychology. It was discussed by brahman teachers, as we see in the older Upanishads, who betray its attraction. Some were dubious about its being a good thing. It might, they feared, make men forget the minder in the mind. Thus the teacher Kaushītaki says: "Let no man try to find out what speech is, let him know the speaker; let no man try to find out what seen-thing is, let him know the one who-sees . . . what doing is, let him know the doer . . . or pleasure and pain, let him know the experiencer . . . or going, let him know the goer . . . or what mind is, let him know the knower." This was not, of course, of interest for Everyman. It is the teachers who, in such matters, get affected, and ultimately Everyman, more or less, through them. This is just what happened in Sakya, in Buddhism. You cannot read the sayings, or "Suttas," without seeing at every turn how the speakers, or at least the editors, had become preoccupied with this matter of mind as a system parallel with that of body, and how, as the Brahman teachers had foreseen, the man, the mind-er, gets pushed aside, and mind, or mind-divisions put in his place.

This pushing aside came in time to be expressed as: The "man" cannot be "got at" (*upa-labbhati*) really and ultimately (lit. in the highest sense); we can only speak of him as so many *dhammas*—that is, things-as-presentable-to-mind, possible experiences, bodily and mental. This looks like an implicit denial that there was any real mind-er beyond the minding. But still later, viz. by the fifth century A.D., this is indeed what Buddhist teaching descended to: "There is no doer, only doing; a way, but no wayfarer"[1] and the like. Now this is known as the doctrine of Not-self (*anattā*).

It may be you will find that Buddhists and Buddhist propaganda will not define the doctrine like this. The learned may say: There is no denying here the empirical self, the self that is a complex or product of all we experience. It is only the metempirical self, the ultra-experience-self, that is denied. To this I would say: Let us not make apologetic distinctions, taken from our Western modern vocabulary, in a literature where we find none made, none held to need the making. You will not find parallels to those terms in them. Let us discuss just what we find.

The propagandist will say: *Anattā* means non-egoism, unselfishness. To this I say: That is a purely modern interpretation. Use the old term for an idea you will not find worded in the Piṭakas, if you will. But do not think to find *anattā*, as unselfishness or the opposite, in so many terms, *there*. Egoism and altruism are even for us modern terms. And so far from "selfishness" expressing indulgence in our worst self, as with us, you can only hope to understand early Indian and Sakyan thought if you see in the quest of the self not a very detestable[2] tendency, but the noblest religious pursuit of man. I have yet to find out

[1] Buddhaghosa, *Path of Purity*, III., p. 609; and *e.g. Dīgha Nikāya Commentary*, I., pp. 197 ff.

[2] I have lately read in a novel "self" referred to forthright as "le *moi* haïssable": the detestable I.

when and why arose our tendency (when once we began to see in "self" a noun, and not only an adjective for "same" [its oldest use] or a pronoun) to use "self," by preference, in a depreciated sense. "Selfish" and its noun do appear as always so used. But for Samuel Johnson "self" as noun does not exist; in Shakespeare there is for the adjective and pronoun no condemnation, unless prefixed to an anti-social term.

It was perhaps Sir William Hamilton, with a culture including Kant and Maine de Biran, who, at the parting of the ways of psychology from philosophy, definitely made "self" a noun for us: "The self, the I, is recognized in every act of intelligence as the subject to which that act belongs." Here at least the new noun is made quite unmoral, dissociated from both egoism and altruism. Of this pair of terms the latter is of the last century only, and the former, as "egotism," only meant for Johnson a lapse of good style in speech and writing.

We were still a long way from the old Indian point of view belonging to the time when the Śakyamuni began to teach. We still, in our popular use of the noun "self," are influenced by the preoccupation with the meaning of "selfish." To get at the Indian point of view, an approach at least is made if, for "self," you *mentally* say "spirit," and then "Holy Spirit." I shall return to this.

There is one other interpretation of the term *anattā*, which is now, an eminent layman tells me, taught by the Church or Sangha in Ceylon. This is, that *anattā* means "a state of non-independence, non-absoluteness. No group or material is independent of others; the fact of continuous mobility makes an absolute state in nature impossible." [1] I mention this as an illustration of changed values, of changing values, revealed in Buddhism under its manifold changed skies. *Attā* has come to mean, not the very

[1] Dr. W. A. de Silva in *Religions of the Empire*, ed. by W. Loftus Hare, London, 1925, p. 155.

man or self alone, as it meant for India during and after the birth of "Sakya." It has come to mean essence in general, or "own-being": *svabhāva* (a word not found in the Piṭakas). *Attā* has come to imply an entirely static state. But this is just what I find Gotama seeking to correct and expand, substituting, for "being" in the Man, "becoming." Not only had matter its transiency, not only mind; the man also was ever changing. But fundamentally *his* changing was an ever-becoming, from which decay, waning, was alien. *His* youth is of "the Immensities, the Eternities." The fact that this change in values, whenever it began, has come over Buddhist orthodox teaching in Ceylon is of considerable interest. It may betray discontent with the miserable repudiation of the reality in the man, of the something More in him behind body and mind, a repudiation which is patent in Buddhaghosa, and also in opinions I have received by letter from Buddhist monks. But here we are concerned, not with any such modern evolutions, but with that well-spring which was in the original mandate.

The Suttas offer a curious midway position in the shrinkage of the full Indian concept of the self, as at once Deity and potential man. At the same time, this midway teaching is a mixed teaching. If you become a reader of the Suttas this may leave you baffled. It has left writers on Buddhism baffled, and they have too quickly leapt to the conclusion that "the Buddha told men they had no souls"—stated to me once in so many words by a very competent (English) preacher and writer, but crudely misrepresenting the Suttas, let alone the Founder and his first men. It is impossible to deal exhaustively here with this mixed position, but if you will always remember those Suttas as taking final written shape under circumstances of changing values and then of changed skies, if you will further remember that a mission gospel, simple and direct in its first appeal, becomes more and waveringly manifold as, in its growth, it sweeps in some of the environing culture of succeeding generations, you will admit that complexities and inconsistencies become inevitable. And hence it is that, in the Piṭakas, you will find passages, *especially metrical passages*, upholding the Upanishadic teaching about the reality of the man or self. You will find popular teaching inconsistent with the denial of such. Just as you will also find passages revealing (*a*) a mainly negative affirmation about the self, (*b*) a preference for using mind and mind-terms instead of "man" or self, (*c*) a few passages indicating an unwillingness to admit the existence of a "self" at all. Under (*c*) it is not clear, whether the "self" who is not conceded is the Divinity in man, or the very real man or spirit himself.

But you may now be saying: Have done with so much preamble; tell us if there be any pronouncement of the Śakyamuni himself about the self which may be reckoned as dating, like the First Mantra, from the start of his teaching? There is, and here it is.

Take up the Vinaya, where we left it at the end of that Mantra and its supplementary matter. Or turn first rather to a few pages later (p. 116).[1] We here see Gotama, sitting near the roadside, asked by some men of his own class (*kshatriyas* or aristocrats) whether he had seen a woman? The little story, crudely mistold, probably from a shadowy memory of what he will himself have repeated, shows that a woman had made off with some properties of theirs. He was still unknown as a teacher, but not, as we saw above, unknown as a very earnest student. If they address him as "the lord, the adorable one," and not as just *kumāra*, the class appellation, this but shows the editor busy.

The brief reply is a very precious survival betraying something historically true, since *it would never have been interpolated later*. "What have you, kumāras, to do with

[1] Text: *Mahāvagga*, I., 14.

a woman? Were it not better that you were seeking the self?" They admit this is true, and he says: "Sit down then and I will teach you Dharma." Here the historic interest ends, for, alas! what he is said to have taught is a little set piece, such as is often given in similar response elsewhere, and which, as a New Word by a new teacher of his genius, is unthinkable.

Now translators have, in every case known to me, rendered "self" here in the European modern way, not in the early Indian way. Namely, by "yourselves." The Pali is not "selves," nor is there a "your"; it is just the sole singular noun "self" (*attānaṃ*). "Self" was then and there not used in the plural, nor with a pronoun. We do find "*me attā*," but this is not "my self"; it is "for me the self," *i.e.* in my judgment. Translators have willed, and rightly, to see a religious allusion in the reply. How for him at this stage could there be any other fit reply? Bespoken was he, I repeat, in all he said. But they have seen it with eyes of Christian tradition, namely, as meaning the losing or finding, *i.e.* the saving, of "one's soul." And this is not wholly wrong; on the contrary. But *for the Indian* this would mean the finding of God within you, the losing of God from within you, of God Who is the Self of you, your true highest self. If we deny this, we must wipe out the whole preceding religious teaching of India in force before and during the day of which we speak. In that teaching, the quest of the highest Self is enjoined *in the very words* used here by Gotama. "What is here in this Brahma-citadel that should be searched out, that one should want to understand," is the older saying; later it is repeated: "This Self" . . . a number of titles of Deity follow, including "Becoming" (*Bhava*), . . . "assuredly one should desire to know, he should be searched for."[1] And others could be cited.

We can get yet further into the Indian religious outlook

[1] *Chānd: Up.* 8, 1, 1; *Maitri*, 6, 8.

of the day, if we see in Gotama's reply an instance of that play on words which the Indian was so fain to use. Thus: in the religious teaching of that day the word "man" (*purusha*) was used as synonymous with "self," with Divine self. "This shining immortal Man in the body, he verily is this self, this Brahman, this All," etc., etc.[1] Early in the growth of Sakya this use of man (in Pali *purisa*) was dropped, while the use of "self" as connoting the Divine mystery in the man was retained for a time, and so we get in our passage the word "self." But earlier, it will have been likelier that the saying was repeated with the word "man," changed later to "self." How apt, then, does the reply become: "What have you, gentlemen, to do with 'woman'? Were it not better you were seeking 'Man'?"

Now turn back to the end of the first utterance. After a few words on the coming-in of the five friends, inserted here, among the many rules and their sanction, to show a start made with the monk régime in alms-getting, we come abruptly upon a second Mantra. Vinaya is not "history," and we can place this more plausibly after the episode just discussed. For we can then imagine the five co-workers both hearing him tell the episode, and add the solemn *caveat* which is the very kernel of the Mantra. Not even for a Buddhist is there impiety in this rearrangement. The Vinaya compilers took certain venerable Sayings and embroidered them on to the Story of the Rise of the Order. It was natural from their point of view to wish to begin with talks to the first "converts" only, who came to be looked upon as monks *from the first*. After that came lay converts. This order, in view of the greater prestige assigned to monks, is hierarchical rather than historical.

As to the Mantra itself, it is conceivably what he actually said to the kumāras, or is at least a part of that. And I have called it mainly a Warning, because with the new

[1] *Brihad. Up.* 2, 5, 1.

interest in the study of mind (known later as Sānkhya) springing up, there was special need of enforcing what the inquirers about Gotama should *not* "seek as the Self." Body, of course not, but neither was the man, the self to be found in mind. Mind was not mind-er.

Here it is: "The seen-thing (or body, *rūpa*) is not the self. Were now this seen-thing the self, it would not conduce to hindrance; it might get to say: Thus let (my) seen-thing become for me; thus let (my) seen-thing not become for me. But inasmuch as the seen-thing is not self, therefore does seen-thing conduce to hindrance and does not get to say: Thus let (my) seen-thing become for me; thus let (my) seen-thing not become for me. Feeling is not the self. Were now this feeling the self, this feeling would not conduce to hindrance; it might get to say: Thus let (my) feeling become for me; thus let (my) feeling not become for me. But inasmuch as feeling is not the self, therefore does feeling conduce to hindrance and does not get to say: Thus let feeling become for me; thus let feeling not become for me." ('Hindrance' is also 'infirmity.')

This wording is now repeated for "perception" (or consciousness, *saññā*), for "activities" (or plannings, *sankhārā*) and for mind (or survivor, *viññāṇa*). Then:

"What think you of this: Is seen-thing permanent or impermanent? It is impermanent. But the impermanent (thing), is it unwell or happy? It is unwell. But that which is unwell, impermanent, a changing-thing: is it now fit to consider that in this way: 'This (is) mine; this one I am; this one is for me the self?' It is not. Therefore here whatever seen-thing, whatever feeling, perception, activities, mind there be, whether it be past, future, present, belonging to the self or external, gross or subtle, low or excellent, far or near: all body . . . *all* mind should be viewed as it really has become, with right wisdom, thus: in these words: 'It is not mine; this one am I not; this one is not for me the self,'

"Seeing this, monks, the Ariyan disciple who has learning holds in no worth either seen-thing or feeling or . . . mind; holding in no worth he wanes; through waning he is set free; knowledge comes:—'as freed I am free!' He understands: 'Destroyed (is) birth! Lived is the holy life! Done the-what-should-be-done! No hereafter in thusness!'"

"What think *you*," reader, of this? For myself, I would say this: The concluding paragraphs are for me a gloss inserted by the monk for the monk. It has nothing in it for Everyman. It is no word in a world-gospel. A world-gospel brings to men a More in their life, something fraught with an unfolding of a richer fuller manifold for them as alive, in whatever world they may be living, and not pointing to just riddance, the done-with, the waning out.

Next, there is much stumbling about among attempts at an analysis of that which in the man is invisible to men—his inner world of mind. Here the primitive Indian analysis of man has survived in the word *rūpa*, literally, shape, but used always as object of sight: "seen-thing." The other part, the "more" in the man: *nāma* or name has, in the new Sānkhya vogue, got split up, split up, not in the Sānkhyan way, but as affected by later academic teaching in Sakya alone. And this way is not so much four factors making a whole;—it was not so atomistic—as four names for man's inner world. Centuries later it was stated that these *khandhas*[1] were expressly selected to show there could not be found, in any term for that inner world, any residual self![2] Late they certainly are, later, that is, than the century we are now considering. Nor can we fitly hear an inspired missioner setting out with a Mantra of this quasi-scholastic phrasing.

[1] Sansk: *skandha's;* literally, heaps; usual translation: aggregates, groups. Words for "process": *pavatti*, *vīthi* seem to have been found later.

[2] *Path of Purity*, III., pp. xiv, 564.

And as to the little twice-quoted "tag" about "mine" and "for me" and "I": here we may see an actual saying still surviving from early Sānkhya, brought in, as it always is in the Suttas, as something from without. In Sānkhya it is used to assert the detachment of the real self or "man" from all that (as *we* say) his "organism" would be busied about in a corporeal state. That self was too divinely pure for such intermixture, was just passive.

But in Sakya—that is, in its later development—a very different interpretation came to be given, and it is one that both Buddhists and European writers have held to. This is, that since the visible shape is not the self (or divinely potential man), nor is mind (the later equivalent of "nāma") the self, *there is no self!*

This inference is, on the face of it, so curiously unjustified by the text as it stands, that we are compelled to see in it something that has grown out of causes we do not at once take into account. For it suggests that the self is to be entirely comprised under and within the body and mind, if it is to found there at all. Thus it would be correct to say: I pull my typewriter to pieces, but I find in it no writer, *therefore* typewriter does not include a writer—that is, if the writer, to exist at all, must be part of the machinery. If, however, the typewriting person be not included in the mechanical matter and process; if she be somehow "other" than either, then the conclusion is incorrect. Now the Indian thought of the day held that "she" emphatically *was* "other"; held that the ways of man were distinct from the man. We saw it protesting against the idea of seeing in thought the thinker, etc. Yet the nun Vajirā's analogy of the chariot and no man is based on this very muddling up the chariot-maker and driver with the matter and viability of the chariot.[1]

You are so used, in this our day, to see the mind-er merged

[1] *Kindred Sayings*, I., p. 170. Cf. *Milinda Questions*, p. 34; *Sakya*, pp. 369 f.

in the mind, to see the residual "man" or spirit or soul consigned to metaphysic or to the pulpit, and made an unworkable factor in every-day culture and science, that this Buddhist inference does not fetch you up with a jerk as something illogical. Nor, for that matter, will you find that the denial of the man, as user of body and mind, is ever based on an inference from just this Second Utterance. It is oddly passed over by both Rhys Davids and Oldenberg in their general treatises. And I have not met with it in any Buddhist propaganda compositions. The latter usually take their stand on a trinity of terms as the base of their theoretical teaching (parallel to the "sīlas" as their moral teaching), to wit: all things (and therefore man) are *anicca* (impermanent), *dukkha* (ill), *anattā* (not self), and claim that these were the teaching of the Founder.

Or even when the Utterance is not omitted, the rendering given of *anattā* is misleading: thus "Body is soulless, mind is soulless . . ." But the word *anattā* is not adjective, qualifying *rūpa*; it would then be *anattaṃ*. The Pali is in the masculine singular: *anattā*; this can only mean "not-the-Self (or soul)," or "not-one-who-has-a-self." Do you see the difference? Suppose a group of men, a staff, and you seeking their master. You pass them in review saying what? Not "you and you and you are masterless," but "you and you are not the master." You would not imply, if none of them was master, that the master was non-existent!

You may here say: May it not have been part of this New Word on which you harp, to say that the current teaching was wrong? That, in the First Utterance, we get the positive New Word; in this Utterance the New negative mandate? This is a clear issue, and one we must get put right straight away.

Do you know of any religious reform which has persisted and grown as very worthy, in which the prime reformer attacked the very centre of the current faith? Not in anything external, however important in men's eyes, but the inner heart of it? Did Jesus attack the Jewish faith in God or the moral Code towards the "neighbour"? Did Luther attack the main teachings of Christianity, or John Wesley those teachings as taught by the Anglican Church? "The antecedent improbability," as I have quoted elsewhere from Edmond Holmes, "of a great teacher breaking away from the highest and deepest thought of his nation and his age is very great. The great teacher is always a reformer as well as an innovator . . ."[1] And whereas he will be the former in regard to abuses, he will be the latter in expanding and bringing to finer flower that which is, for the best minds of his time, the Innermost of their faith. To read in the Upanishad teaching that which we see was in it that Innermost, and then to imagine a man like Gotama of the Sakyans trampling upon it is to libel him unspeakably. You will note he was at no pains to say: "But the self *is*; it is he who thinks, who speaks, who acts, who values." It was so unnecessary to say it; not unnecessary now, were he speaking to us, but unnecessary then and there.

No, the Utterance was not any word *teaching a Less* about man. When we shed that as being impossible in any great New Word, then we are much nearer already to finding out what that word really meant. It was, I repeat, a warning. That it was needed is eloquent testimony to a danger felt to be growing already then: the danger, foreseen, as we saw, by Kaushītaki, of blurring the proceeder in the process, the wayfarer in the Way. This is, in so many words, that which, in and before Buddhaghosa's time, became an accomplished fact. At that much later date we can see the full outcome of the Sānkhyan influence upon the Sakyan tradition. At the time we are considering, that influence was young, but, I repeat, wise teachers were already apprehensive about it. For you surely do not

[1] *The Creed of Buddha.*

see in Gotama's advice to those kumāras a mere sarcasm, bidding them hunt for a will-o'-the-wisp?

But more, the warning was needed because of another cause afoot leading to a yet graver danger. This was the *warning*, in the brahman teaching, that the self, the very man, is becoming, not only being. This great teaching, as we saw, had become infected by the admixture of the idea of decay as being the necessary sequence of becoming or growth: a process we see as true enough so far as just body and mind are in question. Analysis of mental factors was provoking a livelier interest in the physical organism. Both worlds of thought were revealing a more general idea than that of becoming and decay: this was transience or impermanence, including both. Yet more general was the idea of change. But it was the former term "transience" that was in the ascendant, as opposed to the attribute of the Divinely Highest: the Imperishable (*akshără*). You will find impermanence (*anicca*) occurring a hundred times in the Pali records where change (*vipariṇāma, aññathatta*) occurs but once. Out of this idea of transience there grew the notion of momentariness, especially in man's inner world of mind; the unit of experience was momentary (*khaṇika*) in time; but that was a later development.

Such were the mutterings of distant thunder when the second Utterance was first spoken, no more. There was then no need to say: "The self *is*," before "see to it you take not the seen man to be he, still less the unseen mind-ways." There was no doubt that there was a self in the Sānkhyan saying: This (is) not *for me* the self (*me attā*), for the very self is seen *in those words adjudicating about his nature*. Had there been any doubt about it, the early Sakyans could scarcely have "given themselves away" with those two words "for me." Here *is* the self, the man, using mind-ways.

It took a long time before the storm fully broke, perhaps five centuries—that is, till after the writing of the composite work called *The Questions of Milinda*, till, say, the Fourth Council. The midway position in the Suttas is shown thus: The formula you read just now in the Second Utterance appears often; it says only "The self is not body, not mind." Another often-repeated formula called Opinion of the Complex (*sakkāya-diṭṭhi*) [1] is also negative: "only the ignorant sees body or mind as being identical with the self, or as having self, or as 'in' self, or self 'in' either." And a third form of negation only emerges, once in a Sutta, then at the Patna Council, then in the *Milinda*: "The self cannot be truly 'got at,'" *i.e.* cannot be affirmed as being positively this or that; we can only affirm about a complex. But just here and there a more positive repudiation is found: "Empty is the world of self and of what is 'selfic.'" [2] "To say, the self and the world are the same; I shall hereafter become eternal, is a doctrine of the foolish." [3]

You will also find repeated the assertion that all sense-experience, sight, hearing, etc., and its objects, things seen, sounds, etc., are *anattā*. This does not go beyond the Second Utterance. Nor does the assertion "All is *anattā*," for "All" is at once resolved into sense-experience, and thus into body and mind.

The word for Divine immanent Self and human self being one and the same, it is not easy to judge, but I should say that, in the Suttas, it is mainly the former aspect of self that is being dropped. This indicates that, when the Suttas were taking present shape, but were not yet written, the divergence between the growing Order of the Sakyans and the Brahman church was being intensified, a severance similar to that seen in the history of Christian reforming bodies. We never find brahmans protesting against any

[1] *Sakkāya*, i.e. *sa-kāya*, refers to man as "co-complex." Just so we saw worlds referred to as "world co-devas," etc.

[2] A term coined, I think, for depreciating; the other adjective *ajjhattam* was appreciative. See *Sakya*, p. 374.

[3] *Majjhima*, Suttas 43 and 22; *Kindred Sayings*, IV., p. 29.

denial of self by Gotama. But later the brahman belief in and search after the human self became discarded. Immanent Deity had been re-named as Dharma.[1] The growing brahman search for the Self in Yoga is only to be traced faintly in early Sakyan verse.[2] It was mainly to name hindrances that this word *Yoga* was used in the Piṭakas.

But the foot of the downward chute we do not reach till, in the ancient Commentaries, we find the men who recast them in Pali *interpolating* the views of their own day, the fifth century A.D. For instance, we find the compiler of the Digha Commentary, when commenting on the awareness judged wise for the monk in every detail of his "simple life," adding a refrain: "Within, a self for anyone putting on his robe, looking around, etc., there is not." And the wheel of "lives" (*bhavachakka*) lacks any experiencer or agent.[3] The ways, the activities alone are real. The experiencer, the actor, is nowhere.

I should be glad to think you also see in this evolution of *anattā* the downward fall I see in it. Buddhism was too great a mandate to be wholly nullified by its having followed this important side-issue. But, in its outlook as a world-religion, the non-existence in theory of the very man has been a serious hindrance. *In practice* the very man has ever been as real for Buddhism as he is for every true teaching. The very fact that *anattā* is now being explained away, as unselfishness, or again as relativity, shows that this tenet, born of special conditions now no longer obtaining as once they did, needed a new dress to be presentable. Nor would it now be acceptable were it not that our time has seen and accepted the quasi-repetition of a psychology which has no psyche, a science of man's mind without the man. For it is not easy to see the evil attaching to a belief that, in mind, in will, in experience, "I" who have all these am real.

[1] See next Chapter.
[2] e.g. *Dhammapada*, ver. 209, 282.
[3] *Path of Purity*, p. 693.

To the old-world monk of the Piṭakas, the belief seemed evil, and the evil lay in seeing aught but what was worthless in the man: transient, ill, not real. But even for the man of to-day there can be no healthy giving himself to the welfare of others, unless he see in each that self as wayfarer in the Better who, he admits, is modelled on the truth about himself. Them he believes to be such wayfarers, but himself he *knows* to be one. And as such, as valuer, as becoming, "man" is not transient, not "ill," is very real.

See how this wayfarer in the Better, in the More, is revealed behind the brief words of that Second Mantra. See how it makes the inference that man is a Less, because not real, the more grotesque a libel! For look! I will, as "I," to be better in body, in all the possibilities of body. I will, as "I," to be better in mind, in all the possibilities of mind. But whereas each of these, as it is, expresses me as I try to be, it at the same time hinders me. The very Man in me wills to be a much better than they suffer me to be. Nay, were I a paragon, a saint, still would they suffer me to be just so much, no more. Not for this earthly vehicle to make the music of the spheres, to see the vision of perfect being. Yet to this I aspire, in this I believe. Verily, then, is this hampering body, this limited mind, not the very "I" who can so aspire, so believe. Wayfarer am I to the Beyond. Rafts are these, that I just grow by, but when the hour comes I shall lay aside for better vehicles. Long is the wayfaring, but my right of way is not in earth only, nor is yours. Let you the self and me the self take hands and wayfare together. Alone neither will fare nearly so well. The true self in me and in you, seeking the More—we can no other—here are worthy companions!

Take, too, from the last utterances other words, where again we find the wayfarer in the More bound for the Most, the Highest: "So long as the disciples achieve no mere perfection of this side only, making a midway ending, so long may their growth be looked for, not their decline. . . .

Verily they who now and when I have passed away will live having self, having dharma, and no other, as lamp and refuge, they will become that deathless Highest[1]—so they be willing to learn": [2]—how have we not here again the very man, wayfarer in Becoming, content with nothing short of the uttermost reality yet awaiting him as man!

[1] I read the unique compound *tamatagge*, as *t'amata-agge* (*agge* as Magadhese neuter singular).

[2] *Dialogues*, II., 108 f.

CHAPTER VIII

THE WAYFARER'S GUIDE

LET us now revert to our little group of missioners immediately after the First Mantra on Ends, Middle Way and the Man choosing had been uttered: how, according to the record, were they occupied?

One only of the Five is recorded as being through it so enlightened as to need no further teaching—Anyā Kondañya. Of the other four we read that they were further instructed in pairs, first Vappa and Bhaddiya, and then Mahānāma and Assaji. Each pair becomes successively as enlightened as was Añyā. And while the second pair was being coached, the other three are said to have gone about for alms. The instruction given is in both cases called a *dhammiyā kathā*, or dharma-talk. And the men, as enlightened (this is *my* expression), are severally said to have had arising in them "unstained flawless vision of dharma"—namely, that "whatever is arising-thing, all that is ending-thing." Moreover, they are severally described as "having *dhamma* of the seen, *dhamma* of the won, or attained, *dhamma* of the understood, *dhamma* of the wholly penetrated-into, as having lost perplexity and doubt, as having won confidence, and as not being in dependence on others with respect to the teaching (*sāsana*) of the teacher." And then the three sections ask in turn for *upasampadā*, or "the towards-consummation," the technical term for enrolment in an Order, meeting with the response thus worded: "Come, monk(s)! Well declared is *dhamma!* Walk according to Brahma-life for right endmaking of ill."

One thing here is clear: we are not reading a record in

words which give a frank, naîve telling, with eyes newly opened, of something new, just as it happened. We are in the world of the fixed stereoscopic phrasing, phrasing to be found repeatedly in the Suttas, but especially in the first part of the First of the Four great Sutta Collections, the Dīgha. There, though not there only, we find conversions worded in the same terms. The original oral telling had been entirely forgotten; and refrains of carefully worded orthodox values had been instituted as the standard version.

In the next place, we look in vain for a single word of reference to the Middle Way, whether of Becoming or eightfold, fourfold, or tenfold. Instead of that, it is *dhamma* here, *dhamma* there, with *brahma-chariya* as apparently its issue in conduct, and with the *attha* of the Mantra figuring only as its negative equation: "ending of ill." Discounting these two points, and coming to the central term: why is "dhamma" brought here thus markedly to the front, and not there?

And not here only. A few pages later we come to a record telling of the Founder sending out disciples on mission tours, probably a few years after the start of his work. There, where we should have looked to find the mandate given them as "the Way," it is again just *dhamma* and *brahma-chariya*.

The Mission-mandate is as follows: "Freed am I, monks, from all snares, from them that are divine, from them that are human. You too, monks, are freed from all snares, from them that are divine, and from them that are human. Walk, monks, a walking [1] for the welfare of the many, for the happiness of the many, out of compassion for the world, for the good, the welfare, the happiness of devas and of men. Let not (any) two go singly.[2] Teach, monks, *dharma*, lovely in (life's) beginning, lovely at (its) middle, lovely at (its) end, both (its) meaning and (its) wording; show forth the wholly perfect purified God-living. There are beings

[1] *Carātha carikam* (pronounce *ch-*).
[2] This has hitherto been wrongly translated.

with eyes little dust-dimmed (who) perish from the not hearing of *dharma;* (as) learners of *dharma* they will become (grow). And I, monks, where lies Uruvelā the army-barracks, thither I will resort for the teaching of *dharma*."

The mandate is, you will admit, not quite worded as we should have expected. An echo of the Hesitation-scene is there, you will note. But why is *dharma* (Pali: *dhamma*) made to usurp the central place?

Let us connect this message with those first activities. We are in both in a world, not of historians of the Faith, but of registrars of the birth and establishment of the Order of Monks. Nearly the whole of the Vinaya is an account of the inception of this and that Rule. But at the beginning the register gives an account of the commencement of the Order itself, and naturally seeks to show how promptly the first monks got into their stride over the alms-business, and also how they were engaged upon *dhamma* from the very first. For them, in the days of compilation into a *Pariyatti* or body of doctrine, and of revision of the same, the word *dhamma* had, among other meanings,[1] *come to stand for just this compilation.* It was quite natural for them, whether or no the message was orally worded from the first as "dhamma," to maintain it as the right and fit word. "Teach *dhamma*" had come to mean for them "teach the Gospel." Yet, as registrars of Vinaya, they were not *chiefly* concerned with the world-significance of that Sending-forth. Their real subject is the bringing into their register a reference to that sinister shadow constantly dogging a celibate sodality, the "Devil," whom they were wont to call Māra. The legend they give makes him twice taunt the Founder as to the falseness in the claim to freedom from all ties, for himself and the monks. It is owing to this that the Mission-mandate gets inserted also in the Collection called the Māra Suttas.[2]

[1] The later scholastic fourfold meaning of *dhamma* is (1) *pariyatti*, (2) cause, (3) quality, (4) non-substantiality. In Tibetan books the number of meanings has increased to ten.

[2] *Kindred Sayings*, I., iv.

And in this connection I hold it very possible that the little Sakyan community only decided to become a definite Order of *samaṇas*, or recluses, or almsmen (*bhikshus*) *when these mission-tours were started.* Great religions, like charity, begin at home, where the new teachers are known and trusted by fellow-students and friendly neighbours. When longer walks into Anga, Kosala, Ujjeni were planned, it would be probably needful to go in the already accepted garb of the "holy man," who owned nothing, but gave, of his inwardly owned best, in teaching and—this grew apace later—produced "merit" in those who made "the labourer worth of his hire." They would then be confronting strangers, and would have to appear, as missioners, at all costs men who were in their object above suspicion.

But whereas *dhamma*, for Vinaya and Sutta editors, meant mainly formulated doctrine (and does so still), it obviously could not have meant this for a Leader discussing with his first co-workers at the outset what they were to believe and to teach, nor even in those very early mission tours, as the thing to be taught. Not that this seemed to the editors so "obvious." We actually find Gotama made to define *dhamma* in a way only possible in a day when the major part of the Piṭakas were so far compiled as to be in nine named collections. Thus he is made to say: " . . . some who have learnt *dhamma*—that is, the Suttas, the Prose-and-Verse, the Catechisms, the Anthologies, the Udānas, the Thus-Saids, the Jātakas, the Miraculous Things, the Miscellany. . . ."[1] Only one thing perhaps seemed "obvious" and this was that he was omniscient, as to the future as well. And that editors had such an aggregate of doctrine in mind when they revised the Missions-mandate is clear from the two terms we have already noticed: "meaning and wording,"[2] terms that could only refer to set pieces of fixed standardized diction. There is another striking phrase in the Message which, at first sight, may also

[1] *Majjhima*, Sutta 22.
[2] *Sa'ttha sa-vyañjana*, above, p. 115.

seem to imply later editing with a "Scripture" mentally present: "*dhamma*, lovely at the beginning, the middle, the end . . ." as if a very Bible were meant. But this is not so. That the original meaning was forgotten is clear, for Commentators explain it variously; for one it means "moral code, mind-training or concentration, and wisdom"; for another it meant "moral code, the Way, Nirvana." As I see it, the three periods refer not to a body of teaching, oral or written, not to any product of man, but to the man himself, to man by whom the message was sent, through whom it was sent, to whom it was sent, the man who came to be so much ejected from Buddhist formulas. It was in man's youth, in middle age, and in his closing years that *dharma* was pronounced to be lovely: *kalyāṇa*:—we cannot render it exactly, but it is thought to be kin to the Greek *kalos*, "well" in sanity, both morally and æsthetically beautiful.

And there is yet another pair of terms you will find often linked with *dhamma*: it is "come-and-see-ish" (*ehipassika*) and "not-time-ish" (*a-kālika*). It is likely that these had not come into use when the missioner mandate was given fixed wording. The former may be likened to an invitation to hear preaching. The latter is more baffling, and is, I hold, wrongly taken by Commentators to mean "immediate effect, instant fruition." If we note that the word for time (*kāla*) was only used for duration in earth-life, and that other terms were applied to life in other worlds, it becomes possible to see in the term the meaning: "not limited to life on earth only." [1]

We now return to our question: what was this *dharma* or *dhamma*, so patently given place of honour, save in those two First Utterances? You will by other writers be probably told, it is the expressing in one word that which, in the Two Utterances, is expounded in many words; just doctrine, the Teaching.

[1] *Sakya*, p. 413.

Before you feel satisfied with this reply, I would ask you to imagine a Leader of a new religious movement telling his men to teach, using just those words. We do not find Jesus telling the twelve, or again the seventy, to teach the "Sermon on the Mount," or "the New Commandment." I do not wish to press a parallel, but I do hold it, as likely, that to say "Teach *dhamma*!" did not mean Teach the Doctrine, or the Truth, or the Teaching, but "Teach what each of those disciples knew *dhamma* meant. Something as vital for them as was the "Say: the kingdom of heaven is at hand!" for Peter and the rest. It was too early to say "*dhamma*" if this was an equivalent of "Gospel." And if the original word used was "the Way," *dhamma* would not have been editorially substituted for it.

It is as interesting as it is regrettable, that a decision, ascribed to the Śakyamuni before he began to utter any public word, found no place in these Vinaya records. This may well be because the new Order was in no way implicated in the episode. I refer to a little Sutta of the sixth book of the Saṃyutta.[1] The Founder, just after the "enlightenment," while at the Goat-herd's Banyan, decides to honour and worship no earthly teacher, but *dhamma* alone. And he hears a *deva* approving of the resolve. It is a fragment that has undergone embroidery of a Buddha-cultish kind, for it is not the humble, earnest will of an untried teacher that is made the theme, but the swagger of one who votes himself to be needing no teacher. But the core of the Sutta is of the first importance. It is often said that "Buddhism" is distinctive in this, that it is a religion with no supramundane mandate; that the Founder bows the knee neither to an external God, nor to the immanent Deity of his day. What, then, of this record? Gotama is not proposing to revere a yet unspoken, unembodied "doctrine," nor is there evidence that any notion of "Nature" or cosmic law was present to

[1] *K.S.*, I., p. 174, § 2; = *Anguttara*, II., p. 21 (text); *Gradual Sayings*, II., pp. 22 f.

him. A Something it is he is placing where his country, before his day and during his day, placed That Who is Highest: *Brahman, Ātman.*

Wherefore by one desiring the Self, longing for the Great Self
The Very-Dharma should be held in reverence . . .

How have not Buddhists ignored these Suttas! Let me say at once that, in the Saṃyutta version, we have "desiring weal" (*attha-*, not *atta-*), which *may* be the right reading. But the Burmese *t* and *th* are easily confused, and it is to be noted that the Commentaries of both Nikāyas pass over the term in silence. Again, most would read, for "the Great Self," "greatness": *mahattam, v. l. mahattim.* But whereas to "long for greatness" is here inept, the inflection *-attaṃ* for *attānaṃ* is met with.[1] Here the metre requires it.

I am not saying that this is to be read in every mention of the word *dhamma* in the Piṭakas—far from it. But if you ever read say, for an hour, consecutive pages in the chief Upanishads, and then similarly for an hour in the Suttas, you may very likely come to say that, just as the word Self (*ātman*) is an outstanding feature in the former, so is *dhamma* an outstanding feature in the latter. *Ātman* does not always mean just the identical emphasis in the former, nor does *dhamma* in the latter. But the contrast is there and is as such most significant. Somehow *dhamma* has come to have the weight *Ātman* had, much as "*Ātman*" came to have the weight "Brahman" alone had.

Now take the closing scenes of Gotama's life and one of his last sayings. You may know it: "Live as they who have the Self . . . who have *dhamma* as a lamp, as refuge." He is also recorded as saying: "It may be, Ānanda, it will seem to you all: the Word is one of a bygone teacher; we have no teacher (now). But you are not so to consider it. *Dhamma* and *vinaya* which I have taught and revealed to you:—*that* when I am gone is your teacher."[2]

[1] Cf. *Grad. Sayings*, I., p. 228, *n* 2; and for *attaṃ* see *Dhammapada*, ver. 379.
[2] *Dialogues*, II., p. 171.

Comparing these passages with the "worship" Sutta, it is possible that what he said was to name only *dhamma* as his successor in "teaching." The editors would see to it naturally that Vinaya came in too. Anyway, it emerges that *dhamma* stood for something who, or which, was held to be efficient *as teacher and as guide*, both in the beginning for the yet lonely Messenger setting out to help, and also for his orphaned family, as he lay dying.

We are now getting beneath the superstructure of *dhamma* as so many "doctrines," or as articulated teaching, meanings which run throughout the Pali literature. They make the word very baffling *if* ever we forget the building that went on over the ancient ruined city. Take two more references: Gotama is said to spring a general statement of cause and effect on an interviewer with the words: "Let be . . . let be . . . I will teach you *dhamma*: This being (given), that becomes, etc." [1] This looks much like "I will teach you a (or the) doctrine," especially as, in an earlier Sutta, we find Sāriputta the leading disciple, identifying the way of cause and effect with "dhamma." [2] Again, we find Gotama asked, "What is this *dhamma* which your disciples, when trained therein and finding comfort, confess as the base of Brahma-living which they prefer?" [3] And, indeed, in yet another Sutta of this Collection, we meet with the more fundamental antithesis in *dhamma*: the positive and negative forms, used, in the unusual plural, to mean right and wrong teachings.[4]

For there is one thing that *dhamma* (with or without *a-dhamma*) meant all the time in India, and that is "right." It meant other things, too—meanings which you will find in both the Upanishads and the Piṭakas. You will find it meaning custom, standard or norm; [5] you will find it meaning, usually in the plural only, just "things," and not

[1] *Majjhima*, Sutta 79. [2] *Ibid.*, Sutta 28. [3] *Dīgha*, III., No. 25.
[4] *Majjhima*, Sutta 22. The Commentary so explains them.
[5] *Kaush. Up.*, 2, 1.

material things only;[1] you will find it virtually meaning "law"—virtually, since law is that which king or other judge pronounces as "right" (cf. the French *droit*, meaning both), or as "truth" (*satya*);[2] you will find it meaning "duty" in the singular,[3] and "duties" in the plural;[4] you will even, in an Upanishad appendix, find it mean, just once only, "a doctrine."[5] But as meaning "right," with "wrong" implicit or explicit, you find it in both literatures, though in both very rarely. And with the same verb: "walk," a figure for "living" no less here than in the Bible. *Chare dharman!* (he should walk according to *dharma*) is the brahman teacher's admonition. *Dhammaṃ chara!* is the Pali Jātaka equivalent. And so also in the old Dhammapada verses:

. . . "*Let him walk by* dharma, *the right faring,*
Happy the dharma-*farer rests both in this world and other worlds.*"[6]

Again, the opposites "(were there no speech, neither *dharma* nor *adharma* would be made known)"[7] can be met with in Pali:

Verily dhamma *wards the* dhamma-*walker*:
dhamma *well practised brings along happiness*:
this is the advantage of dhamma *well practised*;
not to disaster goes walker by dhamma.
Not are they equal: results of dhamma *and* adhamma:—
adhamma *leads men to hell, but* dhamma
makes a man win the bourn that is happy.
Hence let desire be well wrought in dhamma,[8]

verses which, shorn of the obviously later gloss that follows, have for me the taste of very old Sakya. Here be it noted is *dhamma* conceived not as something the man guards; it is *dhamma* who guards the man, and guides him. Compare with this the verse in Dhammapada:

Surely the Self protector is of self!
Surely who else could his protector be?[9]

[1] *Chānd.*, 2, 1, 4.
[2] *Brih.*, 1, 4, 14.
[3] *Taitt.*, 1, 11, 1.
[4] *Chānd.*, 2, 23, 1.
[5] *Mait.*, 7, 9.
[6] Ver. 169, etc.
[7] *Chānd.*, 7, 2, 1
[8] *Theragāthā*, ver. 303, 304.
[9] Ver. 160.

And this:

> *In that he settles cause of other men*
> *by* dharma *and by fairness, not by force,*
> *warded of* dharma *that sagacious man*
> *is rightly named " he who on* dharma *stands."* [1]

But when we have got to this, that an ancient, important meaning of *dharma* is right as opposed to wrong, and that this may be figuratively expressed as guiding and protecting the man who walks by it, we are not "there" yet. Such a meaning is well rendered, not only by "right," but also by the word "norm," which I decided to use some twenty-odd years ago. "Norm" is healthy mean, or average, and suggests nothing beyond a good maintenance of worthy levels. And I have said that for me religion is very vitally something more than that.[2] When it only recognizes upkeep as against decline, it is doing good moral routine work, but as a religion its knell is tolling.

Always in *dharma* there has lain, for India, latent, if not patent, the sense of the "Ought to be, because it is better." You will not find *dhamma* identified with *sīla*, the moral *code*, the basis in Buddhism on which to build, save as recognizing that basis, and that the basis is *due to dharma*. So we meet with the two words in Asoka's Edicts.[3] *Dharma*, as noun, is from the verbal root *dhṛ*, to bear, support; it is bearing or thing borne, as is *karma*, doing or deed. And the bearing is to be understood as "bearing in mind," "heeding," and "what ought to be heeded." As to the "ought," I have seen, in a Pali Commentary, *dhamma* defined as "doing what ought to be done." As to the "better" I have so rendered the affix *vara*, common in later Pali as meaning "elect," "excellent." This is in the translation of the short anthology called Khuddaka-pāṭha (little texts), first book of the Sutta-Piṭaka.[4] *Vara*, the Aryan equivalent of our will-stem (*val-*), means choice,

[1] *Dhp.*, ver. 257.
[2] Above, p. 105.
[3] Below, p. 313.
[4] *S.B.B.*, VII., *Minor Anthologies*, I., p. 149.

elect. And "better" is for the chooser the relatively "choice" or better.

> *Such is the* "dhamma-Better" *that he taught.* . . .
> *Man of the Better, who the Better knew,*
> *who gave the Better, who the Better brought,*
> *Incomparable, he* dhamma, *the Better, taught.*[1]

Is it not in this "ought to because better" that we see Gotama, in the word *dharma,* giving to his world and his day that which teachers had been feeling after in the idea of all things as becoming? The notion of transience (*anicca*), which ousted "becoming," is a pitiful monk-wail beside this idea of man's becoming That Who he potentially is. But the age was *leaning to that notion,* and because of it man was in sore need of something protecting, warding. The age was beginning to lean away from the indwelling self as divine, and because of this man was in sore need of being reminded that the Self was no merely static concept, to *know* Whom was all-sufficient. Man's best self was dynamic, was to be known as an urge to the better, as will to the better, as mentor of the better, as Dharma: That Who he should be, That Who was leading on, was guiding, was mothering, That Who was ever at hand, unfailing mighty Ally.

How rich was not India, had she but grafted on to her world of the Immanently Divine this *Dharma*-guided man's first teaching! How little need had she, in reality, of a world-shirking monasticism, when she had been shown, that to know the God-in-man she need no more to shrink away from the Highest; that she needed no more to fear;[2] that

[1] *tathûpamaṃ dhammavaram adesayi*
. . . . . .
varo varaññû vara-do varâharo
anuttaro dhammavaram adesayi.

[2] *Katha,* 4, 12. *Taitt.,* 2, 4 and 9, etc.: "then does he become one who has gone to no-fear." *Îśâ.,* 6: Now he who on all beings looks as just on the Self, and on the Self as in all beings, he does not shrink away from him. Or *Bṛh.* 4, 4, 15: who sees the self as Deva clearly as Lord of what was and what is to be he does not shrink away from him.

in Becoming That Who she was, there lay before her the happiest of wayfarings. The Upanishad verse :—

> *Know thou the Ātman in the chariot riding,*
> *the body is that chariot,*[1]

Sakya expanded with :

> *Straight is the name that Way is called, and free*
> *from fear the Quarter whither thou art bound;*
> *Thy chariot is the silent runner named,*
> *with wheels of righteous effort fitted well.*
> *Conscience the* [illegible] *canopy*
> *is heedfulness :* [illegible] *is,*
> *I say, and right view he who runs before.*
> *And be it woman, be it man for whom*
> *that chariot waits, by that same car*
> *he verily to the beyond will go.*[2]

"Conscience," is it? I hear you say, is it not conscience that is really meant by *dharma*? Why has this not been said?

It is well said, and for me conscience—"this Deity in my bosom—"[3] is not far from *dharma*. This is not so much the duty to be done, as the premonitory sense of duty, or the thing due, due from me as a self or God-in-man. But the word here is *hiri*, literally "shame," and interpreted as "shame, not at what others will say, but at what the man within himself feels when confronted with wrongdoing."[4] Here we have but the half-truth; in conscience we have also the impulse to embrace the better, the well-doing. Moreover, it is of interest that, in proportion as *dhamma* became reserved to mean teaching formulated, the terms *hiri*, and that other shame: *otappa* come forward. But neither is conscience a term really worthy of us. It is not enough to be *con-sciens*, aware inwardly. We may be silently aware that a fence of so many feet is before us. We need more to make the jump over it. When our great

[1] *Katha*, 3, 3.
[2] *Kindred Sayings*, I., p. 45; *Minor Anthologies*, I., p. xviii.
[3] *Tempest*, II., p. 1.
[4] *Bud. Psychol. Ethics*, 2nd ed., p. 18, *n.* 1.

word "will," brought into religion by Jesus, comes into its very own, then shall we find a better word than conscience.

But let that act of a virtual placing of Dharma where had been the throne of Deity conceived as in man, the highest self, and as Brahman, the spirit of prayer, not be overlooked. Nor let it be, in its edited form, taken merely as the self-establishing act of an all-wise teacher. Its deep significance, as well as the original meaning and history of the word *dhamma*, has been too much neglected. Writers seem oblivious of the change in the meaning of the word.

Nor need we ask, why do we get the essentials of Gotama's teaching in so scrappy a fashion? No great religion has yet started with a ready-made code, unless we try to see all that in the issue of the Ten Commandments of Israel. We shall err, if we see in Gotama and his first little "club," a deliberate attempt to assail the Brahman established church and its teaching. As a non-brahman teacher—and such were not unknown—he was attempting to teach, not private pupils, but Everyman, certain things which he will not have found duly taught, even to the brahmans' pupils, but which were to some extent recognized in that teaching as worthy. Thus the Upanishads had sayings on the choosing of boons (*vara*), but very little on the *man as the chooser at every turn in his way to salvation*. They spoke of a "way" leading beyond death, but not of that Way as ever involving the wayfarer's own choice. They taught that man was ever becoming this and that, but they did not grip the fact of his essential becoming as the way of effecting Yoga, union, of the minor self with the Great Self. They taught that some one was "dear to you because the Self was dear," but did not make clear how great a basis of true brotherhood lay here. They recognized, in *dharma*, duty, duties, but they did not hear in *dharma* the still small voice of the "Dear, the Precious Self" Whom they, in other noble words, called *Antarayāmin*, "he who within makes to go," and Savitar, divine urger, inspirer.

We need, if we would understand, to forget the far later rounded-off epitomes of a religious cult become utterly divorced from its source, estranged from it in foreign lands, such as the Piṭakas give us. We must see that religious world in its Indian cradle.

CHAPTER IX

THE WAY IN THE WORLDS

In most books, shall I even say all books, on Buddhism, wherever written, you will not find the Way much associated with any world beyond this world of earth. In one Way-formula it is so associated, but this is little quoted. This evasion may be due partly to the scanty fragments in the records of genuinely early matter, partly to unfamiliarity with those records, partly, and perhaps chiefly, to the Way getting edited as those Eight Fitnesses or Rightnesses, and, in general, to the absence of submitting all the Pali scriptures to historical criticism. A favourite word, preferred to Way or Path, when Buddhists get on to a prospect beyond this earth, is one that also means wayfaring: *saṃsāra.*[1] And had the Middle Way not got tied up with the word "eightfold," teachers might have gone to work more intelligently by showing that the Middle Way is itself a faring on, a *saṃsāra,* but is the *right* way of faring in that *saṃsāra* which is our life considered as a whole. Much more would this have been the case had the Way as man's "faring on in Becoming" not been dropped out. We should then have got unity with breadth in Buddhist expositions. But writers have immediately spent themselves in discussion of the "eightfold," a set of attributes very desirable in themselves (if not exactly exhaustive of the holy life), but which do not bear on them, as does Becoming, the hallmark of a faring that is not limited to this one little span of life alone.

[1] Pronounce *sangsâra,* both *a*'s as in "father."

There came another term into Buddhist terms of life, of life as a whole, which does maintain the aspect of Becoming, but only as something vilely depreciated. The West is less familiar with this, and some may have wondered why, in Kipling's *Kim*, the dear old lama keeps up a refrain about Way and Wheel, the one appreciated and sought after, the other the fate of the foolish. This term is the later figure, the "wheel of becoming" (*bhava-chakka*).

There is no finer symbol within symbol in Sakya than the Wheel. You will find the legend of it in the Dīgha story of the magic Wheel,[1] and in the title given to the First Utterance, the "Turning the Wheel of Dharma." It was the ancient symbol of a king's conquest, and became carved on countless Buddhist erections, a symbol of the faith, parallel to the Cross and the Crescent, symbol of, not worldly, but spiritual conquest. Before the legend was so interpreted, before the symbol was so used, it may well have stood for the graphic sign of the Way, this lending itself not well to graphic presentation. In either case, the Wheel of the legend, being well in touch with earth, moved forward as does growth. But as the decadent symbol of a decadent teaching, it stood for a man's many lives as aimless revolvings, where *bhava* had come to mean, not onward rolling, but mere sterile recurrence. The Way had then ceased to mean the long, long faring through opportunities essential to the man's becoming ever more and more till the Most was reached. The Way had come to mean just that short cut to the utter passing out from life into the nirvana in which India had come to believe, the brahman seeing in it absorption into brahman, the Buddhist, a waning out of life-as-man-knew-it into an ineffable somewhat. "Who in the self finds joy and delight, finds light . . . he has become Brahman, he attains the Brahma-nirvana. Yea, this do the rishis

[1] *Dialogues*, III., Sutta 26.

attain when sin is destroyed, duality is got rid of, the self is tamed, even they who rejoice over the weal of all beings." [1]

When this Ixion-wheel of rebirth cuckooed out the original Wheel in Buddhism we do not know. I have as yet found it in one Abhidhamma Commentary and Buddhaghosa's *Path of Purity*, in identical contexts both probably by that writer.

Between the original idea of the Way and the later idea of the Way, as the short cut out of life in this or any world, we have the Way conceived as stages of "ways" and "fruits," with which we have dealt. Here the first Way and fruit came to be judged as about the limit for the laity. This was not a definite tenet, as we can see in a controversy at, or after, the date of the Third Council: "Can a householder attain the state of the arahan?" [2] But the new orthodoxy is not disposed to concede that he can.

If you can now compare the opening of the Housefather chapter in *Kindred Sayings*, II., with Sutta 143 of the Majjhima, and with the Kalāra Sutta of the former work; [3] you may discern how there had come to be one confession of attainment for the layman in the first stage of the Way ("stream-winning"), and quite another for the arahan or man in the fourth stage. And you will note a special teaching as reserved for the *religieux*, not given to "white-robed householders," a teaching in which the learner is taught to "train himself not to be the creature of this world or of any other world." [4]

This should bring home to us how, while not holding in doubt that death, save for the arahan, is but the threshold of another stage in life as we can conceive it, the monastic Sangha, after the early teachers had passed away, concentrated its training in the finished "making-

[1] Bhagavad-Gītā, V.
[2] *Points of Controversy*, V., p. 1.
[3] *Kindred Sayings*, II., p. 38.
[4] *Further Dialogues*, II., p. 303; not a literal translation. See next page.

to-become" of arahans on the life that was then theirs on earth. Hence for them, the Way, especially when they had settled down to their Eightfold business, became, at least for the elect, a road of a few score years only at the very most.

Now I would fain lead you to think, with me, that this truncated Way was very far from being the Long Trail as I hold it was when taught by the First Men of Sakya. To bring you conviction—and I am not asking you to take my word for it—you may need to read at some length in the translations now published. You may not once find any *assertion* that the Way is an indefinite number of opportunities afforded to the Wayfarer for a gradual becoming along a More towards a final Most. How could it be asserted, with editors holding other views? But, on the other hand, there is a pretty big obstacle in the way, hindering you from siding with the monastic ideal dominating the Suttas. It is this:

If the teaching of Gotama and his men had been one of training men against "laying hold of this world or other worlds, or of letting the man-as-persisting depend upon them,"[1] then we should look to find in the Piṭakas practically nothing about life in other worlds, save echoes from the brahman teaching of the Upanishads, adduced only when there was necessity to do so, coupled with such folklore of an other-world kind as is in the Jātakas. The attention and interest of both laymen and learners in the Order would be diverted from dwelling on such subjects. The founders would have turned a cold shoulder on all curiosity of a kind now labelled spiritualistic. And we should find no heed paid to a man's fate hereafter as depending on his conduct now. We should not have found any teaching of a tribunal awaiting him just after death, as an immigrant whose advent was welcome or unwelcome to the inmates of his new world. We should not

[1] A more literal rendering of the same citation.

find the first men seeking access "psychically" to that world to cheer or warn men here by what they learnt. We should not find the Founder welcoming and conversing with visitors from that world. We should not find that between Upanishads and Piṭakas a very cosmology had evolved, unknown in the former literature. *But it is just all of this that we do find.*

Let us consider in brief detail "this that we do find." And first what have the Piṭakas to say that, in the matter of a "cosmology" of other worlds, and of rebirth in them, is much more than we find in the Upanishads?

You will not find much on this in learned works as yet that is likely to help you historically. Thus Buddhist teaching on worlds will be found associated with that in the Purāṇas, Hindu works, assigned to a date after A.D. 400, or about 1000 years after the time we are considering. I have as yet seen no work carefully comparing Piṭakan world-teaching with that in the early Upanishads.[1] In the latter we have a number of fragmentary vague allusions to this and that god of the Vedas; to creation as by one of these, or by Brahman, or by the One Self; to death personified; to the man as being guided after death by one not-of-men; to a dispersal of the outward man at death, but to the very man or self going according to his deeds; to a "way" through the worlds towards a goal; to man as praying "to become immortal"; to man as having the prospect (or hope, *abhyāso*) of happy or unhappy survival in return to earth, according as he has "lived pleasantly here or the reverse." Reincarnation, as we call it—as India does *not*—is not mentioned in the Vedas, but it emerges in Brāhmaṇas and Upanishads, and even rebirth as animal begins to show its face, while return to earth-life as woeful is here and there shown.

And that is not all. I have not in them found any

[1] Cf. the wish in W. F. Warren's *Earliest Cosmologies*, New York, 1909, p. 99.

belief in an other-worldly personally administered system of awarding, or adjudication, awaiting the man after his leaving earth, or other whereabouts of life. You may know how prominent a place is given to this in the Zoroastrian records, the product of a religion at least as old as that of the earliest Upanishads. And there is practically no belief in these of the man of earth as being warded by those of other worlds. The guidance alluded to above is perhaps the one exception: "Now whether there be cremation-obsequies, or not, they pass over . . . there is a man (*puruṣa*) not of earth (*amāṇava*), he leads them to Brahman. . . ."[1]

The creeping in of rebirth as animal is of interest, since no religion worthy of the name owes its origins to folklore fancies, and Upanishad teaching, not being intended for the Many, did not seek popularity though such doses of powder in jam as were the fables, with a moral, called Jātakas, so much indulged in by the more popular preaching of decadent Sakya.

Let us now inquire whether Sakya made any contribution in quantity or quality to these somewhat fluid ideas. My work in this field has left me with the conviction that the contribution was a more *definite* belief in this and that other named world, and in these as being, one and all of them, within man's Right-of-way, as destiny certainly experienced and to be experienced; that wherever he was in that right of way he was still "man," using body and mind; that a tribunal of awarding awaited him; that they among whom he would next be reborn were watching his progress with approval or disapproval, and were at hand to inform, to protect him and even to learn of him, if he had anything worth their learning. Herein I would say that this contribution is only less vague than that of the India of its day. Indefinite it is, unfinished, a patchwork, but less so than the teaching it found.

[1] *Chānd.*, Up. 4, 15.

It has puzzled some: this cosmology that we find in the Suttas as it were ready-made, so much fuller than anything of the kind in the Upanishads, and the solution has been to put Buddhist teaching much later than that literature. But in putting "Buddhist teaching" as later, writers have made this identical with original Sakyan teaching; and this is where we have "slipped up." We have failed to see that the Buddhist teaching of the Suttas is the later thing of changed values, and that, during the century or so of Sakyan teaching preceding this, interest in, and to some extent knowledge of other world-conditions had been strongly prevailing, and *finding expression in the oral sayings of the day*. When a man's interest is much wrapped up in a subject, and he is anxious to persuade others of the interest it has for them, he will speak of it, he will come to write of it. It will bulk largely in his writings. And it is this interest in life as taking him through many worlds during an indefinitely long period of time, a time not yet expired, to which the Suttas are attesting from first to last. That is to say, it is not stated as just a teaching that is not to be neglected, much less is it declared as a new teaching. But now here, now there, men are told, unfalteringly, that the unworthy life, or phases of evil conduct mean for each doer purgatory hereafter, that the worthy life, or good conduct leads to the "happy bourn" (*sugati*), to the bright world (*sagga, svarga*). Nor does this retribution, or this reward to ensue, in any way suggest the operation of a mechanical causal order, an impersonal world-way. It is twice told, not as an allegory or parable, but with the simple emphatic clarity of something true, that a man has to appear after death before a *deva*, "Yama," to be held responsible for his conduct on earth and hear the judge's verdict. Yama in the Kaṭha Upanishad is a personified Death, rather than a judge; in the Sakyan cosmology he is but one of a group, called Yāmas (controllers, restrainers), with a chief

Yama, inmates of the next world. The man is encased in a new body, since he can move, speak and also suffer, or again enjoy, in a physical way. But no claim is put forward that the man is not real in his new encasement, nor irresponsible for what he did on earth. Nor does he as "brand new" plead ignorance. He recollects what *he* did and pleads carelessness. But it is the individual responsibility for his acts which is driven home with much emphasis, albeit the word "responsible" is lacking.

The teaching, I said, is not given as just allegory, but it is accompanied in one context by one, in another by two allegories. The repeated figure is that of messengers come to warn. This figure, famous since then, and may be yet earlier, as Death's messenger in the first grey hair,[1] is, I believe, here only, told of three messengers: old age, illness, death, less worthy for me than Longfellow's three singers:

God sent his singers upon earth
With songs of sadness and of mirth,
That they might touch the hearts of men
And bring them back to heaven again.

These three messengers of the Anguttara-Nikāya[2] are, as I have shown, increased to five in the (therefore presumably) later Majjhima version.[3] Again, there has been inserted in the Dīgha version a fourth messenger, the world forsaker, as you will also have read.

The other allegory is peculiar to the Majjhima tradition, where it occurs thrice. "As there were two houses with doors, where a man with eyes to see standing in the midst could see men entering and leaving, moving along, moving about, so can I who am clairvoyant (lit. who have deva-sight) see men faring after death according to their deeds."[4] Then follows the tribunal and the messengers.

That Everyman will have listened to such teaching, was

[1] See the interesting article by Richard Morris in *J.P.T.S.*, 1885, pp. 62 ff.

[2] *G.S.*, I., 121 ff. *Sūpra*, p. 46 f.

[3] Sutta 130.

[4] Suttas xxxix., lxxvii., cxxx.

needing such teaching, appears from the recurring allusions to his flocking to Gotama, on the latter's tours, to ask what he, as known to be what is now called "psychic," could tell concerning the after-death fate of this man and that woman, whom they had known. The answers are given readily, but in sadly vague or stilted terms, evidently framed by editorial piety as makeshifts for things of a forgotten long-ago. "Now at that time the Bhagavā was wont to make declarations as to the rebirths of such followers as had passed away among the tribes round about on every side, saying: Such an one has been reborn (arisen) there, such an one there." Again: "Of those of Nādikā, Sālha the monk had attained 'release,' Nandā the nun as devī would not return to earth, Sudatta was a once-returner, Sujāta would not incur purgatory," and so on. As would be expected, it is only those of the Order, the first two, who have either won, or will be near to "nirvana."

Thus we have, on the one hand, a public ready and eager to hear of things of the More than just this life's concerns; on the other, we have teachers able and willing to tell what they had come to know about that More. "Psychic" power was then, as now, abnormal, but it was not a monopoly of the Founder. The brahman Moggallāna, ranked by the "church" as his twin leading disciple, is recorded in the Commentaries as having expressly exercised that power, that he might witness, seeing and hearing, the circumstances in the new life of several persons, and so bring a living force to aid in his warnings and encouragement to his listeners. Panthaka Minor was noted for a very abnormal phase of psychic power. Anuruddha, and to a less degree Sāriputta, were also psychic, and there was a tradition that others were so gifted. Ānanda was not; when the vision of a deceased visitor is told him, and he recognizes who it must have been, he is said to have "made a good inference."

But there is more of this "obstacle" to body out. The degree to which the Suttas are records of *devas* visiting such psychic men and women on earth, and especially the Śakyamuni, is not yet grasped by the European reading public, nor, for that matter, by Buddhists themselves, for whom most of their scriptures have been known through a virtually dead language. It was not till 1910, with the publication of the second volume of the *Dialogues*, and 1917, with that of the first part of *Kindred Sayings*, that English readers could get their picture of the world, in which Gotama and his first men taught into better, truer proportions. But such books trickle very slowly into the world of readers, and by that time writers on Buddhism had formed already their somewhat malproportioned picture, and given it to the popular reading public. And so much did this picture make the Sakyans out to be a set of quasi-rationalists in a world of Hindu fancies and "superstition," that I have even heard a fairly cultured man say: "Buddhism did not hold with a future life, did it?" Certainly it were hard to trace, in our writers so depicting, any belief that, in such passages concerning "the unseen" as the records they knew recorded, there was aught beyond pious myths inserted orally to magnify the wisdom and superhumanity of "the Buddha." They might say: Such *deva*-visits are told as befalling the Buddha without others being present, hence the repeaters and compilers might insert just what they thought made for that sort of edification.

As to that, it might equally be said, his being apparently alone would be rather a voucher for the truth of the visions, since only he could have told—as indeed we find him telling Ānanda—and he is repeatedly extolled as a truth-speaker. We can, anyway, let these two arguments cancel each other. It is rather this that I would again dwell upon, so important do I hold it for getting at the right perspective in our reading of the Piṭakas. You have, in them, an older and a younger stratum of recorded matter. In the older, the leading man (with his helpers) is largely occupied with not this world's inmates only, but with those of at least two other worlds: the "next" world and the Brahmadeva world. These inmates are not a mixture of angels and devils, but for the most part persons we should call gentlemen: they are courteous, attentive, wishing man's welfare, deprecating evil-doing, welcoming man's interest in their worlds, welcoming his coming if he be worthy, guarding their world against undesirable immigrants being loose among them. And they show greater will-power than have most men, are radiant and handsome, are governed by a ruler and his "Cabinet"; moreover, in due time, they, too, come to die, probably to pass back to earth.

The greater will-power, resembling that of the few abnormally "psychic" men, is chiefly shown in the way of gaining access to another world. There is herein no question of coming down or going aloft for them, nor of the latter for such men; all that came later into Buddhistic belief. The transit was effected "just as a strong man stretches out his flexed arm, or flexes his outstretched arm; so X vanishes thence and is manifested in Y." (I suspect we have in the latter clause, for "vanishes," a corrupted word, and that it was originally "without interval, *i.e.* of time or space, immediately." For there was obviously no possibility and no need for X to vanish.[1]) You will find, for men, a "going aloft" in translations of Suttas, but the text does not warrant it. Even in the Jātaka, where King Nimi is driven to see purgatory and then the deva-world, the *deva*-chariot goes in both cases onward, not down or up. When men were worthily interested in other worlds, as were the first Sakyans, the idea of worlds as co-penetrating in space seems to have been the conviction, and it was only when religious interest in the worlds waned, that the aloft and the below became prominent.

[1] For the frequently repeated formula see e.g. *Kindred Sayings*, I., p. 179 (*S.* I., p. 141). It is literally "in, or as to Brahmaworld vanished": *antarahito*. The word as *antara-rahito* would mean "lacking interval," and is possibly more correct.

Further, we read of five groups making up the *devas*, or happily acquitted immigrants of the next world: (1) the world of the Thirty (often wrongly rendered as Thirty-three), *i.e.* of a Ruler and thirty councillors, the ruler having the dynastic name of Sakka, Shakra, (2) the Tusita ("delighted") group, whence man's Helpers are reborn on earth, (3) the Yama group or judges, and (4, 5) two groups of very intriguing titles, but left by records quite vague: "they who delight in creating" and "they who dispose of the creations of others." That they come last does not imply superiority; it would mean, if anything, merely a minority. But a world of artistic æsthetic activity seems indicated as being part of the life to come, no less than it is part of life here.

And all these five divisions are, *i.e.* were originally, just as much one and the same world of life as is the earth, to wit, *svarga*, the lucky, happy world of the worthy. Purgatory, too, will have been as it were the prisons of this same world. As to the very little-understood "Peta" world, the inhabitants of which appear as expiating sins by intermittent suffering, I would not speak with any certainty where the records themselves show but much half-forgotten tradition. As a fact, all these seven, not to mention one more rarely cited division—that of Asuras—you will find alluded to as if they were each and all different worlds, a looseness which betrays the relative indifference with which the monkish outlook had come to look upon any but just this one life.

Of the Brahma world we have a number of sections that are scarcely more than names, and a few names, variants of the word Brahma, not the impersonal source of all, the Brahman of the Upanishads, but personalities: Brahmā Eternal Youth (Sanatkumāra), Lord of all (Sahampati), and Baka (-crane), etc. Also certain attributes *e.g.*, in an old Dhammapada verse:

Feeding on rapture like the Ābhassara devas (*i.e.* radiant).

But access for the psychic was possible to them, too, and they, too, came near to man anxious to teach and guide helpers of men. Yet further, "Tat-uttarim," were other worlds of *devas*, of whom older Suttas speak tersely. But I would not see in these the other more scholastic attempts of the Sangha to draw up a scheme of worlds of abstraction, corresponding to that which they had made of "Jhāna or Dhyāna," when they had dropped from Jhāna all that had been originally worth while. When I tell you that one of these abstractions was Asañña, or the being void of intelligence or perception—the word is elastic—you may agree that to stay over these is not worth while. It is the older stratum of values that I am describing, not the later word-structures of logical may-be's.

Jhāna, in its earlier meaning, is emphatically of the older stratum. We find it in the Upanishads with its somewhat younger twin, *samādhi*, but as of relatively minor interest. The former word means "brooding" or "musing," as distinct from what would be called meditating or reflection; the latter is best rendered by concentration. You will have often found it said that India has owed much to "meditation," whether this was India's Buddhist past or her other cults. But do not be misled by this into confounding what Europe means by meditation with what India has mainly meant by it. I find, for instance, several "synonyms" given for *our* "meditate": "ponder, weigh, resolve, study, consider, contemplate, turn over and over in mind." There is in these too much of what we also call "threshing things out." Nothing of this would in ancient India have deserved the name of meditation in any commended sense. Jhāna (or *samādhi* = "concentration") was far better to be described as *access*, *communion*. These were sought in Yoga or in Jhāna. Yoga was a seeking the ideal Man "within," a silent solitary communion with the Better-than-I. Jhāna was also a communion, but not with the better Self "within"; it was with better men without, but in the "unseen," by hearing, or by seeing too. "They *are*," the Śakyamuni is recorded as saying, "they are, these deva-sounds and sights, they are not things of nought."[1]

I am not saying that he was not also valuing the quiet beating out of matters into clear ideas and clear wording. But this is described by other words: *paṭisankhāna*, *paṭisañcikkhati*. And you will come across these less often than Jhāna.

You cannot read long without coming upon Jhāna. It is not in itself taught as a saving or sacramental doctrine, yet it is everywhere commended, and in many contexts is shown as a cathartic preparation for the development of psychic talents. These are, after the Jhāna "stages," enumerated as (*a*) different kinds of *iddhi*, *i.e.* "the wrought," such as levitation, etc., (*b*) deva-hearing, (*c*) thought-reading, (*d*) recollecting former "lives," (*e*) deva-sight. A sixth, called waning of three or four latent evils called *āsavas*, is, as I have shown elsewhere,[2] a gloss of a religious, quite different nature. I have called (*b*) and (*e*) clairaudience and clairvoyance, and have been criticized for doing so, but without being shown *how* I am wrong. These gifts are so often everywhere misused, that perhaps criticism is but natural. Christian readers of the Bible will concede what a potent channel for help they are there shown to be, from the boy Samuel to Elijah, listening with shrouded face in the cavern mouth, to Isaiah at his moan "Woe is me!", down to Jesus, who both heard and saw, as human man, to St. Peter responding to his vision, and hearing, to St. Paul, who both saw and heard, to St. John in Patmos. I should call all these clairaudient and clairvoyant, worthily using great gifts, and guarded therein because of the worthy use.

The opening book of the Third Piṭaka expressly speaks of Jhāna as a "'way' (or method) made-to-become for access

[1] *Dīgha* I., Mahāli Sutta.

[2] Cf. *Sakya*, on "Abhijñā."

to the Rūpa-world," *i.e.* the Brahmā world. By this no "translation" of body or spirit is meant, but the hearing, with or without the seeing, anyone of that world who might be at hand to be consulted. A Sutta speaks of a monk who has attained the devas (*deva-patto*) as one who practises Jhāna. Another speaks of the happiness won in converse with devas by one who is practising Jhāna. Gotama was said to frequent the "deva-seat" in Jhāna, and to be met with, "musing in the wood." Delight in Jhāna [1] is said with reference to Sāriputta and others, men and women. And when Moggallāna exercised in benevolence his gifts,[2] he first mused in Jhāna.

Yet it took me years to see this original purpose in Jhāna emerging in the Piṭakas. This was because no one saw that the *prescribed formula* for Jhāna belonged to that later stratum of values. It has no word about the access sought. It is only a method for gradually eliminating from the Jhāyin, or practiser, in succession, all active work of mind (application and reflection or pondering) and all affective, *i.e.* emotional, states, till he is reduced to a "pure alertness and equanimity." If the result is to be a rapt quasi-trance about nothing at all, this may conceivably have been beneficial as a rest-cure. But there is nothing to show us that the lives of Sakyan monks were so strenuous, physically or mentally, as to need one, nor is there a vestige of it among the things explicitly needed. But if we heed these left-in references just quoted, we can see that the qualities of alertness and of indifference or neutral feeling were *precisely what the listening psychic must develop* to hear "the still small voice," or see the elusive vision.

But values changed, and the monk ceased to be longing to commune with those other worlds, which had become for his outlook so many prolongings of the Ill that was life. He had no quarrel with the large corpus of Suttas and verses about devas, for it was easy so to teach these, as

[1] *Jhāna-rati.* [2] Above, p. 182.

showing one and all how the Man of compassion on the worlds of devas and men was sought out by both. But he so altered his Jhāna formulas, that they either abruptly left off as just preparation, like a ladder against a wall the top of which it does not reach, or he superimposed further formulas of practice in certain mental abstractions—absorption into a concept of bare space (or ether), of bare mind (or consciousness), of bare nothingness, of bare neither-sense-nor-non-sense (or-intelligence), in which it is, for me at least, impossible to discover any religious progress, either from anything in the records, or by pondering. We even find the following sentiment imputed to the unfalteringly Compassionate One: "that as this and that one having died you should ask the tathāgata about the matter, truly a worry is this to the tathāgata" . . . an echo (and imitation?) of the Hesitation episode, but not of that maturer feeling, which will have seen that it was the bereaved who were "worried," and needed him. Nor is the remedy he proposes more free from a suggestion of editorial handling. The dharma-mirror, by which each was to ascertain for himself, is just the later formula: Buddha, Dhamma, Sangha, and faith in these as guarantee, that, at all events, the believer need have no fear of purgatory—a substitution of faith for "works" that is alien to the main teaching.

So habitual a jhāyin was Gotama in his life, that even his dying is recorded in terms of a back and forth in these Jhāna formulas. It is just possible that Anuruddha the psychic was present, who alone could have recognized that the dying leader was already in contact with another world. It is possible that the all-but-forgotten tradition, when intoned and droned in its present wording, may have been effectively impressive. At the same time it is woefully crude. The compiling hand is here out of tune, out of time, with the day of the passing out of the greatest of jhāyins.

The fact remains, that rightly to read the Piṭakas we must recognize, in the sermons and the emphasized tenets, the ecclesiastical values of a monasticism which had turned from all sympathy with and hope for this or any world, as "becomings," not of advance in wayfaring in the more and more, but of a mere round of births, illness and dyings. And at the same time we must look as we read for much testimony left-in, either as subserving the growing Buddha-cult, or just from piety, or because here and there a revising editor was privately one loyal to the older tradition, or from all these reasons—a testimony to a deep and active interest in the original Sakya to the things not of this world.

How, indeed, should it not be so, when we come to see how truly a teaching of the More in and before the man was the Way of Becoming! How could it ever be reconciled with such a central teaching to see in man the creature of earth only? As well might we look upon the schoolboy as always a schoolboy. The old parts of the Commentaries are far from sharing such a view. Not only is Gotama the surviving consummation of myriads of lives, but each saint is recorded as having lived as man or woman in other worlds, and there used well the afforded opportunities of the Worlds-wayfaring. It is man who is wont to contract his own dimensions and shrivel his destiny. The great teachers are they who bid him come up on the hill and throw wide for him the worlds, saying: Behold your right of way! Live greatly!

It is the man they summon. It is true their call is for all men, but it is a blurring, a diluting of that call to consider it only in terms of all men. In every other call, social, ethical, political, it is well to think racially, to see men, world-citizens. But in religion, the message is *to the man*, the warding is *for the man;* there is in it, even though a man give himself as a bridge for others to pass over, no oblivion, no annihilation for the unit. In the lowest specimen, in the most tragic earth-life, there is the divine potency, there is the Way of the worlds. And to develop that potency of perfection earth-life can be nothing further than just one opportunity in many of training. Too heavy is its handicap, even in the worthiest, to permit of more. Hence the vista, in religions, of other worlds. And perhaps in nothing is Sakya more vindicated as a growing beyond its parent teaching of the Upanishads than in its closer touch with other worlds, its much converse with them, its more definite bodying out of the what and the how of them, patchy and still vague as is all that has come down to us. It is by this closer original other-worldly touch, that we can explain the new phenomenon of this cosmology, not found before. And to the waning of that touch it is, that this phenomenon has remained isolated, undeveloped. The kindly watchers of other worlds spoke no more.

CHAPTER X

THE FIRST MISSIONERS AND THEIR TEACHING

WHAT was it that Gotama and his first helpers were banded together to teach? Have I made this at all plain? I see it as this: Man—I mean, the very man as expressing himself through body-with-mind—is, in the things of the very man, a chooser; he has the choice between free play of will and restraint of will by rule. Life is thus a perpetual movement in decision. In deciding he is in process of becoming what he was not exactly, before he decided. He is better or worse. He wills to be what he deems is better; it is of his nature to be seeking, through many "betters," a "best." He is not seeking alone. He is aware of an inner monition to do or not to do. He can see that other men are self-urging, are restrained, even as he is. He values them as also inwardly guided, if they will to let themselves be guided. According to his heeding, or his spurning this inner guidance, he will, after death, enter upon that "better" which he is becoming, or he will enter upon that "worse" which he is becoming. This entering-upon is just another stage, and there is more to come. Thus he is as a wayfarer in a way, a long way of many "becomings." He is with other wayfarers, on a like adventure, like but not uniform with his; each is chooser, faring according to his choice. That inner guide he called "the Self," one with his self, yet transcending it as was the teaching of the day. Or he called It "dharma" —"that which ought to be,"—shifting the emphasis from the "self," and lending a new weight to the word "dharma."

This is for me what writers have called, with their own differing interpretation, the Secret, or the Message, or the Gospel of "Buddhism." It is not an imaginary picture. Had I space, it could be shown implicit yet a ground-wave in Sutta after Sutta. Now and then it is on the surface. So it seemed to me, when, after years of prentice work spent on making the Abhidhamma-Piṭaka completely accessible, I was drawn into Sutta-Piṭaka-study. The thing that perhaps most struck me was the reiteration of a man's varying fate, and adjudicated fate, at death, as the result of his life here, the newness of the impression being largely due to the way in which this is almost ignored in the Abhidhamma, and to some extent by writers on Buddhism.

More usually the message as sketched here is not on the surface. And that is partly because, when the Suttas took their present form, values had become not Everyman-values, but monastic values, partly because, with doctrines become by that time long formulated and established, by a Sangha or "church," the ever-new universal fact of the man as having, if he but heed, a divine inner guidance was no longer made the keynote it was in the beginning. The Sangha, the Doctrine, as in other creeds, was telling him what to do. The Inner Dharma had become a worded, a formulated "Dhamma."

But when we search for the beginnings, we no longer find man's religious life thus ordered by a cult rounded off, so to speak, as compared with other cults. We find something which was given as a New Word *within* the best religious teaching of its day, a word opening up a fresh light, a deeper force in the established creed. Deity as immanent had been accepted, and was beginning to inform the moral sense with a new warmth. Then came this New Word irradiating the accepted and the new with this saving power *for the Many*: "You are not just being, you are becoming; your becoming is That growing within you; your becoming is a matter, not of ritual of just knowing; it is your very living. In the other man That too is becoming. You are each and all in the long way of becoming toward That Who you are."

Only thus shall we avoid the mistaken wonder of pioneers who deemed they had found a unique "religion," so on all fours in its silences with modern Rationalism, that they were tempted to force the likeness, by slurring over the features not consonant with that conclusion. We must fit Gotama's message into the religious framework of his place and time; we must not interpret it in the light of the Hebrew framework of our own tradition. No quarrel is, I repeat, recorded between Sakyans and Brahmans on the subject of Deity, or of Deity as immanent. Had this been quarrelled about, much would have been made of such records in the Pali scriptures. The matters we there find criticized in brahmans are quite other; they are the brahman pride in birth,[1] in the monopoly of being celebrants and mantra-reciters, in faith made to crowd out "works."[2] The Sakyan mission was out "not to destroy, but to fulfil," to enlarge and enhance the accepted faith-in-God of their day, not by asseverating or denying, but by making it more vital. It was brahmans who became the leading disciples; it was brahmans who are recorded as honouring it no less than did certain rajas and certain merchants.

"Becoming," pictured as a Way wherein man grew in wayfaring, was a popular theme, lending itself to applications in scores of ways. But I am far from thinking it monopolized the missioners' talk. It takes a very outstanding kind of teacher to do full justice to a new theme, even as working under a leader. And be it remembered that the five, who alone are named as with that leader from the first, had been with him inquirers for some time

[1] Esp. *Further Dialogues*, II., Nos. 84, 93, 95, 96, etc.
[2] Esp. Tevijja-Sutta, *Dialogues*, I. (XIII).

into what the active world of Vesālī was discussing and indeed teaching. These ideas and practices will have affected them all in different ways and degrees. And whereas the central theme of the Way of Becoming will have been agreed upon, these other ideas will have blended with it more or less according to the individual teacher.

I will here repeat what I find those ideas and practices linked with central theme will have been. They may be comprised in three groups: a new interest in man as being not just (*a*) visible person and (*b*) that inner man called both "name" (*nāma*) and "self" (*attan*), or *par excellence* "man" (*purisa*), but man as being distinguishable, not only into *c*, but also into *a* and *b* the inner world of "mind." And further, that this inner world was orderly and consecutive in its going on. It went on by those inevitable sequences which men saw in the outer world, whereby, for instance, the twirled firestick always resulted in fire; the unfed fire always went out; sound seed in good soil with moisture always became plant and fruit, and the like. This nascent psychology of India (which came later to be called, not *chitta-vāda*, or *mano-vāda*, viz. mental lore, but Sānkhya (in Pali Sankhā [1]), was attracting much attention, as we can see from the early Upanishads. The brahman teachers were able to harness it and for a time maintain it as a useful mental discipline. Early "Buddhism" also harnessed it for the same purpose, but before long it was the mental discipline that harnessed the annexers, and made them its slaves.

This new interest in mind is not usually linked with interest in the thoughts of man as *causal*. That this is not done has led to our interpreting the immense obtrusion of "causal law" in the Piṭakas *from our Western point of view*. When we here speak of "cause and effect," causation, causal law, we at once think of the physical universe,

[1] Through it disciples were referred to as *manobhāvanīyā*, "mind-developers."

of suns and seasons, of forces and resultants. But India at that time was not interested in the material world scientifically—that is, in and for itself—as the West has been for a few centuries. No one, of course, can fail to be interested in the world of matter as playing upon our senses, as our source of bodily life, our main source of dangers, and of what we can get out of it. But this is not the disinterested scientific interest which observes, compares and at some stage says: Given this, that comes to be; from the stopping of this, that is stopped. It was only in connection with the interference with matter in order to heal, that India made her observation of things physical into a causal science. It was the healer's medical diagnosis which, as Theodor Kern pointed out years ago, very possibly suggested the analogous way in which the "four truths," or certainties were presented by both the Śakyamuni in the first utterance and also by the compilers of the Yoga Sūtras Commentary of a somewhat later date. To this I have referred.

If in reading the Suttas you will note, in some books, the frequent preoccupation with things as "conditioned," or caused, you will find that these things are of the inner world of man. Take the first Collection, the Dīgha-Nikāya, in Suttas dealing with causes: "I have said that becoming is the cause of birth . . . that grasping is the cause of becoming."[1] Again: "Envy and self-regard: what is the cause thereof . . . what being present, are they also present?"[2] You will find yourself able to cite many more. The Commentators, being more discursive and exponential, have not seldom recourse to natural phenomena, but only as subsidiary to the study of man and his mind. The freshness of this new outlook upon an ordered cosmology somehow "within" (it was linked with the heart and blood, not with the neural system), a microcosm, yet embracing everything, will have been profoundly stimulating. Europe felt

[1] *Dialogues*, II., XV. [2] *Ibid.*, XXI.

it as such when the new science of "mental philosophy," "philosophy of mind,"[1] "mental physiology," then "mental science" and ultimately "psychology," was coming to birth during the period, say, 1690–1830. Very slowly was the child, the "science" of mind-processes, weaned from its mother, philosophy, and it is only of yesterday that psychology has become a term of current talk. You are too young to have felt anything fresh about it. But I recall the inspiring effect made on me when first reading of this internal world as no less causally ordered than bodily functions. And if we admit this, our own recent stimulus, we can better discern what it will have meant for India, where there was so little specialization in knowledge, that the one word *vidyā* meant religion, philosophy, science and art in one body of knowledge and tradition.

You will see how this great dual interest of the day was making itself felt, not only in the early Upanishads, but also in the assigning a fixed wording to the first Sakyan Sayings. I am convinced that those first missioners did not teach in fixed sayings. It is only when a teacher represents an old revered tradition, that he impresses Everyman with formulas, intoned as were (and are) all traditional fixed sayings or "mantras." If he has no such credentials, he must talk, simply, directly, with utmost personal conviction. He must win his hearer to his own way with the "What do you think?" which survives in so many Suttas as a survival of this method. But you will see no less how often that new interest in causality and the mind has been used by compilers to make plausible the earlier Sayings, which will, in many cases, have been lapsing from memory, nay, which will have, here and there, been about views and terms, which had become "out of date," and even discredited. So thickly are the cause-and-mind-analyses smeared upon the old sayings, that it is not easy,

[1] The Chair of Psychology at University College, London, still bears this title.

in the Suttas, to find any of the direct man-to-man speech left. Mind, for instance, must be adduced under four heads; sense under five or six, and becoming is, where it is not put up and stoned, smothered in a list of causes and effects. I cannot hear either the Founder or his men talking like that. Can you?

Another preoccupation that will have been much on their tongue was the possible and desirable work of communion between earth and other worlds. Into this I have gone in the last chapter. You will not get far in the Suttas without coming upon reference to "Jhāna." It does not follow that this later emphasis is identical with the earlier interest in "other-worldliness." This interest, as I have shown, had waned for the editors. And their waned interest has given to us their own stunted ideas of what was to be sought in Jhāna. But the first men, as we have seen, were ministering to a great popular need for that pulling aside the veil, which the late War stimulated for awhile in Europe, but which has drooped again. After-life had become a pressing reality of more than priestly interest, and here were men teaching a Way of coming-to-be, which involved many lives in many worlds as man's right-of-way. And of these few men, some could hear and see as most men cannot. Let us be quite frank about it: Sakya, at and just after its birth, was a spiritualistic religion. The Founder especially was hymned in what are possibly very old verses as one

Who free from evil, lusts all quenched,
And rolling back the murky veil,
And pain gone by and weariness,
He sees both this world and the next: [1]

the man-who-saw, and saw the worlds as two houses, men going and coming.[2]

Finally there will have been in their talk that which bulks so largely in the Southern Buddhism of to-day: morals

[1] *Dialogues,* III., XXX., 1. [2] Above, p. 181.

and the more than morality which we may call either ethics, or religion, as concerned with the fellow-man. I have seen or heard "Buddhism" spoken of as if it invented morals for India! This will, as most now know, not hold water for a moment. Truth and uprightness, filial piety and honesty, chastity and sobriety may all be found in the Vedas and with a stressing of right and wrong, of aversion from "evil" (*pāpa*), reverberating through the Upanishads; you will find them if you search well. And you will find, too—and this is made very emphatic—that nobler ground of ethics than the not doing wrong to the other man lest he do so to you, to which allusion has been made: the holding the fellow-man precious because he, no less than one's self, is, as we might say, a shrine of the Holy Spirit, or as the Indian would say, the Ātman, the God in and as himself.

But I have said, "if you search well" of a purpose, for it is none the less true that morals and ethics are not the very serious preoccupation of the Vedas or the Upanishads. In them you will find nothing whatever rivalling in moral earnestness the long first Sutta of the Dīgha-Nikāya. Nor need you stop there. The code against murder, dishonesty, sex-wantonness, evil speech and inebriety—it is compared to the earth as a basis of good life—runs through every Sutta of that first section, the Section on Morals, and culminates in the last, the 13th Sutta, with the great Tevijja, where the moral life is shown as the essential preparation fitting the man for companionship after death with devas of moral life, and without which neither faith nor ritual is of any avail. Buddhism is not, never was, just morality, just ethics, as some have said. But there is all the difference between the stress it laid on these as compared with the absence of stress in the preceding scriptures. Early Buddhism lost the fairest jewel of its first message; but it never lost the early insistence on the Life, the Conduct as being of the essence of true religion. There is as much call for, and need of faith in Buddhism as in any other world-religion, but, for it, faith without works is null and void.

Nor will the teaching of the importance in the moral life have rested with the bare framework of the five *sīlas*, or moral habits, which South Asian Buddhism has ever made such a sacrament of initiation. The clothing this skeleton with a more positive vitality you will find in that first Dīgha Sutta and in one or two more contexts. The "Thou shalt nots" are there made vibrant with the positive warding of other lives, of other men's goods, and the like.

But you may say, Is there not a going beyond even this? Have we not heard of a fourfold practice of willing men amity, pity, friendly joy and poise, called the Divine States, or Abidings? Yes, you will find these incorporated into several Suttas. They only begin *at the end* of the Sīla Section, nor are they anywhere brought into any main statement of doctrine. They are in their way unique, for they are efforts in what I have called not telepathy, but televolition. A man, if he be full of amity or good will, may try *by willing* to infect someone else therewith, who is lacking in it.[1] Similarly, he may try to infuse pity into the callous, happiness into the man whose is not yet the joy that belongs not to mere external well-being, the even balance into the man flustered and distraught. To attempt this is as open to anyone, who is himself not empty, as it was then, and he may find the results surpass his expectations. The last mode became unworthily valued in Buddhist teaching, as meaning only a self-steadying after an orgy of willed loving-kindness, etc., but it is as televolitional as are the other three.

Another way in which Buddhist teaching has weakened this intensive ethics is the formulating the practice only in terms of a *universal* radiating. This is very well for a climax in expression and intent. But men were not then,

[1] With no word for "will," "thought" is used, with the verb *pharati*, to suffuse.

any more than now, so strong in will that they could benefit anyone but themselves, when aspiring in this universal way: "he with amity-consorted mind abides suffusing one quarter . . . the second, third, fourth quarter; so above below across everyway by everywhereness the entire world . . . with abundant expanded immeasurable unhate, un-ill-will suffusing abides he, etc." Actually, as we see in one or two later descriptions, a man was to practise his benevolent intent on individuals. A house, a street, a district is then taken on. But the scriptural formula is only in the catholic terms quoted, and this may be the reason why you will never find Buddhists, in writing, inculcating the only way in which to make the practice altruistically efficient.

I cannot here go into the evidence I find sufficient to show this very notable new word in ethics as not belonging to the original message of Buddhism.[1] The evidence, in brief, lies mainly in the teaching as "intrusive," as not counted in with the teachings expressly stated to be central, and as pointing to a teacher and his following who were explicitly brahman. It is a thousand pities that nothing has survived to show Gotama's band taking over this teaching. All that we have is a Sutta telling of its disciples, asking Gotama's men, whether the latter taught the four practices as they did. They make no mention of a leader. And the latter are made to speak as if the practices were as integrally theirs as they were the inquirers'. Old scriptures do not show us such things in process of becoming. They tell of what has come to be. Corporate pride in after years would forbid the Sangha to acknowledge how it strengthened its ethical position by the annexing of that nameless saintly brahman's gospel. I do not judge the annexing was after Gotama's day. I can see him welcoming a teaching which was so essentially one of man as in process of "becoming" seeking to foster "becoming" in another. At the same

[1] See, in *Sakya*, the chapter on "The Warding of Man."

time, the "man" in it is so vital, as valuer, as willing, as directing will, as reaching out to fellow-man, that I am not surprised it was not suffered to come into certain teachings, pronounced as central, which you will find are in every case worded in terms, less of "man," than of "mind," with the man left out.

These teachings are referred to, in the Sutta dealing with the last weeks of the Founder's earth-life, as *dhamma's* which "have been taught, are to be learnt, followed (or practised), made-to-become, expanded, so that this God-life may be prolonged, for the benefit of devas and of men." [1] They are then listed as

Four Presences of Mindfulness,
Four Fit Endeavours,
Four Ways in the Wrought (*iddhi*),
Five Faculties,
Five Strengths,
Seven Parts of Enlightenment,
Worthy Eightfold Way.

Of these I shall have something further to say later. My point here is that, in this list of lists, the "man" is implicit only; it is ways of mind that are made explicit. In the four Brahma-vihāras, or Divine Abidings, the "man" is engaged upon the fellow-man; as person, in what was, and is still for us, a mysterious way, he was to have contact unseen with person. Even the universalized formula always begins with the individual: *so:* "he," or *so bhikkhu*. It is the man-as-agent wirelessing to the man-as-recipient. It is fairly comical to read how Buddhaghosa, a thousand years later, when dealing with this, tries to illustrate the televolition by way of the man-as-unreal. He has left televolition in the lurch, and is persuading the man lacking in amity that he can only feel hostility not against a "man," but against a bit of body or a phase of mind.

[1] *Dialogues*, II., p. 127, § 50.

"With whom, good monk, are 'you' angry?" Yet all the while he is appealing to *the man-who-is-angry*, not to the anger, not to *his* bit of body or phase of mind. Buddhaghosa would have said, he was only using conventional modes of speech; that there was a deeper sense, by which the man was known only in terms of mind, indeed, was no more than that. Nor would it have offended his monkish outlook to know both himself and all men as herein perpetually telling lies in their talk; life was just that!

But that, in the Brahmavihāras, the man is seeking after the Self, the better self in the fellow-man, is just that which will have commended the teaching to the Śakyamuni, who started his mission with that. Would that we knew more of his welcoming it!

Such were mainly the subjects of current religious interest which will have been brought into and around the main teaching of the Way of Becoming by the first missioners: mind, ideas as distinguishable from the very Man, and as occurring in causal order; Jhāna or musing, and by it access to knowledge of other worlds; the vital religious importance of the moral life, and the moral claim on each man and woman of the fellow-man.

That the Way, especially as Way symbolizing Becoming, will have been for leader and first men the topic ever in the front is, alas! not well borne out by the Suttas. If you would see it stressed as an "eightfold" formula, you should consult the last part of the Saṃyutta-Nikāya, where in the "Great Section" that List of lists, quoted above, is dealt with in detail, and where you will find the Way placed, as is fit, not at the end (in numerical progression), but at the start. Here eighty or more little Suttas are each and all stating it. But not in any vital way—merely as a *cliché*, a catchword. It is given as the Founder's first mantra: the man as in a way choosing; it appears as the last mantra spoken by the Founder on his deathbed; and, as we saw, he was called, when he had gone, by the man who then could best know, the Man of the Way. Yet how have we not to look to find him made to teach the Way as what it meant for him: the great adventure of life. You will find it so taught in only two passages known to me: Sutta 107 of the Majjhima-Nikāya and "Tissa" of Saṃyutta-Nikāya III. Even in the latter there has been much editing with scholastic terms.

In the former, Gotama is asked by a brahman whether with his good guidance he brings all his disciples to the ultimate goal, and if not, why not? The reply brings out (1) himself as just shower of the way, (2) the man shown as having to choose his way aright after the showing. And the living force of the talk is yet there. "What think you, sir? Suppose a man came asking you the way to Rājagaha . . ." Read it; and the other: Tissa, Gotama's cousin, is depressed, or bilious, or both. Discounting the mind-analysis with which the Kinsman's healing begins, we just get, in all too few words, the adventure of the Way before him in its ups and downs, with the eventual sighting of the fair land of uttermost desire coming into view. Here, too, is living fire left in, but it is at the end, when comfort and courage are driven into Tissa with magnetic shocks of will, brotherly hands it may be laid on him gripping: "Rejoice, Tissa! Rejoice, Tissa! What need is there for you that I preach, that I come to your aid, that I instruct you?" (Do you not see what, as man-becoming, lies before you, that you in the long run *must* come to attain?) What would we not give for more of such Suttas! But they have been let die, and the formula alone caps the Saying. Yet read them! "Becoming" you will scarcely find: the three "becomings," used for worlds,[1] and the three quests: "sense-desire-quest, becoming-quest, God-life-quest,"[2] the latter two being now made divergent (!) and the Way which must be made-to-become if a man would

[1] *Gradual Sayings*, I., p. 45. [2] *Ibid.*, p. 44.

understand all three. But note the compound "Way-culture," lit. "making-the-Way-to-become"[1] how near are we not here to the conversely stressed "Way of becoming."[2]

If, then, we can find in the Suttas, taken, of course, as a whole, and not in the "Great Section" Way-chapter only, such an atrophied teaching of the Way, will you be saying that I am mistaken in assigning such a foremost place to it in the first years of the mission? I would not be swift to answer in this matter. My convictions herein have been the slow growth of years—can I expect another to adopt them in a moment? I believe more firmly now than ever, that the Way of Becoming was, and remained for Gotama, the central message. I am not in the least deterred when I read, in Vinaya and Sutta, how the Buddha of the legend appears under the Bodhi-tree, as much bedizened with the coils of the Causal formula of how "ill" comes to pass as is the parting guest hung about with garlands in India. Truer for me than seeing him cumbered with a gospel of causation, rejected by him as unfit for Everyman, is it to recall the last sentences of the first Mantra, even though they may be a gloss: "Not till I had made the Way to become, did knowledge and insight arise in me." But I would only expect you to be ready to come in with this my view after much leisurely reading of translations of both scriptures and commentaries, including *The Path*—the Way, it should be—*of Purity*. Then will you see how, for all the fossilizing of the Way or Path in a formula, for all the contracting by monastic hands of its age-long length for Everyman, the Way, the Way comes echoing, re-echoing down Pali literature. And you will then maybe concede we have in it a subject originally as central and become as traditional as was for the early Christians "the kingdom of God is within you."

As to those subjects contributory to that of the Way, is

[1] *Magga-bhāvanā Saṃy.*, V., 49. [2] *Bhava-magga.*

it possible to associate them severally with the name of any one or more of the first men?

This is a most pertinent question. But it will be well to take first a wider survey of them than I have yet given. We may distinguish four groups among them: (1) the first five; (2) the fire-worshipping group of three brothers each with a band of pupils; (3) the Brahman group of eight, three of them brothers, and (4) the Sakyan group of seven, who came in from Gotama's own country when he was already established as a teacher. Besides these groups, there were one or two names that stand out: the two Panthaka brothers, who were Vaisyas, or of the merchant class; Gavampati, "lord of kine," a dim, mystic figure, disciple probably, yet choosing rather the silent exemplar of the life of lonely thought than active converting; and Kappina, a northern raja like the Sakyas, whose coming in we have in Commentaries only. Between the first five and the influx of the second group the Vinaya inserts the conversion, and indeed the (very mythical) attainment of the state of "arahan," by fifty-five persons, and the conversion and ordination as monks of the thirty kumāras whose inquiry led to the reply we found so luminous for the original message. But we never hear again of these, save once only, in a work dating from three centuries later, of one, namely, the first "lay" convert Yasa. With the exception of Yasa, they are nothing more than names, or not even that: they are just "friends of Yasa." And it was probably the felt fitness, of investing the first nucleus of their Sangha or church with the highest sanction of personal and doctrinal authority, that induced the editors of a later day (and perhaps repeaters also) to see in those sixty men so many consummate saints.

The second group is of no little interest. You will only find them in the Vinaya[1] and the "Elders' Anthology."[2] They appear as fire-worshippers, brothers Kassapa (a

[1] *Vin. Texts*, I., pp. 118 f. [2] CCIII-IV., CCX.

brahman name), of Uruvelā, Gaya, and "the River" respectively, and may well have been among those Indian converts to the symbolic significance of fire, which developed in Persia soon after Zoroaster's day, in a more pronounced manner than in Vedic observances. You can read of these converts in Professor Williams Jackson's *Zoroaster*,[1] and especially of one, the brahman Kangran-ghācah, a name in which it is possible to see Kassapa with a personal name, (? Kaṇha = Krishna) prefixed. In the Vinaya you will read of Kassapa and Gotama entering into a sort of competition in *iddhi*, as psychic will-power was called in India, a contest which is probably mythical as being incompatible with the spiritual eminence of both men, especially of Gotama. (A competition with a different object is recorded in Dīgha-Nikāya between Gotama and a rishi or ascetic of Vesālī named Pātika.[2]) The fact that communications between these men dwindled down in course of long repetitions to such a level reflects little credit on repeaters, teachers or editors. It is in the Vinaya account that we come upon the title *arahā* (rendered by our time as arhat, arahat, arahant, and arahan: all forms are grammatically permissible), as implying not merely a world-forsaker, but also one of psychic power of this or that kind. It is very possible that Kassapa, no less than Gotama, had this power, but I do not "see" the latter exercising it to bring Kassapa under his power, and in making a bid for the support of the King of Magadha, Bimbisāra. The entry of the Kassapa brothers with their disciples into the infant company became a tradition of importance sufficient to have attached to it a record of a third Utterance known later as the On-fire-Sutta. Doctrinally it is not of the interest of the first two Mantras. It seems somewhat superfluous as an address to men already classed as "ascetics" (*jaṭilas*, men of braided or tangled, matted hair, a specific term for *samaṇa*), as giving them no word of fresh outlook. And I incline to

[1] Macmillan's, 1899, pp. 84 f. [2] *Dialogues*, III., 1 ff.

think it may owe its origin to some injunction spoken by the Founder when first sending his men, as only then become *samaṇas* or monks or "almsmen," on mission tours.

"Uruvelā-Kassapa" won for himself no distinction in the Order beyond the fact of that very useful rally; it is for that he finds mention in the Suttas, and Anthology, CCX. Yet so notable a man will he have been, in gifts, influence and experience, that we may suspect the bottom of his tradition has somehow tumbled out, has, it may be, been intentionally discarded. Kassapa (Sanskrit, Kashyapa) was a common name of brahmans, as you may see from the Suttas. But it is not only that. It figures in early Indian literature as the name of a mythical rishi, even of divine powers, connected especially with heat. Into that I do not here go, but heat, inner glow expressed in *tejas*, of which both fire and the sun were outward visible signs, lived on in early Buddhism. And it is possible that the Kassapas, with their fire ritual, possibly of Persian origin, were responsible for it.

In one other way is there room to suspect their influence. The triad: deed, word, thought, with or without the affix "action" (*kamma*, Sanskrit, *karman*), is frequent in the Suttas. As a triad it is not a feature in earlier Indian literature. With the prefix "good" (*hu-* Indian *su-* Greek *eu*) the triad is perpetual in the older Zoroastrian literature. With this prefix the terms occur in pre-Buddhist literature, but not as a triad. In Pali the prefix is also occasional only, and not in the triad. The Kassapas may be responsible for the triad appearing in Pali. And monastic Pali being more occupied with "bad" than with "good"; the Persian triad will have got sundered from its prefix. But beyond a suspicion that there may have been this connection we cannot go.

There must have been some reason for their appearance in the Sakyan tradition as a triple school of, so to speak, free-lances, out of touch with the main body of North-

Eastern brahmans, with fire as their central symbol. And whether they were propagandists of Zoroastrian religion, or whether they were just a branch of Brahmanism, worshipping Agni, the fire deity, or Deity-in-fire, they may, when joined with the Sakyans, have never ceased to worship a personal conception of the Most High, rather than an impersonal indwelling Dharma-monition. Here possibly may be the reason why records of what the brothers taught are limited to the brief verses assigned to each in the Anthology.

Or is the reason this: that although these three brethren of the fire were psychically gifted and pious worshippers, they may not have been eager missioners? Psychically gifted because they could "see" the other-world visitors, alleged in the record to have waited upon the Founder, and the results of his own visits to other worlds. This power in them pales in the account, because of the sole wish in the recorders to magnify the one Superman. But that power, in a disciple, counted little for revising-editors, when unaccompanied by the teaching zeal of a Moggallāna, to whose psychic power full justice is done, even to caricaturing exaggeration.

It is only too clear, in the Vinaya narrative, that we have the artificial attempt of revising-editors of a much later date attempting to body out certain all-but-forgotten memorized sayings, in which entered experiences of which they themselves knew nothing, and wherein their one concern was the over-dominance of their Great Man. Their tradition had inherited a certain code about worlds unseen, and they quote it in due order. They also proceed to leave in the undignified addenda by expounding monks, such as the ruler of the next-world Indian devas as a laundry-carpenter, fruit and flower as gifts to Kassapa, etc., all totally out of tune with the bulk of the records about the Founder, yet all to be left in as belonging to the old, forgotten things of the first oral revisings. And these "Jaṭilas," associated therein with their cult and with those experiences for which the later Buddhist world no longer cared, save in so far as their Buddha's potency came into relief, fade out of the picture of the first men.

I come to the third group—that of brahmans not associated with any ritual: Sāriputta, or Upatissa, Moggallāna or Koliya, Chunda and Revătă, brothers of the former, Koṭṭhita, Kacchāna, Puṇṇa and Kassapa, distinguished as Great (*Mahā*). It is impossible in this little book to give in any detail even the slight references to each of these eight found in Sutta and Anthologies. And yet it is perhaps especially these who, as cultured brahmans—we do not know whether any were teachers or celebrants, and with none is the term *tevijja* (versed in the three Vedas) coupled —bore with the Founder the chief labours in the mission-field. But you may take it from me, to be tested by such reading as you may do for yourself in translations, that not one of them stands out in the scriptures as specially associated, either with the central subject or with those other subjects: causation, mental analysis, musing (*jhāna*) or higher morals. Kassapa and Revata were incorrigible recluses; but not necessarily turning away therein from teaching, for Kassapa appears with a company of disciples. Revata's verses have an eloquent apology for his amity towards all. Puṇṇa appears only to depart as a daring missioner to an outlying district where, unknown and unprotected, he met his death, Sakya's first martyr.[1] Kacchāna is mentioned as a skilled exponent, but he, too, went afield, founding a branch at Avanti, a place not easy of access. From that branch has come down a little treatise of doctrinal exposition not included in the Piṭakas, albeit commenting on some Suttas. It is called the *Book of Guidance*, but it is not translated.

Kassapa, too, about whom and his distinguished wife—ex-wife, I should say—the teacher Bhaddā Kapilānī, there is much interesting commentarial narrative, would not

[1] See also, p. 220.

spend his old age with his Leader, returning only in time "to bury Cæsar."

Koṭṭhita appears as the sagacious catechizer and as the catechumen with that other eminent teacher Sāriputta. Their catechism, the "Miscellaneous Sutta," should hence be highly informative, yet has the hand of the reviser been busy with it, making it hard to see in it the stamp of those first utterances. It is chiefly interesting as showing the best early instance we have of the influence, on the early teaching, of that keen, crude psychology known as Ŝānkhya. You should make a point of reading it, aware always that whereas we have there two of the very first teachers, and that the new analysis of mind as not "the man" was deeply interesting them, their talk will have passed through many revising hands. Do not see in the talk anything so irrational as the one teacher coming to have ignorance purged by the other. The very reasonable tradition is, that the two comrades drew up together a catechetical scheme for learners, as associated with and endorsed by the sanction of their two names. This may not yet have been quite correctly handed down, but it is at least plausible. Read it in the *Further Dialogues*;[1] it is well rendered, especially in the way it keeps the "man" on the stage, in the talk on his mind. Actually the word man does not occur. There is the adjective implying agency: "one-who-is-wise," and there is the pronounless verb, as in the Latin, e.g. *sapit, percipit,* also implying the agent. A less careful translator might have slurred over the agent, and might also have written "what" enjoys, not "who" (p. 210), as I have seen done elsewhere. That the enjoyer (of sensations) is actually said to be the mind, not the man, shows the influence of the new analysis, already here talking in terms of process only, without proceeder, and making a dummy man of the mind, just like our own psychology.

[1] Vol. I., No. 43; cf. *Kindred Sayings,* IV., pp. 272 ff.

Read, I repeat, but take these *caveats* along: Note the original word "become" twice omitted by translators: (1) "in understanding we have to develop"; this is, literally, "*paññā* should-be-made-to-become," the very word applied elsewhere to the Way. (*Paññā* is not a term of intellect or mind; it belongs to Indian religious terms; and is the growing, the making-become, the developing, of the very God-in-man, of the Divine nature.) (2) "Becoming" is called "rebirth." The question is, "How many *bhava's* are there?" "Corporeal," again, for the Rūpa world is quite wrong; sensuous rebirth (the *Kāma-bhava*) is corporeal as well. Again, delete "Ecstasy." There was nothing Bacchanalian about jhāna or musing. It was just carefully prepared listening. I have gone into this.[1] And remember that "heart" is just *citta*, a purely "minding" word.

It is a strange thing and a tragic that, of all the first men, the one who alone is recorded to have won the Founder's praise as "turning the dharma-wheel as I do,"[2] the wheel, that is, as Way-symbol—should not appear in the Suttas as linked explicitly with the Way-teaching, that is, with the becoming or growth of the very man. Even his younger brother Chunda, known otherwise only through three discourses and a visit, shows this teaching in the little poem named after him:

Good hearers grow by hearing: hearing is growing in wisdom:
By wisdom one comes to know the Good: known Good brings happiness along.
Seek ye as lodgings lonely spots: walk in the liberty from bonds.
If there ye come not by what ye love, dwell ye as cenobite,
The self well warded and the mind alert.[3]

Here is none of his brother Revata's fervent amity to enrich the quest of the better man; it is so far the poorer; the whole gospel is not there, but the well-spring is, and in the four ślokas much is said.

[1] Pp. 186 ff. [2] *Ibid.*, p. 82 and elsewhere.
[3] *Psalms of the Brethren*, ver. 141–2.

Sāriputta, eldest of the three, is oftener met in Sutta than anyone save Ānanda, and many are the topics in his talks and questions. Yet in emphasis there is but one of them I have found linked with him three times, and with him only. It is not on any of those four contributory subjects, with which we should like to link names of first men. It is on a point of Brahmanic teaching of his day, a point which that growing vogue of mind-analysis was about to take by the throat and, in Buddhism, ultimately to strangle. I mean, the reality and function of "the man" as distinguishable from his mind and body. It is a parable:[1]

A few of the chief men—Sāriputta and Revata, Moggallāna, Kassapa (Mahā) and Anuruddha—are enjoying the moonlit evening in Gosinga Wood. Ānanda approaches. "Come along, Ānanda," calls Sāriputta, "welcome! Fair is the wood in the clear moonlight, with deva-perfumes methinks wafted around. In what manner could a man make the wood (more) beautiful?" Ānanda votes for one who knows the Sayings and is good. The others being asked, Revata the recluse is for meditation, calm and musing; Anuruddha, for clairvoyance; Kassapa, the ascetic, for one endowed with the virtues brought about by the severely simple, ascetic life. Moggallāna's reply is unexpected and stimulating. "When two men of the Order are conversing on the *higher dharma*." We should have looked, perhaps, for Anuruddha's reply to come from him. Higher dharma, *abhidhamma*, we do not associate with Moggallāna, nor, for that matter, was any specific study, such as developed into the third *Piṭaka*, then dreamt of. We must here be up against *an older use* of the term—the use I went into above. If that be so, we have him saying what we might call a talk about conscience, or about God. How far more likely is this than that he meant anything like the dreary catechisms of the Abhidhamma books!

[1] *Further Dialogues*, Sutta 28.

Finally Moggallāna rounds on Sāriputta: "What would *you* say?" And Sāri's son is made to reply: "Take a man who is master of the mind, and is not under its mastery. . . . It is as if a raja or his like, having his wardrobe filled with clothes of divers colours, were in the morning to don the pair of robes he were to desire for early wear; at noon were to don the pair he might desire then; in the evening, the pair he might desire then. By such a man were Gosinga Wood made (more) beautiful."[1]

Now the occurrence of this parable thrice is no evidence for its being a genuine early saying. It is the *emphasis* in the parable, an emphasis which did not appeal to the later outlook, that makes it impossible for the saying to have come in later. *Then* the man became held as only to be known as and in mind. You can see this in the Miscellany Sutta, where the mind has been put in as doing precisely what, in the parable, the man alone can do: estimate, desire, choose. The mind, *i.e.* the minding, is just the estimating, desiring, choosing.

That the parable is associated with Sāriputta, and with him only, is evidence that, whatever else he believed and taught, the "man" was for him very real; the Way will have been, for him, the Man in the Way.

But there is one other subject, this time one of those I have grouped as associates of the central teaching, which *is*, seldom, associated with Sāriputta, but with varying context. This is that uniformity in our inner world which we call causation or causality. In a Sutta of the Majjhima-Nikāya Sāriputta is made to deliver a very monastic discourse, which he winds up with imputing to the Bhagavā the saying: "He who sees causal happening sees dharma; he who sees dharma sees causal happening."[2] This would appear to be a confusion in traditions of different sections of repeaters. The Saṃyutta repeaters had this

[1] The word "select" in the translation is not in the Pali.

[2] Sutta No. 28.

saying of the Bhagavā to the doting disciple Vakkāli: "He who sees dharma sees me; he who sees me sees dharma."[1] Or else I have overlooked where he is made to say the former saying. I do not believe he will have said, can have said, either saying. Or that Sāriputta delivered that discourse. With him, causal happening would be shown rather as the way in which man *strives after his good,* believing in his own transformation into the better thereby, as the effect of the cause. He would not have harped on ill, as he is here made to do. He is again met with on the matter of cause and effect in Saṃyutta Suttas:[2] those termed *Sectarian Teachers, Bhūmija* and *Become,* but you will see him shown, not as having made the subject peculiarly his own, but as a pupil in it of the Bhagavā, quoting him and being instructed by him. (The last-named Sutta is a tragic instance of the Founder being made, by monastic values, to show "things as become" in a repellent light, instead of beacons of hope and growth in man.)

But the most striking way in which Sāriputta's name is linked with causal law is in the Vinaya account of how he was brought into the new company of Gotama's men. Assaji, of the first five, was the intermediary. Sāriputta and Moggallāna, young brahmans studying under the brahman sceptic or sophist Sañjaya, are in quest of the best way to *amrita*, the "immortal," the conquest over the power of death to frighten, bewilder, depress, a quest so much worded in the Upanishads. Sāriputta meets a very radiant Assaji (whom he apparently knows). Who, what has brought him light? The reply, given with diffidence, is that the samaṇa Gotama can assign its cause to any and every effect. (This answer is put metrically.) Light comes to Sāriputta that every caused thing is as such a stoppable thing. And he and his friend come in.

It is to me little short of amazing that Buddhists appear to acquiesce in this as a true account, and that Western

[1] *Kindred Sayings*, III., p. 103. [2] Pp. 27, 30, 35.

writers follow them, in so far as they accept the records, uncritically. It is not that we have here again the monk's contracted view of the mighty promise in causation, or uniformity of sequence. It is that we have the man of the Way-gospel seen as a man who saw his central gospel in the fact of this inner world-causation. It is also, in the assumption, that simply to hear of a teacher whose causal knowledge is all-embracing makes a man hearing of it realize that caused things can be stopped. There is too far a cry from the one fact to the other. The little episode does not hang together in itself, or with *the first utterances*; it is a patchwork. There will probably have been *some other teacher* for whom inner causation was as central as was the way of becoming for Gotama. And, further, the line of verse, destined in much later times to be used as a Buddhist inscription (it never, I believe, recurs in the Piṭakas), will have here been inserted long after in a more than half-forgotten oral record. I am far from rejecting the episode, nor can I reconstruct it save in the most tentative fashion. I have so tried, and you will find the attempt in my *Sakya*.[1] I do not make Assaji out to have been a teacher of causation in religion, but I do see in him the pupil of one. And if that teacher came in with Gotama, it may be that to him is to be assigned the noticeable thread of psychological and religious interest in causality in Suttas and Abhidhamma. Assaji does not figure as a strong teacher.[2]

We now come to the fourth group of inflowing members: the Sakyan kumāras from Kapilavatthu, Mahānāma, Anuruddha, Bhagu, Ānanda and Devadatta, together with their

[1] Pp. 125 ff.; also *J.R.A.S.* 1927, p. 193.

[2] There are certain named teachers of that day repeatedly referred to in the Suttas (e.g. *Dialogues*, Sta. 2; *Kindred Sayings*, I., pp. 90, 94), who are mainly quoted as being anti-causationists, especially Mokkhali and Ajita. I have gone into their views a little in *Buddhism* (Home University Library), Chap. IV (*b*). Since they, with the exception of the Jain Nāta-putta, were of the nature of "sophists," and do not come into direct contact with the Sakyan missioners, I have not held it pertinent to go over the ground again.

valet-barber Upāli. The story of their leaving home, and why, to join their kinsman's company is given in the Vinaya less for its intrinsic interest than because of Devadatta, for it is inserted under Dissensions in the Order. So far were Buddhists, at least in India, ever feeling the high importance of making a consecutive history of their tradition, even when writing, with a good medium for it, had been lit upon.

The Devadatta plot seriously threatened the continuity, or at least the unity, of the Order. It was dramatically interesting, with a leader almost rivalling in gifts the Founder, and his name lived to have heaped upon it the sort of obloquy the Christian Church piled on that of Judas Iscariot. But as affecting the process by which the Founder's teaching became diverted into a doctrine dominated by monk-values, its influence was, I judge, *nil*.

Nor do the Sakya nobles appear to have identified themselves with any of those contributory subjects, causation and the rest. Anuruddha became famous for his clairvoyance, but he was of no weight as a teacher, and repeatedly appears as living in seclusion with two friends, Kimbila and Nandiya. It is the Founder, rather than he, who "holds the floor" in a discourse on their common gift.[1] Mahānāma too appears as a devoted learner rather than teacher.

We have seen Ānanda's testimony to Wayteaching in his cousin, but albeit he is often spokesman in Suttas, he is not shown insisting on that, or on any other one subject. The personal and devoted attendant of Gotama in his old age, more loyal than any to him to his last breath, and famed for a wonderful memory, he was in no way so gifted as to be a real brother to Gotama as Sāriputta will have been till death cut short his help. The phrase "beloved disciple" is not so true as, for him, "beloved master." It is quite unsupported by the texts, and is probably a carelessly made Christian parallel.

Upāli has had fathered on him a repute in "canon law,"

[1] *Further Dialogues*, Sutta 128.

that is probably a result of confused tradition. I can give no proof for my view that, in the master of Vinaya, prominent at the First Council and elsewhere, we have a cultured disputant of the Jains, whom Gotama converted to his teaching.[1] Nor do the three Upālis of the Anthology help me out. But I cannot but think that had the good barber developed into a learned Doctor of the Rule, the transformation would have found mention in some Sutta. No such transformation need be assumed in the Jain's case.

Rāhula, Gotama's only son, who is recorded as bidden as a child, by his mother, to follow his father, when the latter returned to visit his home, and Nanda, his half-brother, play no part either as teachers. The former makes brief entrances as questioner, and is credited with becoming arahan. But he won less fortunate reputation as a liar,[2] in the rock-edicts of Asoka, striking link though it be between inscription and Sutta. The silence about both in the Sutta telling of the passing[3] makes me think that either both, especially Rāhula, had predeceased the Founder or, more likely, had given up the life in the Order. There may have been many such, and who can quite blame them? Yet one more kumāra from Kapilavatthu was Bhaddiya. The Commentarial tradition makes him leave home with those others; the Vinaya leaves him out. A "simple-lifer," he would seem to have found happiness in that life-in-other-worlds implied in what "jhāna"[4] brought to the first men. That he taught any subject does not appear.

I could mention many other names of "first men" and also of first women, but it would too much inflate this book. To the latter I tried to do justice many years ago. They were probably "there" from the first, as sympathizing hearers, ministrants and even as teachers. Where and when is not woman interested in the New?

[1] *Further Dialogues*, Sutta 86.
[2] *Ibid.*, Sutta 61 and below, pp. 230, 314.
[3] *Dialogues*, II., Sta. XVI.
[4] *Psalms of the Brethren*, CCLIV.

The new, *c'est son métier;* it's her business, is it not? the looking for the new; the tending, the fostering of it in the new man, her child. It is perhaps only in defence of that New that she is ever really conservative.

Concerning those women and other first men a list of what we might call diplomas survives in the first part of the Anguttara-Nikāya, which may have been drawn up even before the Founder passed away (I am not suggesting he had any part in it). It is instructive for us, both in what it says and in what it does not say. For instance, the order of precedence, which meant much in Buddhism is odd. Our alphabetical order was here, in oral tradition, unused. Seniority in years can only have counted in the first name Añyā Kondañya, for Rāhula *precedes* Ānanda, who must have surely been his elder. Nor does seniority in esteem account for Koṭṭhita being placed long after the names and diplomas following after the first five names of high repute. Omission, too, of the names of the more prominent women-poets and of the yet more famous nun Vajirā suggest that these were not yet nuns. Again, of the special subjects for which I have sought to find special teachers, *not one* in the list is famed for teaching religiously or psychologically, causation. Koṭṭhita is associated with one of those subjects, analysis—in other words, Sānkhya. We have seen this. Kacchāna is also an analyst here, but in exposition only. One woman, Nandā, and two men are associated with jhāna or musing; these are Doubting-Revata and Subhūti. Yet is it only the Commentaries that have preserved Subhūti for us as a notable "jhāyin."

A word on just one other: Kumāra-Kassapa, whom I have found once included in the inner circle about the Founder: he is the protagonist in a striking and exceptional Sutta of the Dīgha-Nikāya added at the end of the second section and, by one scholar of repute,[1] held to be of a Jainist source. It is a championing of the very man, the

[1] The late Dr. E. Leumann; the Pāyāsi Sutta, Dīgha, XXIII.

"soul," against a materialist's attacks. In the list he is called "chief of the varied preachers," and the Commentary ascribes this fame to the many ingenious features he used in that argument. For me it is more likely that he won repute as a champion of the very man or soul, but that the word *atta-* was by the later authorities, who were famed as "Analysts," *i.e.* of the "man" as only knowable in "mind" (*citta*), changed to *citta*. *Citta* means both "mind" and "varied." The Commentary recognizes only the latter meaning, and I admit that, by commentarial standards, it was a great thing for a preacher to be a Boanerges with figure and parable. I am not satisfied with that *citta* (or *citra*), but must leave it unsolved.

One thing we must recognize in this list[1]—about the Way there is silence, let alone about "becoming." One would have thought that for a disciple to win fame as teaching after the example of his Leader, who was called, as we have seen, by Way-epithets,[2] would have brought recognition. Sāriputta taught so, as the Founder is said to have admitted, yet his fame is "chief of them who have wisdom." Does this silence mean, that Ānanda and I are wrong, or was it because the Way and what it stood for were *no longer even then held to be central?* Was that doomed word "becoming" banishing the Way, once linked with it, to a secondary place?

[1] *Gradual Sayings*, I., pp. 16 ff.

[2] Pp. 116 f.

CHAPTER XI

THE PARABLES AND THEIR HISTORY

LET us cast about and see if it be possible to get from the scriptures what those first men did really more expressly teach, as possibly differing from what came chiefly to be taught. And I in seeking am not asking you to consider the many discourses addressed to monks of the Order, of which the Majjhima-Nikāya is the more special treasury: the "sermons" beginning in the stereotyped way you see in the first Sutta: "Thus have I heard. The Bhagavā was once staying near Ukkaṭṭha in Pleasant Wood at the foot of the King-of-the-Sāl Trees. Now there he addressed the monks saying: Monks! Sir! those monks responded. Bhagavā said this: The root method of all things, monks, I will teach you; to that listen well, attend, I will speak. Even so, sir! . . . Bhagavā said this . . ." We have in these, here and elsewhere, not so much heart-to-heart talks from man to man, as carefully compiled paragraphs with a special way of "refrain" or recurring phrase, evidently adapted by compilers to aid oral learning, before anything was written. And adapted, I venture to think, later than the prose in the many Suttas in the Third and Fourth Nikāyas of prose followed up by verse.

Our natural tendency is perhaps the other way. We tend to see in the verses ending a Sutta a sort of moral, as in a fable, or the little climax winding up a Shakespearian scene in verse. Now here prose and verse do not always fit very well together, and at times the verse betrays an older stratum of Indian thought than the prose. Take, in the Anguttara-Nikāya (Nipāta 3), the Sutta *Dominance*. You will find the reference to the self as guide of conduct worded *in the verses* as "the inner Witness" in close conformity with the Shvetâsvatara Upanishad:

> *the inner self of all,*
> *The overseer of karma, in all abiding,*
> *The Witness . . .*

but you will not find it so expressed in the prose.[1] And had I space I could give other instances. Look, then, carefully at these mixed Suttas, to see this older teaching peeping out. I am not saying that in either verse or prose you will get the very words of the first men. They did not try to help the Many *in mantras*. They can do that now in Ceylon and sister Buddhist countries, because for centuries preaching monks have accustomed congregations to the nasally intoned shlokas, which mean for folk the voice of holy tradition. But we seek to make alive again those first days, when the first men had before them the creation of a new vital message, of new Vedas. When those discourses were compiled, the message was then no longer new, and the authority of a "church" was editing its "right" way of teaching.

Can we get any nearer to what they will have said? I have ventured to think we can do so with some likelihood of success if we watch sayings arising out of the unforeseen, the unprepared sayings prompted by this and that man questioning the man. To these I would add a careful pondering over that common feature in talks addressed to popular audiences: the parable and simile. I do not mean that only the first men used these. Far from it. But this kind of teaching, not being drawn up in set affirmations or denials, and bringing in analogies from what the teacher sees in things about him, are clearer pictures of what he was valuing when he spoke.

As to the individual questions, quite a number of Suttas consist of replies to such. It is only in these that there survive any personal traits in a Founder, whose worshippers

[1] *Gradual Sayings*, I., pp. 131 f.; and Introduction, p. xvii.

have in their piety done so much to obliterate for us the warm, living individual. I drew up a lengthy list of them in my *Old Creeds and New Needs*,[1] and will not go at length into them here. I have only space to sample. In the brahman's question quoted above[2] (Does he bring all his learners to final salvation, and if not why not?), the reply is very precious, for it is one of the only two left in the records given in terms of wayfaring. And the questioner is made himself to answer his question, with the "What think you as to this?" To a wayfarer the brahman can indicate the way to the city, but the wayfarer must, heeding or unheeding, himself decide which turn to take, now here, now there. Way-showers are we both, not more. Again, a feeble old man, pleading that for him the sight of Gotama and his men is very "chancy," begs for good words of help. "Ay, you are weak indeed," is the reply, "in your body. See you keep well in the 'man' (the self, or as we might say, the soul)." In the text the word is, "in the mind." But Gotama would know, that it is only when the very man is master of the mind that this ceases to be a mere reflection of the state of the body. He will have got behind the mind. But alas! his after-men did not get there, and we can see the Sutta undergoing the sort of editing I have suggested. It is ominous herein, that the monks about Gotama are by the old man called "mind developers" (*mano-bhāvanīyā*), a term we find now and then, and indicative of how Sānkhya was spreading (*K.S.* III., pp. 1 f.).

Once more, and this time in an informal debate with a free-lance *religieux*, or "wanderer," in which query and answer go on briskly, the latter asks: "How far can a man make real the world as entirely happy?" Most writers on Buddhism would say, his reply will have been that the effort were impossible; the world is never entirely happy. But the reply *is in the affirmative* and also to the point: "In so far as a man in musing comes into intercourse with *devas*,

[1] E. Benn, Ltd., 1923, p. 65. [2] P. 204.

and goes on conversing with them," [1] a reply quite in keeping with that which I have claimed above as the original object of the quietly alert state, here adduced, called jhāna.

Note, too, any Sutta, like this one, where we have Gotama, ceasing to be the respondent, and turning on the questioner with a word *ex abrupto*, question or otherwise: "Have done with debating past and future knowledge! I will teach you something: 'given that, this comes to be; the rise of that makes this arise; if that is not, this comes not to be; the stopping of that makes this stop.'" Here we have the Founder himself propounding a teaching of causation; does he go on to make it a living gospel? The records have surely led us to expect it. But no! The wanderer is very puzzled; is at a loss to follow the "this and that"; he switches off to another subject and Gotama is acquiescent. For me this has the appearance of a true memory: the trying on of a teaching by way of causation, put as it should be put, in general terms, terms unmet with till we find them ascribed, here and elsewhere, to Gotama; and the proved sterility of such a teaching, as such, in religious discourse.

See, lastly, in the very important Tevijja Sutta,[2] how Gotama is questioned, and then is questioner, on a subject very vital for him: the Way to reach the Better, not here only, but in the hereafter. You will not get at the heart of the matter here, if you see in it anti-brahmanic teaching, or a mere satire, or an attack on faith. The vital point is, that with knowledge and ritual there *must* go a life led in conformity with the life as lived by that Better man, those *devas*, intercourse with whom after death is reasonable aspiration. And his questions pour out: If a man stood this side this river, wanting matters on the other side, calling to that bank, Come hither! Come over! think you, for his invoking, it would come? And think you to reach companionship with worthy *devas* by just calling

[1] *Further Dialogues*, Sutta 79.
[2] *Dialogues* (XIII.), Sutta 13.

upon the great gods? Or by lying down and sleeping? Or tying your limbs? Or doing things of which they disapprove? Would that we could strip the Sutta of all that in it voices later values, of all the "set piece" with which it ends, and have it as once he spoke it!

The similes you will probably find a delightful study, and the translations of them for the most part vivid and true. I began to urge students to take up the study of them twenty-five years ago, and a little later drew up, with too little time for the job, a thematic index of them.[1] For a more detailed consideration of them you can consult twenty-three pages in *Sakya*. Here I can only say, in brief, how impressively for me they can be shown as throwing into relief now the older, now the later more monastic teaching. I do not ask you to assent to this straight away. Detailed study is necessary, and that may possibly leave you dissentient. I will cite such parables as seem to me to be *likely* to have been on the tongue of the men who taught what I hold was the real first gospel, and then I will cite from such as I think *those men will not have taught.*

The first group belongs to life looked upon as an adventure of hope and faith, and upon man as in that adventure becoming a More; upon man as the very real, and master of his spiritual destiny. The other group belongs to life looked upon as something to be dreaded and got rid of (by "life" I mean life-in-a-body, in some world), and upon man viewed as a less, as not-real.

There is, first of all, of course, the symbol or figure of the Road, and of what goes with road-life, the adventure of the "open way." You will find two road stories put *at the head* of the great birth-story (or Jātaka) collection. It is the caravan of wayfarers there talked of, and the "caravaner" was a title given both to Gotama and to other "Buddhas." The parables of the wheel, too, and the chariot and also

[1] *The Open Court*, 1908; *J.P.T.S.*, 1907–8. These inspired Dr. Burlingame to publish a book on the Parables.

relays of chariots are all figures likely to be chosen by teachers for whom the essential thing in religion was advance, progress, a world of coming to be. It is, among others, in the chariot similes that you will find a feature common to Buddhist and Christian parables: namely, a bringing home the analogy by an interpretation of details. You will find the best-told chariot parable given above, but there are others, and they are paralleled in the Upanishads.

Then there is the parable of the chariot relays, the only effort in teaching ascribed to the early brahman disciple Puṇṇa, whom I have called martyr. The root idea of swift progress by a method of consecutive religious study, leaving relatively first principles and faring on towards perfection,[1] may well be of the original teaching, even if, as I think, the terms in the present recension are later scholastic insertions (e.g. *parinibbān' atthaṃ* possibly replacing *paramatthaṃ*, etc.).

The idea of stages in progress we also meet with in the noted Raft parable, which the Pali scriptures quote as scriptural. It is in Sutta 22 of the Majjhima-Nikāya, and is cited in Sutta 28. A man on a journey comes to a sheet of water; perils beset him behind; he must get beyond, but there is no boat. He fashions a raft of brushwood, and paddling with arms and legs gets over. Does he then lift the raft on his shoulder and so go forward? Nay, "great service to me this raft has been, but now I can leave it afloat or stranded, and go unencumbered on my way. I have taught you the raft-simile for a laying aside, not for a keeping hold of. Even so do you leave behind what has been for you dharma, much more what is not dharma."

This leaving behind, or putting away "both good and bad" is an Upanishadic teaching, not well brought out there, nor well understood there or here. But under the aspect of "becoming," of growth, it should be clear. A

[1] *Further Dialogues*, Sta. XXIV. Cf. Hebrews vi. 1 (wrongly cited in *Sakya* as the words of St. Paul).

code good for the child is not of necessity good for the adult, or even for the adolescent. But an absolute putting away of "good" is, even for the most saintly man or woman an attainment impossible on earth. On earth we are all, even the best, in the world of striving after the Better, in a world of Becoming. No metaphysic playing with the abolishing distinction between opposites applies here. The utmost we can do is the not being mastered by opposites. It is a weakness in the laudable groping after the ideal we see in the Upanishads, that they make it possible for the saint on earth to get beyond the struggle and reach the Best, the Consummate, even here, an error carried on by monastic Buddhism in its arahan theory. This can only be made plausible by contracting the idea of perfection. I sometimes think that, if those teachers had had to hand the word "potential," their outlook might have been better balanced. The *shakti* (capacity, ability) of a later cult tried to supply the want. They might have filled the want with "becoming," had they brought their groping here to that grip which I see Gotama disclosing in the figure of the Way.

The raft figure underwent a chequered fate, and the reader should watch this. For monastic teaching, it became either the final mode of transport, to the Highest, not typifying just a stage,[1] or it became the average man's way, when the superior man flew.[2]

Let us now follow the idea of Becoming, not in the Wayfaring, but in the nearer figure of physical growth, in the incubating egg, in the sown seed. Here again is a parable noteworthy at least for the "school" called Majjhima-repeaters who reiterate it. Not poignantly tragic, as was the fate of the Jerusalem chicken for Jesus, but full of confident hope, it is in tune with the teaching of the first men. In an earlier stage the mother-hen may be fussily anxious as to the hatching out, but the well-sat-on eggs are

1 *Kindred Sayings*, IV., 107 f.; *The Snake*.
2 *Sutta-Nipāta*, ver. 21; *Dialogues*, II., pp. 24 f.

safe, the chicks "bound-to-become"! So, too, are you, if you have done your utmost in right training, bound to come out into the light! But not if you have not done all you could.

Similes of inanimate physical growth are more numerous, and once or twice come near the Jesus-parable of the sower. Read, *e.g.*, that of the soils (*Kindred Sayings*, IV., p. 221, called "Teaching"). "Suppose a ploughman has three fields of good, poor and bad soil respectively. What think you, headman? If the same quality of seed be sown in all, he naturally begins with the best, though he sows in all, with very different results. So I, with different results, teach dharma, the same dharma to all." The question here has touched on the important matter of a teacher holding something back, and I will return to it later.

Better known and bearing on the growth of the very man is the episode of the brahman landowner, landtiller, Bhāradvāja, who, at the dinner interval of ploughman and oxen, challenges the lonely monk, bowl in his hand, to show he has so ploughed as to earn a meal. A lesser man would have pointed to his mission-work and the merit to be got by ministering to the *religieux*. Other is the reply. "I, too, plough and sow; when that's done I enjoy." "May be so," is the reply, "but we don't see master Gotama's yoke or plough, ploughshare or oxen." Here again the reply has been for better memorizing metrically set:

Faith is the seed and rain the inner spring,[1]
Wisdom for me is both the yoke and plough,
Conscience[2] *the pole and mind the fitted strap.*
And watchfulness for me ploughshare and goad,
Guarded in action, guarded too in speech,
And temperate as to the stomach's food,
I weeding make with truth : release from work
Is that fair thing of innermost desire.
Effort for me the burden-bearer is,
That carries me toward the haven sure.

[1] *Tapo, -as.* I have chosen one of the several meanings of this important term (cf. above, p. 61), the meaning of the season between winter and spring, when the plant world is astir.

[2] See above, p. 171.

Onward it goes, nor ever turneth back,
Whither when we have gone we weep no more.
Such is this tillage, such this ploughing is,
That is the crop of fruit that dieth not:
And he who tills after this sort
From every ill obtains release.

Here is no external work indicated, however meritorious. His work was to show the inner growth or becoming of the very "me," in whose culture "mind" is but that which, as it were, ties "me" to my body, and through that agency to other men.

In this for me impressive parable we have, I believe, very old matter. We have the very man and his becoming made central, and while the back and forth of the toiling teams might, for a modern teacher, call for the idea of concentration on culture of this life only, in the mouth of Gotama the ploughman is merged into the adventure of the Way, into a going on and on, into the longer furrow of the worlds-trail. Here is no making "mind" the central feature, as we see it in the surely interpolated line wherewith the Dhammapada begins. "Mind" is merely a connecting cord. Here is harmony with the parable given above of the man selecting his clothes, his mental investiture. If it be said, Where in the tillage does Dharma, as the inner monition, come in? I would remind you that the man here taught is a brahman, to whom dharma would indeed mean the "ought," but would not mean that aspect of the Divine, the guiding, chiding, better self, stressed by Gotama. He would see that Better Self *implicit in the man himself* who is shown tilling and undergoing tillage.

As to the emphasis laid on the very man rather than mind, I would ask you to note a parable which appears to reverse that emphasis. It comes in the Kiṃsuka, or (?) "Judas tree" Sutta (*K.S.*, IV., p. 124), and deals mainly with the need there is to see, not merely *quot homines tot sententiæ*, but the several ways which this man and that man take, in their becoming. "Who in divers manners hath spoken unto us," is ever true, for men's spiritual reactions are very diverse. The parable is that of messengers swift coming from east, north, west [Note the geographical limitations for India. I do not think there has been omission of "the south"] to a fortified city, and reporting to the lord of the city sitting at its centre. Here is a parable which may be a word of the first men, but the interpretation appended is later, for it is monastic, and I am not dwelling on it, save to say that the master is called "mind," or, as translators prefer to say, "consciousness": *viññāṇa*. Nevertheless, this is not the superseding of the man by mind, that it will seem to you. In that case the word had been either *chitta*, or *mano* (or *manas*) as *e.g.* in Dhammapada. For the first men *viññāṇa* meant, less "mind," than the man-as-surviving-death. As such, he was not worded as "wraith," ghost, soul, spirit, but as *viññāṇa*. He has laid down the visible man, the *rūpa*; there remains the invisible counterpart, his invisible instrument through which he wielded his *rūpa* (there was no word for "instrument"). And by the interpretation, which calls each message brought "nirvana," we see that the parable-teller was concerned not with earth-life only. Hence the parable is not so late but that *the man is still the central fact.*

Parables are usually of the things seen, but when the things are also touched and handled—become, as we say, object-lessons—they may be the more vivid teaching. The Jesus-word "Give me a penny" is of these, and the "He took a little child." The most graphic of these in the Suttas is perhaps the rock-famed one about lying as a sham, when Gotama takes the footpan with which Rāhula has washed his father's feet, half empties it, then wholly upsets it, saying the while how empty, how good for nothing is the deliberate liar. (No modern problem of "Should doctors tell?" comes in to complicate.) Another Sutta gives what, for the hearer, the housewife Visākhā, was virtually an object lesson, the different processes of, and materials for cleaning in her house, the idea being to show that religious festivals are opportunities for that cleansing the inner man which aid in growth. But of the prevailing faith in bathing the body as a sacrament, especially at certain festivals, availing to cleanse the very man, the voice, it may be, of the first men is raised in protest.

Though in this river and in that the fool
May ever bathe, the man whose deeds are dark
Is not made clean. . . .
For him who's cleansed 'tis always festival,
'Tis ever Sunday for the man made clean,
For him whose life is pure always the rite
Is new accomplishèd. See here's the bath for you :
For every creature sanctuary make.
If you utter no lies, and hurt no life,
If you steal nought, have faith and nought begrudge,
What work is left for you to river gone ?
Yea, tho' its waters were as well-spring clear ?

So also Puṇṇikā, or Puṇṇā, slave to the Sakyans' chief merchant-supporter, to a "water purifying" brahman, who is said to believe that,

Who in youth,
Or age ill deeds hath wrought, by baptism
Of water from that karma is released :—
Nay now, who, ignorant to the ignorant,
Hath told thee this : that water-baptism
From evil karma can avail to free ?
Why then, the fishes and the tortoises,
The frogs, the water-snakes, the crocodiles
And all that haunt the water straight to heaven
Will go !

and much more, spoken with an unabashed candour which the Commentary does not seek to explain away.

The best known, perhaps, of all recorded object-lessons is, be it remembered, given not in the Piṭakas, but only in a Commentary: that on the Women's Anthology. This is the quest of the mustard seed to be got from a house where no one had ever died, and it is ascribed to the Founder as a task set an agonized mother carrying her child who had expired in her arms. I hold it likely that we have here a true tradition, but unlikely that we have all he will have drawn from his quiver of comfort. He had so much more than this jejune and stoic solace, which any materialist or rationalist could have administered. Very possibly, however, her vision was too blurred with misery of self-pity to leave her capable of understanding how the little son had run just ahead of her in the long Way, yet would so often be near her had she ears to hear, eyes even to see. To practise jhāna one needed not to become a nun. The eloquent words of world-sympathy put in the Comforter's mouth by Edwin Arnold [1] are no wise within the vision of the commentator. He only repeats the monastic gag we find in the Suttas: If you would not suffer, do not love, which is that teaching of Man-in-the-Less, that shrinkage of our nature and not the expansion of it, that is the hall-mark of the monk. And he confines himself merely to the one good result; the overcoming of that self-pity: "she stiffened her mind from the softness of love." Poor impoverished mother!

I have gone into her case in a translation of the Nuns' Anthology, and have learnt many things since so writing twenty-four years ago. I there made the best case I could for the Buddhist saint's position: the dwelling on a very long memory of lives, and the assurance of present (or imminent) attainment replacing the forward view; on the fact, too, that the few who were ready for that uncharted view, called for a very specific judgment. To that special pleading I here add no repudiation; I say only, it is not now for me the teaching *of the first men*. It is true that the women poets, save only the last two, bear names of contemporaries of those first men. But the verses, in the form they have come to be fixed in writing, are strongly monastic. I even think that, but for much editing by later orthodoxy, they would not

[1] *The Light of Asia.* Cf. *Further Dialogues*, Sutta 87, for a miserable monastic treatment of bereavement and consolation.

have been admitted into the Canon. It is a parable repeatedly told of the Founder, that the man-who-sees sees life as it were two houses, and men coming and going between each. But the consolation given to this and other bereaved mothers in the poems is, not that in a little while the joyful hope of "moving across" will be hers, but that she has been weeping over lost children for ages, and it's time she stopped!

Other object-lessons in the Suttas deal with objects afloat in the rivers by which he will have walked, such as flotsam borne by the current. But I am doubtful that these will have appealed to the first men. In one Sutta, it is true, the Way is equated with a stream,[1] and we have stream in the fourfold Way-division. But to be adrift on a current is not in harmony with the strenuous adventure of the Way. The epithet "upstreamer" (*uddhaṃsoto*) applied to the religious man in general, and to the notable nun Dhammadinnā in particular,[2] is far more fitting. The interpretation, too, is very monastic. "See, monks, yonder great log floating down Ganges. If it ground not, sink not a-midstream, catch not on a snag, nor get seized by men or not-men, nor get caught in a whirlpool, nor rot inside, it will be carried down to the ocean." These being explained are recorded as this and that bank of sense and sense-objects, sinking in lusts, mingling in sympathy and business with men, aspiring to a hereafter with *devas*, pleasure and moral rottenness, ocean being nirvana.[3]

You may say, Surely warnings were needed in a complete gospel and once the band of missionaries was launched as an Order of monks, they would need and look for teaching of a special kind addressed to themselves. And this is right and true. The Third Utterance is of this kind, and so is the very lurid parable or object-lesson of the bonfire,

[1] *Kindred Sayings*, V., p. 302.
[2] *Gradual Sayings*, I., 213, etc. *Pss. of the Sisters*, p 17.
[3] *Kindred Sayings*, IV., p. 113.

declared to be safer for a monk to embrace and scorch himself at than to singe his virtue by embracing a maiden.[1] But we shall err if we see, in inner warnings given to "the staff," the teaching it was at the beginning theirs to give as missioners to Everyman. Yet so much do we find the chief emphasis come to be laid on such inner warnings, that for any one parable suitable for a world-religion I can show you a dozen of monastic outlook and emphasis. In fact, so much was attention directed to these, that we find lists of them,[2] drawn up probably for teaching, for memorizing. The longest is in a very outstanding literary effort (probably a written composition) by a nun, the last in the Anthology, and it refers to some thirty similes or parables, which may be found in the Suttas.

She may be composing a ballad, as Christian nuns wrote plays, or it may be her own experience. Pleading to be let join the Order of nuns, she, in desperation, cuts off her hair, a very Catherine of Siena, and pours forth before her bridegroom her monastic ideal with a very fountain of anti-marriage, anti-world figures.

Like the sharp blades of swords are sense-desires,
Like the poised heads of snakes prepared to strike,
Like blazing torches and like bare gnawn bones. . . .

and so on.

Call ye to mind how it was said that tears
And milk and blood flow on world without end,
And bear in mind that tumulus of bones. . . .
Remember! . . .

she wails many times,

Remember how the parable was told
Of purblind turtle in the Eastern seas
Or other oceans, once as time goes by,
Thrusting his head through hole of drifting yoke:
So rare as this the chance of human birth. . . .

[1] *Anguttara-Nikāya*, IV., 128.
[2] Cf. *Further Dialogues*, Suttas XXII, LIV.

[How did this amazing notion get into the Buddhist teaching on the subject?], and more after this sort. Note, in the poem, her silence about chariot or hen, and eggs and ploughing and such. How, as I have said elsewhere, is not this the outlook of tired vision, grown dull of imagination in failing to grasp *what it means* to be born anew, with youth and energy as fresh as in Eden, and with who knows what more added in the will when the Wayfarer has become a More with new opportunity before him! Yet it is just the other-world opportunity which is condemned, as of necessity an undesirable and fearsome thing. Yet the Jātakas, with their teaching of the evolution, through new opportunity of the will to become, in the man there called "Bodhisat," ought to have taught a saner outlook to those monk-editors.

Do not think I am blind to Sumedhā's (this nun's) forward view. She was no materialist holding that this dreadful thing, life as she saw it, ended with dying. The finest lines in her poem, her sermon, are those of a mysterious, glorious "life" which she has no words to name positively:

> *There is that groweth never old! . . .*
> *This that doth ne'er grow old, that dieth not,*
> *This never ageing, never dying WAY:*
> *No sorrow cometh there, no enemies,*
> *Nor is there any crowd, none faint or fail,*
> *No fear cometh, nor aught that doth torment.*
> *To this, the WAY ambrosial have gone*
> *Full many, and to-day, e'en now 'tis to be won;*
> *But only by a life that's utterly*
> *Surrendered in devotion. Labour not,*
> *And ye shall not attain. Thus Sumedhā*
> *Ended her say.*

bringing over bridegroom and parents to her will. But we see that for her, too, the Way is but the final passing on and out, and that she conceives this only in terms of a very NOT.

I do not go so far as to conclude that any list of similes that may have been in her convent had omitted those parables of hope and growth, in which I see earlier teaching. She had a will to leave home-life, and naturally made her selection to strengthen her special pleading. It is, I repeat, just the matter of emphasis, of "preferential treatment" that lies in these monastic, anti-world similes. Surely not with these on their lips can the first men, seeking to bring a higher, wider teaching about human nature, human life and its possibilities, have laid the foundation of a new world-religion appealing, not to a world within a world, but to every man and woman, to the very man in each!

CHAPTER XII

THE FIRST MISSIONERS: THEIR LIVING AND DYING

We tend perhaps, in weighing the original or not original worth in the sayings, to forget this important feature in all religion, but especially in any religion eventually breaking away from one of older ritual: that the way a new messenger lives his creed is more vital than what he says about it. A priest (in Italy) said once to a lady, so I heard recently, "Does it very much matter, dear madam, what Jesus did say?" He probably meant: Has not Holy Church been ever telling us under inspiration what does matter? But he may have meant: Was it not on an example—"an ensample of godly life"—that he really founded his religion? Was it not the carrying out, "Thou shalt love the Lord thy God and thy neighbour as thyself" in his daily life and death? This must be yet more markedly true in the case of the missioner ancient or modern, who finds himself in a land of alien tongues. His talking becomes of necessity a "silent film"; in purity of life and in warding his neighbour lie his sermons. This barrier will not have so limited the founders of the great religions; none the less, much, very much, will have depended on how they "let their light shine before men."

What, then, the question arises, can we find in the records informative of the life and doings of the first men? Tradition gives the Founder forty-five years of mission-life; the Suttas, even without the Commentaries, are many times the length of the Four Gospels: is there in the former an equal proportion in narrative, and consecutive narrative to that contained in the latter? There is not.

Many centuries, many leagues, come between Piṭakas, more correctly, the pre-Piṭakan epoch, and Gospels; in the former both the felt need and the means to record passing events were not yet come at; writing was known, but used only for brief memoranda; the word was only honoured as the living spoken communication. When, midway between the date of the lives of the two great Founders, India, at last finding materials, took to writing more fully, the Buddha-cult was well advanced, and the chief thing held worthy of record was testimony, less to the influence of the character and conduct of him and his disciples, and more, much more, to the proofs of his wonderful will and knowledge *alone*. It is chiefly these that form the materials of the one attempt to sketch the first twenty years of the ministry. You will find them in the Commentary on one of the later poems of the Sutta-Piṭaka: the *Buddha-vaṃsa* (lineage of the Buddha); a synopsis of it is in Rhys Davids's *Manual*, Kern's *Indian Buddhism*, and E. J. Thomas's *Life of the Buddha as Legend and History*, and I am not holding it worth repeating here. Neither have I space here to set out in detail the scanty fragments of the where and why in scores of Suttas each recorded answer or discourse is said to have been uttered. I will limit myself to the general impression made upon me as reader and translator.

In the first place, for many years there will have been no question of permanent dwelling-places for the new missioners. Monasteries (*vihāras*) were yet to come. This word, mentioned often in the Vinaya's Commentary on the code of general rules (*Pātimokkha*), occurs only once in the Vinaya narratives, and there probably means a cave, on the hillside near Rājagaha.[1] It may also, meaning literally residence, have been used for a group of huts (*kuṭi*), to shelter one, at most two monks apiece. Tradition associates the Founder with a residence in such, and

[1] *Mahāvagga*, V., p. 1.

no more, in his old age. Made possibly of sandalwood, it was called the Fragrant Hut (*gandha-kuṭi*). Between such settlements, matter of quick craftsmanship, and erected probably by pious patrons for *religieux* in general, or for lay-students (*paribbājakas*), either in the open woodland or in an enclosed "park," the first missioners will have toured some eight months of the years, halting at one of them for the "rains." The laity were apparently ever ready, to a sufficient number, to fill each monk's proffered begging-bowl with broken meats; nor was there stinting of material here and there for robes, or of materia medica, or of the larger welcome now and then to come in for the midday meal, where missioners had not, by some failings, dried up, or proved unable to tap, the sources of this hospitable usage. It was only when the larger building came into vogue, such as we read of King Asoka providing, that the later (and modern) custom will have arisen of vicarious begging by a few monks with a more ample apparatus, to suffice for the larger permanent settlement of men who no longer practised the wandering life. In the Vinaya-Piṭaka we see a mid-way state of things: there are both "resident" and "in-coming" (touring) monks.[1]

I am not saying that the monk in Buddhist countries has ceased to go on tour, nor would I speak of the ways of to-day of which I have no first-hand knowledge. The monk of to-day may tour less to teach than to learn what to teach—testimony to this I have just printed in a report on new Buddhist cultural activities in Indo-China, Laos and Cambodia.[2] But in the first days, the new Order was not complacent in accepting alms for the *merit* conferred on the donor by the ministering; those men in return for bodily support gave their new word, to the individual and the group, on the More that there was in the man to become, according as he lived that More in his progress in the Way.

[1] E.g. *Chullavagga*, IV., 4, 4 (*Vin. Texts*, III., p. 6).
[2] Pali Text Society, Report for 1931.

I do not hold that their way was one of roses. The *young* monk was a novelty, a growing vogue. By the popular verdict he should either be a "whole-hog" ascetic or fakir, courting alms by self-torture, or he should be at the world's work, or at least, under some brahman, preparing himself to undertake the same with a priming of current "culture." You will in the Suttas come across this disapproval of youth being unnaturally spent,[1] and in the Vinaya too,[2] where the incoming of the brahman group with that of many "kumāras" spoken of above raises an outcry, and one concerning which a scarcely worthy rejoinder—probably composed much later—is put into the mouth of the Founder. He is said to have said, "Do nothing; all will be over in a week. Great teachers lead their pupils by truth." It is more likely that Rājagaha opinion soon realized that those many students, kumāras and brahmans, had only changed their teacher, and had not committed themselves to any career shirking a citizen's duties. Later monasticism will have wished to present them all as budding monks, and the very rational protest against the flower of world-workers being drained, as by a war, from useful productive labour is made to appear as a foolish popular outcry. The matter is narrated not to serve as history of the Order, but independently, under the subsection—Admission to the Order.

Two items in the matter of residence you may find of special interest. At the mother-settlement of the Order, the "Squirrels' Feeding-ground" in the Bamboo Grove near Rājagaha, there appears to have been an extensive collection of both woods and caves for the nightly accommodation of touring monks, and an official was appointed, a steward, to locate them on their arrival in such a way that members proficient in a special line—repeaters of sayings, Order regulations, etc.—should be lodged near

[1] E.g. *Further Dialogues*, Sta. LXXXII.; *K.S.*, I., pp. 14 f.
[2] *Vin.* Texts, *Mahāvagga*, I., 24, 5.

each other. One section of such are referred to as "musers" (wrongly translated by Rhys Davids as "given to meditation").[1] These will have been men of psychic gifts, who preferred to converse with men of other worlds, and from them to receive advice as to their work, rather than to discuss with their fellows of earth. We shall not faithfully reconstruct the first decade or two of Sakyan mission work, till we see how much the Way was for the first men a Way of the worlds.

The second item is the case of a "close season" for monks habitually otherwise on tour, during the period usually called Vassa (rains), when there was a danger that much "hiking" might lead to trampling the growing crops. The rule will not have been made till the Order had grown in numbers and the incessant touring have not yet faltered. We read of a growing number of cases where, for one week at a time, the rule might be in certain cases suspended, such as permitting a monk, if sent for, to visit his mother or father in illness. One of these cases throws a glimmer on the progressive accumulation of the oral sayings which were the nucleus, first of the teaching taking fixed form, then of these eventually getting written. It is, that if a layman knows "how to recite (lit. recites) a very worthy saying which he knows well," and sends a messenger to say to the nearest monk-settlement: "May their reverences come? they will learn this suttanta, before it falls into oblivion," monks can go, even during Vassa, so they be back in a week. We may see by this, comparing it with the silence there is about any organized reporting by monks on the spot and at the time, how haphazard was, in part at least, the compiling of the great Sutta thesaurus of the Piṭakas.

[1] Rhys Davids (who translated this section) holds, in a footnote, that Jhāna may be referred to, but quotes Mahāvagga, I., i, 3–7, where the same word (also wrongly translated by Oldenberg) apparently means just reflection. Both of these pioneers overlooked the extent to which Gotama himself was a constant muser.

Not unworthy of note, too, is a relaxation of the precise date of Vassa, when a king has willed its postponement, for a month—he is said to have been Bimbisāra of Magadha —"I allow you monks to follow after (obey) kings."

You who read the Vinaya may remind me here, that you find an original injunction forbidding monks to use any building whatever to lodge in, much less live in, and thus limiting them to the shelter of rocky recesses or of trees. Further, that this rule was only relaxed when the foremost burgess of Rājagaha, Sudatta, better known as Anāthapiṇḍika (feeder of the unwarded), watching well-behaved monks, from his garden, approaching the town for alms, offered to put up sixty "vihāras" for them, a work which was accomplished in a single day. Not such huts alone, but four other kinds of buildings are recorded as all at once made permissible, together with the possibly specially treated cave called *lena*.[1]

As to this, it seems, in its abrupt contrast of no lodging and lodging of any kind, suspiciously like a later invention, like our early histories of England made to begin with the siege of Troy. It opens the chapter on monk-residence, and leads up, through a number of petty permits in detail, to the climax of Sudatta's generosity: the purchase at Sāvatthi of the famous Grove called after the vendor Jeta. We can pass it by. But that monks often did make mother Earth their lodging is both probable and apparent, not only when, if need were, on tour, but from choice, and in more permanent fashion. Such were called forester monks,[2] and we have an almost humorous Sutta on them in the Majjhima-Nikāya, betraying that in their manners they will have been found, by monks of a politer way of living, "bounders." Particular instances of such haters of human company are to be found, especially in the Anthology: Bhaddiya, for instance: "constant forester"[3] and many others, the

[1] *Chullavagga*, VI., p. 1. [2] *Araññakā bhikkhū*, Sta. LXIX.
[3] *Psalms of the Brethren*, verses 8, 127, 307–10, etc.

finest poetry in the work being clustered about such a life, in the poems of Ekavihāriya (of a later date), Bhūta, Tālapuṭa, and Kassapa. The last of these even rejects the brotherly invitation of the aged Founder to tend himself, no less aged, in reasonable comfort at Sāvatthi, stating his preference for the wilder life.[1]

Such men among the early company will have given check to the mission habit of the Founders of much touring, who were intent mainly on bringing their new message to all sorts and conditions of men. They were those who were merged in the vogue of the genuine hermit or recluse, which had been growing in India. Such a vogue was not, *never has been, peculiar to India.* That everywhere and at all times the incorrigible solitary may be found is not to force the truth. But if, and in so far as, he seems to be oftener found in India than elsewhere, this may be due, not to any permanent trait in the mixed races of India, but to an intrusive religious cause. I have said elsewhere, and more briefly repeat here, that the tremendous *volte-face* in Indian religious conviction, spreading out from the few—the turning from an externally conceived polytheism to an immanent theism, such as we see in the Vedas and the Upanishads respectively—will have exercised on some men a profound effect, such as we, with our modern eclectic combination of a Godhead both externally and internally conceived, are too apt to overlook. Here and there a man, wishing to realize this, that he as man was at the same time a More than man, nay, the Most, felt it needful to "come apart" and ponder this man-wonder away from men. It was, in the German phrase, a "God-intoxicated" idea, and to such Divine madnesses men have, not in India only, been prone. We need not wonder that to such men it seemed as of no value to be occupied with anything else. And strange phrases about it linger in the Pali: *miga-bhūtena cetasā*, "with a purpose become that of the wild";[2] and "he

[1] *Kindred Sayings*, II., p. 136. [2] *Miga* is any wild creature.

tormenting neither the self nor another, lives as to the seen uncoveting, extinct (as to evil), become cool, experiencing happiness, through the self-become-God." That Commentators explain "God" (Brahma) as "best," or "like *devas*," is no doubt an anti-theistic letting-down of later days, yet is there no real banishing of the Uttermost, the Supreme, in the word best (*seṭṭha*). That the man went out to ponder over this: "I am become Brahman, my Best Self; what as such in my nature becomes ultimately impossible for me?" will, even to us in our day, reveal an overwhelming inspiration; how much more at its birth as an articulate teaching?

A second impression we can get if we search is that of a concordant joyousness prevailing in the first little company of Sakyans. The Founder seems to have led the way: "If any one in this world is to be called a happy man, I am he."[1] And when Sudatta of Sāvatthi learns of hospitality a-foot at his colleague's, the "burgess" of Rājagaha, for the Sakyan men, and calls upon him in "Cool Wood" to pay his respects, the reply to his greeting "Sir, have you slept well?" is also in terms of a man who rests happily.[2] The Vinaya translation (Oldenberg's) speaks only of "peace," but the Pali word is *sukha*, happiness, pleasure, and in the Saṃyutta account I have rendered it "rest happily, having attained in purpose peace,"[3] "peace" (*santi*) coming only just here. I would not maintain that we have here, even were the response in prose, the phrases he will have used:

Surely at all times happily doth rest
The brahman who is utterly extinct .

for he is expressing satisfaction over things the real Gotama

[1] *Gradual Sayings*, I., pp. 119 f.
[2] *Cullavagga*, VI., p. 4.
[3] *Kindred Sayings*, I., p. 273.
[4] "Brahman" was for the Sakyan the very worthy man. The last words = *parinibbuto*.

would not have felt complacent about; the ideal is of the monk. But the aroma of calm happiness—that is for me a true memory. Radiance, not tears, is the impression we get of this man who is seen now and then smiling over long memories of his past, but weeping or sighing never, and whose picture of spiritual growth in the very man was to describe him, not as just at peace, but feeling "an arising of joy, thence of rapture, thence a bodily serenity, thence a happiness making stable his thought."[1] (I find that "peace" plays over-large a rôle in the books on Buddhism by votaries and non-votaries; in part the translation of *sukha* by peace, not happiness, is perhaps responsible for it, as you will find in such passages as those cited.)

Nor do I get a different impression as to his fellow-workers. A teaching mission undertaken out of good-will towards *devas* and men (how do not Buddhists pass over the former!) could not easily proceed otherwise than in ways of joyous compassion. It was apparently their saying, "This happiness by happiness is won," probably in distinction from the tendency in their contemporaries the Jains to win happiness through suffering.[2] The poem ascribed to the converted brigand Angulimāla, aware of the wonderful "becoming" in his life:

Deep in the wild beneath some forest tree
Or in the mountain cave, is't here is't there,
So have I stood and let my throbbing heart
Transported beat. Happy I seek my rest,
Happy I rise, happy I pass the day,
By evil ones unhaunted—ah! behold
The Teacher's sweet compassion shown to me!

was not peculiar to this one man, if we take as a true record the touching testimony paid by the aged king of Kosala to his contemporary and friend, the "Teacher," at their last interview. Comparing the Sakyans with other

[1] *Dialogues*, Sutta ii.
[2] *Further Dialogues*, No. 36; *Psalms of the Brethren*, pp. 40, 64, etc.

religieux, he found them "joyous and joyful, exultant and jubilant, buoyant and fervent, without care or worry, tranquil, with purpose become as creatures of the wild. Surely, thought I, this is due to your teaching!"[1]

A necessary result of this—or shall we take it conversely?—was the harmony and concord among them. The king compares it with political and domestic strife found elsewhere. Pajāpatī the Gotamid, aunt and stepmother to the Founder, has a verse on this (Psalm 161):—

> *Behold the company who learn of him,*
> *In happy concord, with their energies*
> *Aroused, their self firm based, and ever strong*
> *In their advance; 'tis thus to worship right.*

I here introduced the word "fraternity," but no such word is or was there and then. Not even "brother" or "brethren" is truly justified in sound historical translation, nor to call the Company (*sangha*) "Confraternity" as has been done. "Brother," if not "brotherhood," was there, and we find in the Vinaya the monks referring to nuns as "sisters," but it was not the Indian way to call a man "brother," even were he so by blood. The terms of address recorded as used within the Company are, from Leader to monk *bhikkhu* (voc. plur., *bhikkhăvĕ*), from monk to monk, *āvuso*, from monk to Leader, or to senior monk, *bhante*. All are words difficult to equate exactly. The first is literally "broken-meats (man)," and "almsman" comes nearest. Later exegesis saw in the word "broken bonds" (of sin or the world), and hence Buddhists have not taken kindly to the rendering. *Āvuso*, a curiously corrupted form, it is held, of *āyasmā*, is just a courtesy-word, like "sir." "(Your) reverence" is more distinctive, if less accurate. *Bhante* (= *bhadante*), a term of disputed origin, is more honorific, and is sometimes translated "lord." It is a shortened form of an old Sanskrit word, which we have fuller in "Bhagavan." Modern Europe is poor in such courtesy-appellatives. We cannot, save in

[1] *Further Dialogues*, No. 89.

mild ridicule, use "Mister" without the proper name, nor even then is the word in place in archaic wording. The old English "Master," or Master X., is in this respect better, and I have used it much.

To return: if "brother, brethren" be an unjustifiable rendering of *bhikkhu* and of *āvuso*, there is, on the other hand, a word of amity which—I speak subject to correction—the Sakyans appear to have needed, and in needing to have found, and with it to have enriched the spiritual vocabulary of India. This is the word *samagga*, as a noun and adjective for concord, unanimity, in Sanskrit only an adjective meaning "entire." We find it separate and in glowing compounds: "Train yourselves in these things being all in concord, in pleasant intercourse, without strife." "Pure with the pure abiding . . . in concord, will ye put an end to ill."[1] "The company in concord—how far can that be?"[2] "Putting away slander, . . . he lives a binder together of the divided, encourager of friends, enjoying concord, impassioned for concord, delighting in concord, speaker of words making concord." (Here the translator again makes "peace" serve for the right word.)[3]

> *In bygone days, in former births,*
> *Lost ones to those who long had sought,*
> *Kinsfolk and friends to friends he brought,*
> Made them at one *and made them glad.*"[4]

Compared with this efflorescence of the word and what it implied, there is a contrasted absence of the like in Veda and Upanishad.

We see in the Suttas not seldom emphatic commending of the *kalyāṇa-mitta*—that is, of the lovely friend or friendship, a truer translation I now hold than friendship with what is lovely. (Sometimes the abstract form—*mittatā*—is used.)[5] It is even said repeatedly to be, not

[1] *Further Dialogues*, Sta. CIII, CIV.
[2] *Anguttara*, V., p. 74.
[3] *Dialogues*, I., p. 6.
[4] *Ibid.*, III., Sta. XXX.
[5] *K.S.*, I., 112f.; V., 2, 27, 29f.

one half, but the whole of the righteous life, the "God-conduct" (*brahma-chariya*). The Commentary here is unusually intelligent, remarking that the teaching herein required the fit man to assimilate its object, like medicine; also that a monk's life yielded two main results: good friends and the making of the individual man. No hard-and-fast line could be drawn; the two together were the making the Way to become.

It was inevitable that for the monk, life, pruned of nearly all its relations, conjugal, parental, filial, domestic, professional, social, should have resulted in the starved affections developing the two remaining ties: teacher and pupil, and friendship. We read often of the former as a specifically Indian cult; it is not recognized how the latter relation is almost non-existent in pre-Sutta literature. It emerges in such works as reflect the influence of the high worth of man as taught in the early Upanishads, together with that of the development of comradeship through monasticism.

There is, on the other hand, a shadow in the Suttas and Vinaya not less dark beside this sunshine. The much squabbling and bickering met with, let alone the signs of schism in the Order, at first sight seem to cancel out the testimonial of the Kosala king. We read of these as an accepted feature: "At that time monks among whom altercations, contentions and quarrels (there is a long sinister string of such terms in Pali) had arisen . . . behaved improperly towards each other in gesture and word and came to blows. The people were annoyed and angry. . . . The moderate monks also . . ." and the Leader appealed to, admonishes wisely that the squabblers "sit down and resolve to refrain," or some new rule gets made. And there is the outstanding case of the Kosambī quarrelling, where the Leader, having gone to quell the squabblers, is met with the plea that he depart and enjoy happiness, but leave them to fight it out.[1] And wearily he does so,

[1] *Vin. Texts*, II.; *Mahāvagga*, X., 2.

and seeks comfort in a visit to the devoted friend-trio, Anuruddha, Nandīya and Kimbīla.

Well, as to internal troubles of this kind being chiefly met with in the Vinaya, we have to recollect that rules are not made for orderly peace-lovers. Monks are and were very human—namely, of all sorts—and it were unjust to take stock of the manners of a company by its worst members. It is noteworthy that this worst element came to be cited, not as by different names on different occasions, but by the stock word, the Six-set monks, the original six of a certain case being named only once. Similarly, fractious nuns came to be referred to by the one name Thulla-nandā, who may also have been a first offender. It was probably a way, and a quaint one, for giving a rule at once a historical and a general validity.

Further, I incline to think that we should see, in the arising of discord, a feature later than that fine harmony which must so have distinguished the first men, who were out both to teach, but at the same time to live the way they taught. To name the darkest cloud over the Leader's career, Devadatta's sedition: it can scarcely be invention which makes him cite the advanced age of the Leader as a reason why he should have a vicegerent. But I see nothing so reliable in Sāriputta and Moggallāna being mixed up with the quelling of the schism. The former especially I do not see in the picture. No man famed for wisdom would have *needed* the injunction to proclaim Devadatta's debasement in the terms recorded. Namely, that to condemn the man then was no less right than to have praised him before. The recapture, too, of the group of new members by a rival discourse is a fairly obvious invention after a stereotyped model. And surely it is with this dear friend, had he been still on earth, that the harassed Leader would have sought comfort, when flouted by the quarrellers. As the Order grew in numbers, and when such men as Gotama and Sāriputta grew aged or had died, it was ever a growing probability, that the bright dawn of the new movement should become overcast with clouds, the first fine inspiration losing something of its burst of joyous "compassion for devas and men."

But there is more to be said. The first men, mostly brahmans, will have brought with them, in that "compassion"—lit. that "vibrating-because of"[1]—the attitude towards men, towards "the other man," involved in the immanent Divinity of their faith—"most precious is he to me in that he, too, is in potency That Highest Self who is I. As I worship This in me, so do I worship It in him. He is more than brother; he is I. Between him and me is no room for aught beside amity, pity, fellow-joy, equanimity."

> *Since man in all the world self-lover is,*
> *See he to it he harm no other man.*[2]

Of this I have spoken. But *as time went on*, and the growing world of this monk-order came to stand over against the brahman "established church," both from the fact that the teachers were of any class, and also had fault to find in this and that privilege of the brahman, in this and that weakness in his teaching, it would follow, that the very central doctrine of the best brahman teaching would not be gladly promulgated by the new Order; it would follow that the doctrine of the Divine Self would become discredited with the rest. In other words, the man as in himself an ideal in attainment, the value in the man as such, dwindled. As this was happening, the monastic outlook on the world and human nature was growing, an outlook which was cheapening the man, which began to see in him, not divine perfection in the germ, but the beginning of that measuring as a Less that has its echo in our day, when men can write of man's "mean little individual life."[3] Along the gradual way of this downfall

[1] *Anukampā.* [2] *Kindred Sayings*, I., p. 102.
[3] H. G. Wells' *Outline of History*, p. 263.

men would cease to hold each other in worth; self-respect and mutual respect would wane together, and thus even the professedly religious would fall back on the brutish bickerings of those for whom the lofty Indian religious ideal meant nothing.

Born, too, of the Indian ideal of the man as innately divine was that casting out of fear which belongs to the great gospels. I have referred to this under the "Message." It was an outlook taken over by the Founder and his first men from the brahman teaching of the day. That the very man, the man-in-man, bore about within him the nature of the Highest, and therewith the promise of his own consummation as such, came in Sakyan poetry to be called by such a term as "the no-whence-fear."[1] The great adventure of the Way implied toil and difficulties, but the Divine guide was within and the Goal ever ahead. And there was time, for the Way was as long as was the Becoming. The adventure called for courage and stamina, ideas we see in the appellatives for Founder and worthy disciples of *vīra* (hero) and *dhīra*. And the *mā bhāyi* (fear not) of the former is not less characteristic than the "Fear not!" of Jesus. The things in life reckoned fearsome are not so for you if you be not *appasadda* (man of little faith), if you be *bhabba* (man who is to become). The monastic vogue made much of the fearsomeness of life of the world, and a favourite shibboleth was *mutti*, *vimutti*, the *being freed from*. But this will not have been the release bound up with the no-fear of the first men. It was the cry of the world-shirker, appealing only to such, not to Everyman. The message to him was a *freedom-in* the confidence born of the new light thrown on his nature and destiny. Confidence, faith, serenity are all prominent features in the apparently older sayings, features that were slowly borne in on me as I went, in

[1] *A-kuto-bhaya*; cf. *Kindred Sayings*, I., p. 244, where many references are given.

my research, back from Abhidhamma to Suttas. And this common "freedom-in," not "from," and mutual fearlessness will have militated as strongly against internal quarrels in the first years of the mission as they would now, did they yet truly exist, against international strife to-day.

What more have I in this scanty sketch to bid you look for in those years of quiet seed-sowing, wherein befell nothing that was striking, dramatic, sensational, wherein the converse with other worlds was carried on in gentle confidence, overlooked by the lowered taste of aftermen, who wove garish "miracles" into those first twenty years, mostly of a kind which the Founder is said to have condemned. Steadfast in their touring, happy because full of hope and confidence, and because they found Everyman in a way waiting for what they had to tell, fearless in freedom and in concord, recking little of bodily needs, so they were able to maintain themselves in fitness, and minister to each other in sickness: [1] all this does not make for such live recording as does the telling of the Devadatta disloyalty. Not one of the first men made any well-attested mark in oratory. The discourses bear the stamp of later premeditated compositions. The only parables that rise to eloquence are probably annexations from the brahman company of Brahma-vihāra teaching. The trait for which Gotama and his men seem to have been well known was love of silence, avoidance of worldly chatter—a feature which came to be called the Ariyas' state of silence. They were out to teach man as becoming, and that means man as willer, man as chooser, man as potentially divine, and no word had they in their language for any one of these three new mandates, nor for lives and worlds, essential opportunities in that Becoming. Is it at all wondrous if their central teaching is wretchedly worded, even had late editors let their mantras alone? *The life itself:* that was the thing. And we see it in the now fairly well known and

[1] Cf. *Psalms of the Brethren*, vers. 185, 186.

probably genuine talk with the villagers called Kālāmas. We have here, as so often, the question put and the questioners made to assist in giving the reply: "How shall we rate the teaching of one who comes to us (*e.g.* like you) with a new word?" They are advised, not to assent because of any good qualities he may show—because he keeps to tradition, to what they are accustomed, to *what is suitable for becoming*, or because he has a reverend mien. They are to rate his teaching by the effect it will have on conduct.[1] Elsewhere again, the man who would teach must show he lives as he teaches. Seek not to till another's field till you have tilled your own.[2]

This commending a warmer deeper morality as taught by the example of the teacher's own life (as in the later Jesus-word: "For [in washing your feet] I have given you an example") is recorded twice at least of Gotama. We find him bathing and dressing a sick monk grievously neglected by his fellows and, on proceeding to hold an inquiry, being told that the neglect was due to the patient "being of no service to the monks." The rejoinder runs: "You have no mothers nor fathers to wait upon you; if you wait not upon one another, who will do so?" And then the Gospel-like words: "Whoso would wait upon me, he should wait upon the sick."[3] There is another instance of such tending in a Commentary,[4] reflecting yet worse on the ethics of the monastery, where a senior monk, riddled with disease, has been cast out of the vihāra and left lying. And here no indignant reproach follows the brotherly nursing. Both records, I take it, are of a much later date than the Founder's lifetime, of a day when there were monasteries with "dormitories," and tours of inspection of them by a senior. But it is also possible that we have, here too, a surviving tradition, a fragmentary record

[1] *Gradual Sayings*, I., pp. 170 f.
[2] *Dhammapada*, ver. 158; *Dialogues*, I., p, 294.
[3] *Vinaya*, Mhv. VIII., 26.
[4] On *Dhammapada*, ver. 41.

about the tender warding of the man as the Founder's "way" in life.

But that such fostering love was no more foremost in the later values appears from the place assigned it in the records, and from the curiously repulsive way in which the Vinaya editors, not to omit the Commentator, frankly, as if unashamed, narrate the low level to which, in ordinary morality, the Order must have fallen. The episodes should have found place in the Suttas, had the example and the lesson in it been held as part of what was then known as "dhamma." Actually we find the former in the Vinaya section on the monks' dress! and the latter in the talk around a verse about imminent bodily death in a chapter on mind! The rebuke calls forth no expression of sorrow or shame whatever. How impossible it is to see in monks of this kind the men who were the Founder's fellow-missioners, the men who will have seen in each man, monk or layman, well or ill, a precious "temple of the Holy Spirit."

It was yet a far cry to the later day of the healing power which was so outstanding a symbol of that warding of the fellow-man's bodily need we see as integral in the Jesus-gospel. This is not to say that India was wholly unready for such a mandate; there is much to show that she was not, in this matter, very backward. But the Sakya mission had a different object, as I have tried to show, and one for which the Indian religious soil had been getting ready. Healing-"miracles" are greatly to seek in the Suttas, and whereas psychic abnormal gifts have much more importance in the records than writers usually allow, they were very rarely that of "faith-healing." And the exhibition of them for any purpose save that of moral and spiritual education is recorded as incurring the Founder's severe censure.[1] They were rather of a nature for educating men

[1] *Dialogues*, I., 279; but, on the other hand, see *Vinaya* (Mhv. I, where the disciple is ordered to work wonders *as* being the pupil of a great Wonder-Man.

in the "more," the *plus*, that, as in the case of the gifted few, lay within man's possibilities; a more, especially in power of will, such as *devas* were shown to the few as possessing. And you will notice that the descriptive Musing formula (the fourfold jhāna) often is a preamble to a descriptive formula of such gifts. These were collectively called *iddhi* and *abhiññā* ("effectuating" and "super-knowledge"), and are more fully discussed elsewhere.[1] Briefly, they were (1) supernormal movement, especially levitation, (2) hearing like *devas*, (3) thought-reading, (4) memory of former lives, (5) seeing like *devas*, and (6) insight into riddance of latent evil bias (*āsava*). That the older number was five, the last being of a different species, I have found betrayed by a fivefold reference and even a fourfold one (after separate treatment of the first).

Not to be too long, I must put aside these gifts of the few. But they belong, weighed as important, to the true original values. And reasonably so. Those values lay in the More that a man, as essentially in process of Becoming, could look forward to developing, if not now, then when he joined a world of *devas*. The Indian teaching had placed the very universe of the Best, the Highest, the Most within man's nature and said, "This art thou, however much thou now fallest short." Sakya took man by the hand, saying, "Thus and thus canst thou, this being so, become a More, a Better." And abnormal gifts were certain ways in, a part of, this become-more which was the man's birthright and right of way.

Finally, I repeat, the first men, especially the Founder, had the reputation of being, not gifted orators, not eloquent mantra-reciters, but lovers of silence. Confining ourselves to the latter, he lived rather than talked his message; he was a lover of jhāna-converse with other worlds, with visitors, that is, therefrom; and more, he was chiefly fain to speak as man-in-man to the man-in-man, getting past

[1] *Sakya*, chaps. XII. and XIII. Cf. above, p. 187.

all those wrappings, physical, mental, domestic, tribal, professional, national, social, that were often mistaken for the man, to the very sapling of God beneath them. Was the shoot growing? Was the will to become astir? Then he spoke; if not he was silent. His silences have impressed writers and have elicited various replies—that he avoided all but the pragmatic, the practical; that he shunned metaphysic, and the like. We should get rid of modern formulas here and take him, as the Commentaries, often stupid, sometimes discerning, rated him in this matter. He saw the light of promise "shining dimly as in a jar" now in this man, now in that woman, in that child. Then he spoke and helped. Where no light shone as yet, he could do no tending; he said never a word.

When he spoke, how brief are the sayings that seem to be of actual utterances, as distinct from the preachments with more or less pronounced monastic tendency! We cannot sense the wondrous will-power of him that will have made itself felt in every sentence, in the message of those blue eyes.[1] We can only trace here and there, in some hammer-like idiom: "Enough, enough!" "Let be, let be!" or in the frequent gestures that supplemented the deficient stock of will-words, what a living dynamo he will have been,

Who laid his hand upon my head and took
My arm and to the garden led me back
And in compassion to me gave . . .[2]

or who took leaves or dust in hand as object-lessons, or who pictured supernormal will by clenched fist and outshot arm. I say not that this well-spring of energy neglected the equally needful calm and relaxed serenity. The need of relaxing tense lute-strings forms one of his parables,[3] and we find him both as lone muser in the wood and in the

[1] *Dialogues*, Stas. XIV, XXX.
[2] *Psalms of the Brethren*, CCXXXVI, cf. above, p. 204.
[3] *Vin Texts*, Mhv., V., 1, 15 f.

woods "happily resting, filled with compassion for all things."[1] But I confess that the one preponderant conception of him which has been made visible down the ages, of the immobile, cross-legged Sitter, has for me no appeal, and typifies far too much a creed which has come to a standstill, has cast aside its first and central truth, that man's nature is essentially a becoming and he must look to it that he speed up that becoming by the dynamo of his will.

What of the dying of those first men? Did it befit the way of their living? Alas! and fie! on the recorders; save in the case of the one man in whom they centred their real interest, there is virtually nothing to say. One Sutta and (so far as I yet know) two Commentarial passages[2] speak of the two leading disciples as passing away before their leader. But how long before—this we are not told; even though in one place the very month is given, the year of the Mission is not. Of Sāriputta the death appears to have been after the Jetavana settlement was instituted, but such evidence is not "evidential"; so very many Suttas have the stereotyped beginning of "living (or staying) at the Jetavana." Nor does the Sutta, though in its way impressive, record a single feature in the passing. And there is a borrowing from, or a lending to, between it and the great Sutta of the Founder's passing—the reader will note this—suitable at least to this extent, that there is the recorded testimonial to him from Gotama, that he taught (turned the Wheel) as did the former.[3] Of the dying there is but this: he fell ill when at his native village, Nālā, near Rājagaha, and so died, and the news had to be broken. But the grief that his great leader will have felt is made to find expression in Ānanda, of feebler insight. The novice Chunda who brought the news appears solely occupied with the (probably) cremated "relics," so will

[1] *Kindred Sayings*, I., p. 39.
[2] *Ibid.*, V., p. 141; *Jātakas*, No. 95 and 522.
[3] *Sutta-Nipāta*, ver. 557. *Kindred Sayings*, I., p. 242.

have grown, for the editors, the outlook on Man-in-the-Less.

Much more sensational is the curious story about Moggallāna. He is said to have met with a violent end from violent men, the result, uncancelled by his much righteous missionizing labour, of a vile attempt to kill his parents in a previous life.[1] The Suttas are silent, and the strange notion that a saintly disciple has to get permission to die from the Leader finds in them no backing. Of all the rest, "the rest is silence," save only on the Founder's passing. And of that we have in the Jātaka Commentary the unworthy, unsupported "thought" put into his mind, that "My two chief disciples having passed away, I too will pass away." This sort of "thinking" is also recorded in Chinese MSS. of the aged Gavampati, when news of the Founder's death is brought to him:—Gone out is the light of the world; why wait here longer?[2]

That Gotama lived into "the eighties" there is no reasonable ground to doubt. He is said more than once to say this of his age, and to speak of his body as a worn-out cart held together with difficulty. That he may, as to the companionship of worthy comrades of the touring generation, have been bereft and lonely, is as yet ill realized; at least, I have yet to see any sign of it. There appear to have been left Kassapa, who refused to bear him in his last years company, Anuruddha, his cousin, now also old and always a recluse, who left it for the Leader to visit *him*, Kacchāna, at Avanti and Ānanda, loyal, devoted, but not approaching the spiritual level of his great cousin. Of the rest of the inner circle of ten or so we find at the end no sign. They would, were they on earth, be too old to go a-touring, but neither do we find them bearing him company at Sāvatthi, in the Jetavana, where the Founder appears to have spent his latter years.

[1] *Dhpada, Comy.*, X., p. 7.
[2] J. Przyluski, *Concile de Rājagaha.*

I think of him as, amid a company of younger men, who would be more or less on tour, but also were spending much care, perhaps only during the rains, perhaps longer, now that Sudatta had erected many huts, on the fixing orally of the accumulated store of the many Sayings, learnt and repeated by the chief teachers for some thirty years and more. This fixing would include turning many into verse, whereby memorizing was made easier, and recollection too. But it does not follow, either that he remained equal to the work of presiding over such activities, or that the younger men were ever wishing him to do so. Revered doubtless, obeyed when he decreed, and faithfully waited on by Ānanda, he will have been, for younger and capable men, very old-fashioned in his ideas, and as a venerable Nelsonian battleship scrapped for active service.

Nothing else can explain for me the inconsistencies between (*a*) the Upanishadic teaching that we find lurking in his own first utterances, in the Ātman emphases in Dhammapada and early Anguttara and elsewhere, and (*b*) certain Suttas in the Four Nikāyas: *e.g.* the ribald No. XI. of the First, the scoffing at the divinity of the Self in No. XXII. of the Second Nikāya,[1] to mention no others. Secession from the established brahman teaching had been slowly coming on; the arahan theory of the man consummating here on earth was ejecting the man of immanent divinity; the over-against-the-world standpoint of the growing monk-vogue was contracting the long vista of the Way of the many worlds. It will have made his declining years often a tragedy, such as his religion, tending evermore to glorify him as figurehead, and ultimately to make that Figure supersede, as a renascent external deity, the monitor and Witness within, Whom he worshipped, has to this day failed to discern.

Unfit to go once more a-touring from village to village, he must have set out on that last tour, which we find so

[1] *Further Dialogues*, I., p. 97.

pathetically told in the "Great Suttanta of the Passing," under some driving pressure which we are not permitted to see. We are told that, beside Ānanda, "a great company of monks" went with him, but the usual formula is shortened, and the next day's walk is always addressed to Ānanda alone. Read it carefully, and it may be the two lonely old men of that once joyous company will stand out in relief: "Come, Ānanda, let's go on to X. . . ."

How lonely, too, is the little couch, just the spread cloak under the twin sāl trees, the suffering supervening on an indigestible dish of truffles or other savoury mess,[1] given in hospitality, but breaking down the enfeebled powers of digestion, the misery of poor Ānanda, the supreme last effort to tell an inquirer about the Way, the coma, the silent and unseen Wayfaring hence.

How different would have been the record of the last walks, from this village to that, the illness, the dying, had the venerable Leader been attended by the "great company of monks," as he is said to have been! Ānanda appears as the sole ministrant and nurse. At the last breath, Anuruddha is brought on; he briefly tells Ānanda the patient is not dead, but in jhāna; he afterwards orders Ānanda (who addresses his cousin and old friend as a superior) to run on errands (there being no one younger),

[1] This word, into which commentators, Buddhist and European have carefully gone (Franke especially: see the long note, in his Dīgha-Nikāya, p. 222), is *sūkara-maddava*, lit; either soft, or dry, or joy, of pig. A food-compound of pig-flesh (*sūkara-mamsa*) does occur once in the scriptures, in a Sutta of a curiously unworthy kind, where a householder, in inviting Gotama to dine, goes through quite a *menu* in a refrained detail! *Maddava* is nowhere else associated with meat, and I remain of Rhys Davids's opinion, that we have here a dish (not less indigestible for this participant than pork) of a root, such as truffles, much sought by swine, and which may have been called "pig's joy." Such a roo did not know—in our "pignut," the little nut-shaped bulbous roc are liked by both pigs and children. See Rh. D.'s note, *Dialogues*, II., p. 137; and cf. Shakespeare's Caliban:

And I with my long nails will dig thee pignuts.

and then, doubtless summoned in haste by a friendly passing ascetic, Kassapa comes hurrying up, and, a man of strong will and level-headed, takes the lead in the funeral, and shortly afterwards, in the first conclave, which it was obviously the necessary thing to convene.

Do not be misled by the pains the compilers of the Dying Sutta have taken to mask the loneliness of that dying, or the strangeness of that last tour when touring was for him untimely. Especially, by the way, a talk with Sāriputta has been dragged in, a talk which came, long drawn out and evidently "developed" like any symphony *motif*, to be inserted in the Dīgha-Nikāya. Had Sāriputta been on earth at so late a date, can there be a doubt but that we should have found him beside his dying friend and comrade, and not conceding the disposition of arrangements to Kassapa? The Sutta, as Rhys Davids pointed out in detail, is heavy with gloss and interpolation from other books. He only failed to see how lonely and unexplained is the tour, and how the whole composition points to the growth of relic cult. In any case, it was an awkward situation for the Sāvatthi monks, to whom the Commentary shows Ānanda returning, heavy with his tidings, to convene their presence at the Mother-settlement, Rājagaha. And measures had to be taken, in the business of the recording, to dress up that lonely resting-place of the twin sāl trees in the imperial robes of a Superman's passing.

Art, too, helped in this posthumous decoration. You will see many illustrations of bas-reliefs showing a raised couch or bier surrounded with bent mourners, scenes that may well have taken place when the neighbouring town of Pavā came to be told what had happened near Kusināra village. But for the artist, as for those he impressed, it is the *earlier* stage that is represented. You will also see a surprising preference in art, next to the cross-legged Sitter, for the prostrate deceased Figure. In Japan, there may (as I see depicted) be superposed over this in the sky a radiant deity, and that is consonant with the Mahāyāna faith that in Gotama we see an *avatar*, among others, of that Buddha who is worshipped as God. In Southern Buddhism there is no such eternal being; the faith has stopped at the conception of man's reality as a great "No," a "Not." And still the loneliness of the passing is not reconstructed. The artist depicts an ideal, oftener than the truth of an actual happening. But he has to symbolize by the concrete, and thus becomes, for the historic imagination, a lying guide.

As to the, at first sight, curious "jhāna" in which this servant of man, this brother of man, is said to have passed away—I judge that we have here a surviving fragment of deep interest. I have tried to show that for the first men jhāna, or musing, meant access to, or the attempt to get access to, the inmates of other worlds. For the later men it came to mean *only* the requisite preliminary abstraction. But *for the first men* to say "in jhāna" will have meant "in converse with the next world." So reading, the valedictory utterance ascribed to the governors of the two worlds, the Sakka and the Brahmā, followed by that of Anuruddha (who alone could have heard clairaudiently) falls into place.[1] And we have the "down tools!" of this great Labourer attested by unseen worlds, even as we read of the taking up those tools in the first Utterance attested. The fragment will have been, as associated with Ānanda's recording and Anuruddha's fixing in prose, or even in verse, too sacred to get forgotten. But the later values drove, and it became for repeaters, for editors irrepressible to trot out the formulas and much of them, resulting in the Jhāna scale-playing which you find in the Passing Sutta.

I am not blind to the reverence and worship at work in these, to us, strange ways; it is the worsened values betrayed in the treatment that I deplore. We read here of the man in the unseen honouring the very man in the seen.

[1] *Vin. Texts*, Mahāv. I., 6, 30.

In jhāna the very man is recognized as a real entity in converse with real entities, even in the formula, even in the commentary on it—"in a procedure there will be a proceeder." Yet when the after-men of this faith tried to philosophize, they produced the dogma, often called central, that there is no experiencer, that there is no knower, no doer, only doing, no wayfarer, only way![1]

[1] *Path of Purity*, III., pp. 609, 726, etc. Buddhadatta, in his (contemporary) *Abhidhamāvatāra* (P.T.S. ed., pp. 85, 118), echoes this.

CHAPTER XIII

THE AFTER-MEN: THEIR DOINGS AND THEIR RECORDING

We may not be far wrong if we imagine the slowly spreading tidings of the passing of the venerable Founder of the Sakyan Order to have been felt much as was felt the passing of that other venerable living tradition, the Queen Victoria, the Great White Woman, the Great Mother, for many outlying portions of her empire. It was not so much one monarch among others who had gone hence: it was an institution. A vast majority therein had never seen her; a vaster majority had never spoken with her, but she had for so long been at the centre, its nominal, its very respected head. In a relatively little "empire," and to a somewhat lesser degree, this was true of the Sakyan "Teacher"—the "Satthar"—to give him his earliest title.

We shall certainly be wrong if we imagine that those tidings will have been felt by that lesser world as *then* holding the cult of quasi-deification of him which we find in the Commentaries and, to a certain extent, in the Piṭakas. Into the ground and growth of such cults, mixture as they are of sincere tribute to worth, or position, or both, of remorse for opportunities neglected, of faith (*quand même et parceque*) in the very live persistence of the now unseen "man," I do not further go. But that the Buddha-cult was of later growth I find implicitly betrayed here and there, but notably attested in the Vinaya account of the so-called First and Second Councils (in Pali called *paṭhamā* and *dutiyā sangīti*, or "thorough-chanting").[1] Taking only the Vinaya account as undoubtedly the oldest we have

[1] The *Mahāvaṃsa*, perhaps by an oversight of scribes, calls the first *paṭhama-dhamma-sangīti*, the second, only *dutiya-sangīti*.

yet found, and seeing that it was held as soon after the decease as a representative number of members of the Order could be convened, and therefore when the sense of loss and (who will not say?) of remorse was yet keenly felt, we find no expression publicly made of any feeling that the Order had sustained a tremendous (if inevitable) loss; no panegyric of its great Father; no mention of him from first to last as "Buddha," much less as "Sambuddha" (thoroughly wise one). Nor, as to that, is he called either Tathāgata or Sugata, as it were *par excellence*, as is so usual in the Suttas. In the questioning of Upāli and then Ānanda for such evidence as they could best give as to the first utterance of Rule and of Saying respectively, the Man who came to be called the author of every Rule and of nearly all the Sayings *is not even alluded to*. When, in the personal inquisition of Ānanda, he is at length mentioned, it is just to be called *Bhagavan* (Blessed One). There are not even incidentally any words of adoring reference. Bald and jejune the account of that First Council is; the assembly are made to appear much keener about Dhamma and Vinaya, and about Ānanda's shortcomings, and even about the Order's petty economies, than about their loss.

Things are not different even at the Second Council, placed a century later. Preceding it we find the thin end of the wedge of Buddha-cult getting in. Verses are cited where occurs once the title "Buddha, kin of the sun," which is found in the Anthologies. And in the prose, the plural "Buddhas" occurs. But at the Council itself, just "Bhagavan" is used again, together with the older title Satthar, here translated Master (Magister). And again there is the preoccupation with "Dhamma and Vinaya."

It may be said: Do we not read that he named no human successor to himself but just and only "dhamma"? And were not the Councils strictly business meetings? I reply Yes! to both questions. But even at a business meeting loyal members would have made, at least by way of preamble, some reference, at the one event, to that sorrowing loyalty, and some equivalent to our National Anthem at the other event, some solemn *Namo* . . . as we find everywhere in *written* undertakings. I do not speak with any confidence of what may have been Indian usage in those far-off dates. But when you come to learn from the Pali, not to mention the Buddhist Sanskrit literature, how uptowering and overwhelming the cult of the "Buddha" became, how he was "Dhamma" and Dhamma he, how every rule in the Vinaya, even incredibly petty rules, are made of his instituting, how nearly everything his fellow-teachers say (especially if they are women) is either outlined by him or endorsed by him as what he would have said, how the personalities of those individually interesting women and men are made colourless in the devotional glare lit about him, how, finally, even the arid Abhidhamma catechisms are, as dehumanized shells of teaching, made none the less to be all his teaching, not on earth, but to his (unfortunate) mother and other devas in another world, you may agree that the absence of signs of this tremendous cult in those two Vinaya records of the Councils is very significant.

You may say about that preoccupation with "Dhamma," that it is in accord with his own behest. But I would contend that he, with values that had become, as I have suggested, "old-fashioned," had *his own dharma* in mind, not the Dhamma of the recorders. In the Second Council this "Dhamma" is spoken of as something to be "learnt by heart," orally formulated codes of conduct, sayings in prose and verse we now call Suttas, an externalized conscience. *His* dharma was that each man had a *Satthar* within him, the bidding of Whom was communicable and to be conferred about when fit. Not so much of that outside Dhamma had come into articulate shape at the First Council; we read of only four great Pārājika Rules, of only two Suttas or Sayings, and of no Abhidhamma (there may have already existed the heads called Mātikā).[1] And if the compilers give us to understand that there was much more, you will, I hope, be by this time on the look-out for the ubiquitous gloss of editors who sought only to impress, and were void of historical sense.

As to the "historicity" of these two, and also of the third Council of the middle of the third century B.C., certain writers of the past generation have been at some pains to undermine it. Here I am merely telling you where you can follow their arguments, and that only in a note. I judge that the inherent likelihood of such councils, when and where they were held, is a far stronger argument for the truth of the serious affirmations that they were held than are certain silences about, or lapses in, them, good testimony that nothing of the kind actually took place. The denials make a greater strain on our credulity than do the affirmations. Has any church got established without such gatherings, or maintained itself in outward unity without them? Nor does Franke's extraordinary hypothesis, that the last two chapters (in the Vinaya) on the Councils were compiled as object-lessons in etiquette of monkish modes of address,[2] prove that the Councils were not held. The chapters may have been compiled from the oral records which somehow got lost. The marvel, indeed, is that not more records got lost, lost before being written, lost after being written! That existing records of two councils may have been used as good material to recast, so as to show how it was correct to address X and Y—this is possible; but it in no wise excludes the existence of the genuine original records, much less the high probability that the Councils took place.

The very fact, if fact it was, that the dying leader named no disciple, certainly no Kassapa, as one he could trust to carry on in his place, but only the conscience (*dharma*)

[1] See above, p. 27.
[2] *Vin.* I., Intro.; *Vin. Texts,* III., ch. xi, xii; *Dial.* Sta. XVI., Intro. *J.P.T.S.*, 1908.

working in each man and woman, appears to me strong evidence that there was not in him, nor ever had been, the will to institute a "church" of any kind, a Set, Party, Society, Sect or Cult, *least of all* to place any Order, or nucleus in such a society, as being, in prestige or in worth or in nearness of attainment to the Goal, *above the laity as such.* So far as this superiority "hedges in" the Order to-day in the Buddhist countries of Southern or Central Asia or of the further East, so far do I see a contravention of the Founder's will. I see in that will the desire that, whereas man among men could find many lines of advance by way of his natural relations with his fellows, the growth, the "becoming" of him as very man (as "soul" or "spirit") should and could be best left to be forwarded by the divine inner Dharma-monitor, together with the *kalyāṇa-mitta* :[1] the "lovely friend," one or many, acting upon the heedful will of the man. A friend or friends, be it noted, not necessarily always or only of this world, but, it might be (in *jhāna*), of worlds, where the man was at least to this extent a More in that his vision had become longer, wider than that of the child of earth.

Not utterly should those sayings be disregarded as unreliable in which he is shown foreseeing a tragic falling to pieces of the little world he had witnessed growing up about him, fixing its ways and standards *externally*, both in formulated teachings, cenobitic rules, worsening of the high ideal of the man as bearing about in him the Man Divine in potency, worsening the lay life, the home life over against the monastic life, the in-letting of women not yet rightly regarded as each of them the man-in-man no less than each monk, but looked upon as so many "females," weaker in every religious qualification than the "males." One voice alone was heard upholding the deeper view; that of the nun Somā, whose verses are dateless, ageless—the voice of the woman claiming that her true being lay deeper than sex.

[1] Cf. p. 247.

She is taunted:

That vantage-ground the sages may attain
Is hard to win. With her two-finger consciousness
That is no woman competent to gain.

Somā:

What should the state of woman do to us,
Whose mind is firmly set, to anyone
Who, knowledge rolling on, dharma discerns?
To one for whom the question doth arise;
Am I a woman in these matters, or
Am I a man, or what not am I then?
To such an one are you, sir, fit to talk! [1]

Here is surely one after the Leader's own heart! But monastic editing has made out this sorry case for one it deemed all-wise:—Refusing thrice the plea made by his foster-mother, Devī Pajāpatī and many women, their feet dust-covered by the walk, as would-be *religieuses*, from Kapilavatthu out to the Banyan Park, where he was staying, a plea presented [as to the secluded presence of a potentate—think of it! He was not then old.] by Ānanda, he yields as if unwillingly to earnest persistence, but warns his men that he has thereby committed the Order to a measure by which the God-life would no longer be foretold as "long-persisting, the very dharma as lasting for a thousand years"; [2] that its stability had been shortened by one half that term. Other sayings name, one four, another five "things conducing to the blurring, the disappearance of Very Dharma," and others are full of "future perils." The "things" include misunderstood sayings of the teaching, forgetting a saying, slackness in teaching, decline in energy and the simple life, schism and quarrelling. And emphatic is a future peril detailed as the having "ceased to make become," in this line and that, in the man.

[1] *Kindred Sayings*, I., p. 161; cf. *Pss. of the Sisters*, pp. 44, 181.
[2] *Vin. Texts*, III., x, 6.

I am not seeing, in the reluctance about ordaining nuns, anything beyond a monastic re-fashioning of a very old advice, possibly given when the Order was in its first years, and when, under the primal conditions of mission-touring, it was not expedient for women to become literally comrades of the "Road." There is another tradition preserved in the later Anthology, the Apadāna, where Gotama's wife, Yasôdharā, is shown (above, p. 57) speaking about her joining the Order long ago, bringing women with her, and now come, an old woman, to greet him. He is said to have re-visited his home soon after he had launched himself and his men as monks, in the fifth year of his starting as teacher. It is possible we have a mix-up of traditions about Yasôdharā and Pajāpatī, the former being rejected when she applied too early for admission, on the grounds I have given, the latter entering much later, with only a welcome, not a rebuff, to an honoured foster-parent become a widow.

Nor do I see in the tidily drawn up Suttas of the Anguttara, with their fourthlies and fifthlies, sayings as actually uttered by the Śakyamuni. The later writers end their exegeses with a cheerio! as to the Sāsana lasting long, coupled with the hope the "god may rain," blissfully unburdened by any thought that their text or their own expoundings are at all in conflict with the aspirations or the far-seeing fears of their great Founder. Were not the Vihāras grown great still standing, wherein they could sit and write with their brass styles? Was there not at each a Sangha, with or without an Almswomen's quarter, and around, a complacent, compliant laity, giving alms daily, and robes occasionally, and coming on full moon and half or quarter-moon days to be edified? Monks are "above us; all's well with the world."

Yet all the while they were in their very writings perpetuating, adding to "the blurring, the vanishing" of which the Suttas tell! How much they had, in the changed values of their time, come to do this is not yet kept as clear as it should be. There is in their comments plenty of strong moral earnestness; they still retain a vista of the good life as a way of progress, even though they are ever more concerned with riddance than with a positive Becoming-more. And this may serve as blinkers to their readers. But it is the very core that they have eviscerated from the teaching; it is but an empty chariot that they are pushing along. Let me show in citing what I mean. The Commentary on the Sutta-Piṭaka book Paṭisambhidā-magga we are just seeing through press has this: "Wherefore it has been said:

Verily there is just ill but no ill-man;
No doer, only doing exists;
There is waning, but no man who wanes;
Way is, but goer exists not.

All the truths are to be understood as void, from the absence in an ultimate sense, of experiencer, doer, waned goer." [1] Or again, the famous Path of Purity abounds in such passages as: "He (the earnest student), in '*all complexes are empty*,' does not see 'self' in anything . . . nor does he see the self of him ascribable to any state of any one else" (p. 799).

Now let us clinch the teaching recorded of the Man, the Śakyamuni, in combining his first and last utterances; taking "Were it not better that you sought the self?" with "Live ye as they who have the self as lamp, as refuge, who have dharma as lamp, as refuge, and who have no other lamp, no other refuge. . . . With earnestness thoroughly bring to pass. . . .

Full ripe my age, short term of life for me,
Leaving, for you I shall go hence. I've made
A refuge of the Self. . . ."

Enough, Subhadda! Leave all that (sort of talk)! I will teach you dharma: where you recognize the way, therein

[1] P. 193. "The reference is to the accepted authorities in the Sangha. "Waned" is *nibbuto*, meaning lit. "quenched" and hence the frequent rendering "at peace."

will you recognize the religious man in one stage or another of it. . . ."

How in the world are we to harmonize with these the later writings quoted? Here we have their "not-anywhere-to-be-found-'self'" as not only held to be present and most real, as not only *one* saving help to man's faith, but as, with dharma as Voice of the Highest Self, *the one and only saving help*. Here we have not only the Way, but no Way without the Wayfarer, the "goer." How has it come to pass that with these records—and well known they appear to have been to Commentators—such sheer contradictions should be believed in? Buddhaghora, here quoted, cites the Suttas "not singly, but in battalions"; the Commentary echoes the nun Vajirā's verses: "There's nought but Ill that doth arise. . . ."[1]

Some will say, If you will fall in with other translators, and will drop the Indian way of the "self," and will render those phrases by "yourselves as lamp," etc., "myself as refuge," the contradiction becomes much softened. The Way and wayfarer will remain, but the rest will be shown as a teaching of self-reliance—in fact, a positive Agnosticism.

A value such as this makes no little appeal to many at the present day—or should we not rather say, to many of yesterday, for to-day that confidence in the man being thrust back upon himself is tottering somewhat. It may be said to have found expression, for the past generation, in poetry as

Under the bludgeonings of chance
My head is bloody but unbowed.

. . . .

I am the master of my fate,
I am the captain of my soul.

Here we have the rebel, the anarchist, assuming lordship over all that in his life and nature he does not understand

[1] *Kindred Sayings*, I., p. 170.

called "soul": the world in the unseen, the world of feeling; assuming it not because of his worthiness to be "captain," (the sole warrant for rightfully being "captain,") but because he has made something else dominant, and placed his will at the service of that. The something else is the evidence of his senses, and the systematizing of this in science. He may know little of science, but it is there; and the evidence building it up, of which he perhaps does know something, is there. And that for him is the worth in "Captain." Should he come to deepen his idea of the "I"; should he see that "soul" is included in "I," and "I" in "soul," his standard as to what constitutes a "captain" worthy of the name grows. And he will see himself as no more than a man of the rank and file, who, the Captain having been put out of action, is doing his level best to take his place. Now this is the "myself" of the modern European.

If we read this "myself" into Indian utterances of the sixth century B.C., we shall be purblind. In the word *ātmā*, *attan*, those utterances meant, not just our "self," but a *more*, just as we mean, by the word "spirit" or "essence," something actually or potentially more than anything visible or external or average.

If, assuming the Śakyamuni did utter that exordium above—and it would certainly not have been a later interpolation—if he meant by "self" "your actual selves" (as when we say in winter: Do wrap yourselves up!) we may be sure the Suttas would have had sayings insisting on this new and limited and lessened use of the word. Why? Because it would have been so new, so different from the way in which other religious teachers of the day were teaching. And this new way, in foreshadowing the later way in which Buddhist teaching about the "self" was going to take, would have been preserved and emphasized as the head and centre of its divergence *from brahman teaching*. But we find nowhere any saying pointing to such a new divergence. Hence we should see, in his use of "self," *the religious usage of his day*. Of that I have spoken in the chapter on his Message.

Do not misunderstand me! There are Suttas giving expression to a shrinkage, a lowering in the view taken of "self," as being wrongly called eternal, persisting, or real, because all things were "transient." And for me these are the trend which the teaching about the "self" was already taking. But just because they are so different from that exordium, quoted above, do I see in them what he will not have said, however we read the word "self." Who, as a teacher of any worth, would exhort the self to be taken as a lamp, a refuge, if it were transient and unreal? For the teaching of Gotama's day, the man had indeed a captain, was indeed the captain, but it was not the actual imperfect, limited private soldier of the English poet; it was That More in and of him, yet known only as a More, not yet as Most, who, as the early Pali poems say, is "the protector, the upholder, the witness, the noble one, the trainer"; in modern phrase, the ideal, nay, the divine self. There is nothing properly to be called Agnostic or Atheist in this. Nothing is so closely known, so intimately cherished, as the "I," and rightly so, if in the "I" be divined our infinite ineffable possibilities. To have taken Deity into the very heart, the innermost of Me is at once a true Gnosis, a form of Theism. "Are ye not a temple of the holy spirit?"—the Christian here approaches the Indian view. But the Indian view says: Are *you* not holy spirit?

In such a view the unworthiness of "the private soldier" at once stands out, as I have showed earlier. To attain the worthiness of "the Captain" Who he by nature is, he *must become;* his whole life opens up, not so much as a being the Captain, but as a long striving to develop into the Captain. And here we come to the secret that would have brought harmony into the changing values in Buddhism, had it not cast away the very core of the Founder's teaching in the word *bhava*, becoming. I may add, had not the established religion cast it away also: that, too, I have already discussed. The doctrine of the God-in-Man as the Self had become rigid, for lack of this idea of becoming. Men thought they had to choose between a Self who is imperishable (*akshara*) and unchanging, and a self who is transient, even momentary, a series of flashes, a row of beads. Nothing of the kind was required, had but the I, the very man, been, as Gotama urged, *kept apart from body and mind*—these were indeed transient—and viewed as *bhabba*, or *bhavya*: one who is becoming, indefinitely, immortally becoming.

We are ever too European in our valuing the Indian religious mind, and under this should come the early Sakyan mind. Too alien to it is the false humility which can write of man's "mean little individual existence," or tolerate a religion which could bid man rely solely upon himself, where "himself" meant man apart from God. "What miserable mantra is this," would the Indian say, "that you seek to foist upon us? Do not belittle yourselves; realize your Brahmahood, your Divinity. No mere fleeting man of earth are you save as to your earth-body, raiment of clay. Almighty is the Ally, the Kinsman within you. Lose yourself in That (*nir-ātmā*), and you then truly find your self; but apart from That (*an-ātmā*) you are irremediably lost."

Once more, do not misunderstand me! In the current way of speech, in the conventional ideas expressed in speech, the self, as any person distinguishable from other persons, *was* accepted at all times by Buddhists as by all men. They would say: Our denial of the self or man as real only comes in when, on analysing what these words mean, a persisting immortal being, over and above transient factors, is seen in or behind those factors. The word has come down in our tradition as meaning such a More in or behind those factors, that were there such a More in "man," he could be, become, anything he wished. But he cannot wield such power, such exemption from infirmities; so we say no such self is in or of him. And we only permit a merely conventional truth in our use of self or man. The factors, we say, are real, but the name (these two words) merely binds them conveniently together. And it is in the factors bodily and mental that we seek to make-become (*bhāveti*) that man-in-the-More which Indian religion saw in a positive persisting "self."

I am not in this little book seeking to do less than justice to different points of view: my main object is to make clear the historical truth of there having been an original teaching older than this, and of its gradual supersession by teaching which had come to hold the changed values quoted. And hence I comment thus:

Note that the distinction between truth as (*a*) just conventional and as (*b*) "higher" (*paramatthena*), or, as we might say philosophical, is not clearly applied to the term self or man *till the fifth century* A.D. With it Buddhaghosa concludes his Comments on Kathāvatthu I, i.[1] It is possibly in other Commentaries also. It is more tentatively put forward in the Questions of King Milinda (B.C. about 80).[2] That words as such were beginning to be critically weighed—a new thing for India—is touched upon in Dīgha- and Saṃyutta-Nikāyas, much earlier. But that Gotama taught, as we now say, both exoterically and esoterically, is contrary to sayings recorded of him in the Suttas and also to the Jātaka "Bodhisat" tradition. The Abhidhamma Piṭaka *is silent on the matter*. I must conclude, therefore, that in the first and last sayings about the Self, quoted as of the Founder in this chapter, he spoke with a single undivided meaning only. Namely, that to get at the truth of a word, he did not ask the philosophic man to reverse the meaning it had for Everyman.

Note further that, whereas there is in me nothing but

[1] *Points of Controversy*, p. 63 *n.* 2.
[2] *S.B.E.*, XXXV., p. 226 (text, 159).

appreciation for the way in which Buddhism has ever striven after making-to-become a more in human conduct, and whereas the ideal agent practising that conduct was personalized as *arahan* (worthy one), conventionally personalized, their literature has ever shown them consistently busied over, not the *man* so much, as *ideas* (*dhammā*) about him and his conduct. But this was not so in the beginning. Those ideas about him or those factors of him included, of course, all factors or aspects of mind. These came to be distinguished as fourfold—came to be, when the growing Sānkhya swept the rising young Buddhist world under its influence—the man as "coming to know by way of sense-and-feeling" (*vedanā*); the man as "coming to know by way of the word, the name" (*saññā*); the man as "coming to know in complexes, or concretes, or compounds" (*sankhārā*), and, finally, "the man as persisting-with-awareness" (*viññāṇa*). This kinship with life in the unseen hereafter, expressed in the last term, is usually overlooked by writers, because they have seen in it (*a*) only its etymological meaning, (*b*) only what the Abhidhamma compilers had come to see in it. Its older meaning, akin to our "soul," you can find in Majjhima-Nikāya;[1] and also we have seen it in Saṃyutta-Nikāya.[2] And this early meaning has curiously persisted in mediæval books when death and rebirth are the theme. But Buddhist teaching had virtually eviscerated the man who had been "*viññāṇa*" and had seen in it dying thought, as resulting in the thinking of a newly reborn complex. We saw it selected as meaning the man as judge, the lord of the city to whom come messengers of various and true ways to salvation.[3] Had "mind," as just recipient and valuer of impressions, been meant, the word *mano* or *chitta* would have been used, as used they were. That *viññāṇa* is used places us in values other than those of earth alone. But when, in the Abhi-

[1] Sta. 38.
[2] IV., 3, 3 and XXII., 87; *Kindred Sayings*, I., p. 152; III., p. 106.
[3] *Ibid.*, IV., p. 127. Cf. p. 230.

dhamma-Piṭaka, *viññāṇa* is defined, it has become just mind or consciousness, and is so for southern Buddhists to-day.[1]

Thus, considered historically, Buddhism *has not always looked upon* the man as a bundle of transient factors to be trained religiously as factors. Man was for it at one time a persistent somewhat, wayfarer in both this and other worlds.

As to the irrational theory of doing (*karma*) persisting and passing over as substitute for the man, to meet with a mechanically, impersonally determined result, I find nothing in the Suttas to warrant this later decadent view. Do not think I am inventing a fiction. I have but just seen it emphatically taught by a Japanese lecturing as were he a Hīnayanist of the most sectarian set: "Karma transmigrates without its doer." But we have seen that the Piṭakas clearly insist on the survival of the *doer*, who is arraigned after death because of the things done, for which he, and not a new complex, is held responsible (p. 180 f.).

Emphasis on the deed (*karma*) was a new note in India in Gotama's day, due probably to the pains, and discussed *privately* by other teachers (*Brihad*: *Up*. 3, 2, 13). But for the first Sakyans, it was still and ever the man, the *doer*, who, changing yet persisting, was taken into account.

[1] *Compendium of Philosophy*, p. 234.

CHAPTER XIV

WRITING AND HISTORIC TRUTH

I COME back to the successors of the first Sakyans and to the long blank interval of years that intervenes for us between the passing out of the Founder, or at best between the Second Council, and the time when a brief-lived Indian empire had arisen on the ashes of Alexander the Great's blighted conquests in the East. This interval had a duration we cannot fix with precision; the West makes it about 230 years from Gotama's death till the middle of Asoka's reign; the East sees it as nearer 300 years. During that interval the Sāsana, the teaching or "church" of the Sakyans continued to grow in numbers and influence, but in the central portions of India only. Till probably towards the end of the interval there was, mainly for lack of suitable materials, no writing save of a brief memorandum kind on thin metal plates, on which letters were stippled with style of rounded points.[1] These memoranda may have been heads or titles of the kind called *mātikās*, mentioned in my second chapter, thus, *e.g.*

"(the) two strengths: computation-strength, making-become-strength."
"(the) two teaching-ways: concise, detailed."
"(the) two men hard to find:

the first-to-show-kindness,
the grateful-for-kindness,"

or this from another book:

"*the phrase 'agitation':*
the phrase 'occasion of agitation,'
the phrase 'and the earnest struggle of him, the agitated.'"

[1] Cf. Rhys Davids's *Buddhist India*, Plates, pp. 125–7; and my *Milinda Questions*, Pl. II., dated A.D. 76.

In the last triad, you will find the text specifies the amplification *left to the teacher*.

Or the memorandum may have been an outlined lesson called *uddesa*, the exposition, left as oral, being the *vibhanga*, later on, *niddesa*. Thus in the Majjhima-Nikāya we find a few of these *uddesa*-cum-*vibhangas* left in: *e.g.* "A monk should so scrutinize that, for him scrutinizing, the spirit of him as to the external, undistracted unclinging, the mind as to the internal steadfast, he, not grasping after, may not be terrified; there will thus be for him in the hereafter no arising, no becoming of birth-old-age-dying-sorrow." This is the *uddesa* which an able expositor is shown as proceeding to expound in *vibhanga* about twenty-eight times as long (Sta. CXXXVIII.).

We know that the smooth inner surface of certain kinds of bark was used in Asia for writing, but reference to it has not yet been found in Pali Commentaries, with this apparent exception:—In the Commentary on the Dīgha-Nikāya, in a debate as to whether a certain passage should be considered as accepted "text," we read: "and having supplied bark" (*calliṃ upaṭṭhapetvā*), as if they had said, having fetched paper. But it was the leaves of the palmyra palm which, once lit upon by some inventive genius, when or where we know not, but presumably near the sea where the tree is found, will have been shipped up the Ganges (from Orissa, perhaps), ousting the clumsy metal plates. It came, may be, just when the Greek culture, introduced into the north-west provinces, where Greek rule lingered, and in embassies to the Mauryan court, was opening up to India the immense opportunities in speech as perpetuated in space rather than in time, in appeal to the eye more than to the ear.

To us the advantage accruing from this shifting, in the handing on of the man's vocal expression of himself, seems so immense that we have only pity for a race compelled till then to make known, let alone preserve, that expression orally. But India thought very differently. For India the living voice was of that "more" in the man, not of his merely visible shape (*rūpa*); it was, in the mantra, a More speaking through him, even a Divine More, so that speech itself was ranked as divine. Beside this *deus ex machina*, the carved, the written word was a very dead, soulless thing; and it was not till probably our present era that the newer will to write Vedas and Upanishads prevailed. Greece had thought like this once—it was, scholars say, a very Aryan sentiment to resent the written word—but she had given way earlier.

India may be said to have "given way" through the example set by Buddhist influence. The often lengthy edicts which King Asoka had carved on rock and pillar, far exceeding the length of the usual inscription, were not all indited with a professedly Buddhist credal motive, but the Buddhists of his empire were the first to exploit the new tendency, just because they were, in his day and around his new capital, the most vigorously growing movement, while the more venerable brahman "church" would naturally be the "Die-hards" in this new-fangled secularizing of their treasured monopoly of Veda-utterance. What gave the new impetus (under Buddhist patronage) to writing in India it is not easy to say. I seem to see three possible causes which may have all been at work. First, the Greek influences bequeathed by Alexander's partial conquests in the North-West, the Panjab, etc. These must have made many impressions in matters of practical culture, however little India was Hellenized.

Secondly, the new invention of palm-leaf materials. Rhys Davids saw in these the one sufficing cause, and it is certainly the most obvious.

But with it, and contesting its monopoly, there will have been a cause which, while it hindered brahmans from availing themselves of the new means of easy recording, called forth no aversion in Buddhists. For me this must have been the changed values as to the speech and the speaker held by the latter. They no longer (as did their first men, Gotama, and his mainly brahman helpers) saw, in the speaker speaking, the man wording as the mouthpiece of the More, nay the Highest Who he potentially was. Their uttered treasure was with them once for all, in caskets of fixed statements, fixed in verse, and becoming fixed in certain prose "refrains." So, it is true, were the Vedas and many Upanishads, etc. But for the brahmans there still remained, not the spoken word only, but also the speaker. In his mouth the intoned hymn was still the renascent re-animated divine oracle, since in the man there was, as there had been from the first, the very breath and nature of God at work. In the Buddhist outlook this had died out. The speaker was not only, not in any way divinely, real: he was coming to be held as only real in a changing momentary flux of "mindings." And to be able to fix further those caskets of "sayings" in written "scriptures" came slowly to appear, not a degradation, but a positive advantage.

This changed value in the Indian outlook to which Buddhism was coming, to which it fully came perhaps only after it had lost its Indian home, may seem to you a little fanciful. I admit you will not yet find it in other books. But this conclusion of yours and this silence of others may be because you and they find yourselves in a somewhat analogous change of outlook, and hence the transition is perhaps less easy to see as startling as it then was. You may see what I mean, if you will compare the outlook of the great thinkers of the seventeenth century with the outlook of thoughtful writers of to-day. For the former, the study of "mind" was just breaking loose from the study of the man; man was discussed in terms of man and Deity. In the latter, man is discussed (so far as he is incorporeal) in terms of "mind," nor is he in his nature held to be, explicitly or implicitly, divine. Even the religious writer will only hold him to be a son of God "by the adoption of grace"—an adopted child. For the early Indian he was divine by birthright. And this will have been the outlook of the founders of "Buddhism"—of Gotama and his little band, mainly of brahmans—when they sought this "man" and "that man," and gave him in speech word of that nature that was theirs by birthright.

But very different had the outlook on the man become for the Indian Buddhist of the third century B.C. He had forgotten that his founder had confessed to a worship of Deity conceived as inward Dharma, as not only the highest self in man's nature, but as that Self conceived not as static, not as passive, but as ever stirring in man as the Bidding Witness, as our "conscience." He had externalized this term "dhamma," making it a name for those sayings, that code which he had been and was so industriously formulating and memorizing. The well-source had been choked, but the waters were abundant, and the more ducts for these, the better. Hence it came that the teachers, who first availed themselves of the new vogue for writing what they had to say in full, were they of the Buddhist Sangha. (Scholars, I believe, agree that the Jaina sayings were not committed to writing till the fifth century A.D.)

Nevertheless, there exists only a Sinhalese tradition as to when the full writing down of the Sayings was carried out. This is recorded in the poem called Dīpavaṃsa: the Island Lineage, or Chronicle,[1] repeated in the later poem Mahāvaṃsa.[2] The date, reckoning by native kings referred to, will have been about 80 B.C. But the *motive* is not given as the positive advantage in the written thing; it is the negative anxiety to preserve, in troublous times, when want of discipline and good temper was bringing about much schism, writing by way of a *common bond in the Book: potthaka*, rather than in the many individual, often cantankerous

[1] Translated into English by H. Oldenberg, XX., pp. 20, 21.

[2] Translated into English by Geiger and Bode; Pali Text Society, ed. just now out of print, XXX., pp. 100 f.

mukha-pāṭhakas, mouth-text-men. Both Piṭakas and Commentary are here recorded as having been put into writing. The former will presumably have been written in the Pali, which by that time will have become the standardized diction that is meant by the word. The latter, being the free explanation, with embroideries, of the Piṭaka texts, given by the teachers in Sinhalese to Sinhalese learners, was written down in Sinhalese, and only recast into Pali, with doubtless later further comment of his own day, by Buddhaghosa, when he visited Ceylon. Such, at all events, is the record. No Indian record of this kind, enlightening us on similar procedure there, has come to hand. I have found only two signs that the Sayings were not yet written in full in Asoka's time, but were written round about 100 B.C. The *former* is, that the debates at the beginning of the book Kathāvatthu were, when especially composed, "spoken" at the Third Council, about 240–30 B.C. Had they been written, they might conceivably have also been spoken, but we should almost certainly have read that they were written for, or laid before, the Council. The *latter* is the allusions, in the latter part only of the Milinda Questions, to *lañcakas*: inscribed-things, containing *e.g.* "the excellent Anguttara-Nikāya," etc. This will have been an early word for a pile of duly cut palm-leaves, tied into a unity. The word was soon dropped for *potthaka* and *gantha* (*grantha*). That interpolated allusions to these, and to the writing of them, have not crept into the text of the Piṭakas, as is the case in the Jātaka Book, is evidence that the oral text had been fully "arranged," both in prose and verse, both in Rule, Sutta, Vagga and other divisions, before writing in full was resorted to. I have found only one possible exception to this case. In the 27th Sutta of the Dīgha-Nikāya, brahmans are spoken of as *ganthe karontā*, "making books." Yet it may be we have here only a corrupt reading (very easy in Sinhalese script) for "making *mante*," i.e. mantras. This is not forced; "making books" is decidedly so.

See, the Oriental would say, how errors come in, once you put speech into writing. And he is not wrong. He has given way about writing. Yet even in our day he cannot see that printing should insure more of accuracy than the personally written manuscript. Rhys Davids has left the testimony of his fine-minded monk-tutor to this.[1] Anyway, it is certain that a blunder in printing has far-reaching effects, as some of us painfully know, such as one scribe's misspelling has not. The printing of an impression of the new Jacobean translation of the Bible with the injunction, Thou shalt commit adultery, was an error that eluded printer, reader and publisher, being found out by the accidental purchase of a new New-Testament by a London divine, so John Selden has told us.[2] Nevertheless we are very far from being willing, even were we able, to adopt the ancient manuscript method for recording "sacred" sayings, let alone the oral method.

This is not to say that I neither appreciate the oral method nor the extent and degree to which India developed it. We who have not visited her have all heard of the way brahmans have developed and still develop the apparently unlimited human power of retentiveness, of vocal reproductive power. We have only to look at our dramatic profession to seek a parallel. And I do hold that the written word as read, and even as read aloud, can never be for man the living thing that is the memorized recited word, let alone the well-improvised word. Some of us know the difference that lies in speaking to, from reading to, an audience. In the latter case, willy nilly we are become so many words, so many sentences. In the former, we are we, and giving ourselves. But when it is no longer a question of a present living gift of this kind, when it is a matter of faithfully reproducing in words the articulate will, not of this or that repeater, but of the original speaker, who then can doubt but that, in the written copy, if copy it be, we have that which *in the true* transcends all the oral repetitions, however

[1] *Hibbert Lectures.* [2] *Table-Talk*, ed. S. W. Singer.

eloquently spoken, however present be the conscientious will. Take a reciter of a play: should his memory for a moment fail, none but they who also knew the play by heart would know if he altered or omitted a line, unless it were from lines become cultural common property, *e.g.* "The quality of mercy is not strained. . . ." To a certain extent he could alter with impunity. So also could the brahman reciter. And alterations could take root. If you think I babble, glance at the work by Maurice Bloomfield and his pupil, my friend Professor Edgerton, on "Vedic Variants" and count their number! It is ten thousand differences, in a letter, a word, a phrase, a sentence. Now it is mainly oral variations that are responsible for these. And they show that not all the rehearsings of convened brahmans have succeeded in so standardizing their sacred hymns, that variants have ceased to exist.

This we may consider as an opening for change more likely to affect the fixed Sayings of the growing Sakyan centres during those centuries B.C. 500 to 230 than the older brahman organism. The Sakyan missioners were at first mainly brahmans; the teaching was fundamentally their own, and it was on the progressive, the "Radical" side; but this would cease to be the case when monastic and Sāṅkhya preoccupations were tending to see (*a*) man in the Less, (*b*) man in the mind. And hence possibly there may have been a relative scarcity of adherents with finely developed memory.

But there were other openings for changes to which the Sayings were exposed. I have not found these openings systematically gone into, and yet it is very needful when reading the Piṭakas to keep them ever in view. And the not keeping them in view has for me hindered progress in our interpretation of the records as being the palimpsests they so largely are.

Let us draw up, Buddhist fashion, a list of these openings:

1. Apparent absence of any listener to sayings, told off to memorize what is being said.

2. Apparent freedom being for an indefinite interval left to the disciple listening to re-word sayings in his own words.

Under this: the freedom being for an indefinite interval left to the exponent of a discourse, fixed in wording only as to its outline, to expound in his own words.

3. The different Indian dialects in which the teachings would get repeated, dialects in which important terms, *e.g.* "man," might not always have an identical meaning.[1]

Under this: the absence of standardized meanings such as can only exist in a more advanced civilization, involving writings, if not printings, in standardized diction.

4. The fact that no intelligent man is mere automaton. Even though a man, whose business it is merely to repeat, to recite, the Sayings of others, can become approximately automaton, the fact that man, having memorized, has also to expound, and so give something of himself, as well as repeat what another has given, will almost inevitably *tend to bring in changes*, both in selection, in emphasis and even in word or clause. As a result of this, taken together with relative isolation of his circle of influence from that of others, the "versions" *used in that circle* would involve certain omissions, alterations, interpolations.

5. The fact, due this time not to isolation, but to influx from without, that the social phenomenon of monastic life for men of all ages (not for elderly men alone) was all the while growing in attractiveness, and therewith was growing a changed outlook on the "man" and his aspirations.

6. The fact, due to a similar cause, that the philosophical phenomenon of man's mental equipment as a causal orderly procedure, distinguishable from the man as having and using it, was all the while growing in attractiveness.

Let us go over these in the briefest detail.

[1] Note the variants for "bowl" already commented on when Sta. 139 of the Majjhima was compiled.

(1) The nearest the records get to any "reporting" of a talk is the injunction (*a*) to listen attentively, (*b*) to bear in mind what has just been said, together with the frequent Sutta opening: "Thus (has it) been heard for (not by) me." The word for repeater—*bhāṇaka*, literally "sayer"—is never used in the Suttas, only in Commentaries. The earlier term for one occupied with the Sayings and the teaching of them is a curious one: *ajjhāyaka*, "he who does not muse," *i.e.* practise jhāna. You will find this stated in the 27th (Aggañña) Sutta of the Dīgha-Nikāya). There the recluses, who had become cenobites on the borders of the villages (and not away in the woods) make "books" (or is it "mantras"?) and teach them. "Now 'these muse not' is what is meant by *ajjhāyakas*." Thus we have, on the one hand, the man who sought in "musing" to hear the new teachings from another and worthier world, and the man, on the other, who sought to consolidate and further the words that had at some time previous been uttered. *Ajjhāyaka*, in the Vinaya, reappears as *upajjhāya*, or tutor. Here is the prefix *upa*; near, towards, up to, used for tutorial teaching in the word Upanishad: the near séance. But the rest (*adhi-āya*) philologists derive as access, and not from *jhā-na*.

But of any testimony to the repeating, compulsory or otherwise, by disciples, junior or not, of a discourse just uttered, so as to be able more truly to "report" it, we find nothing.

As to the next "openings" in our list, it must be plain to you that there will here have been much militating *against* any standardized collections of teachings, such as you now read in the Piṭakas. It was only very gradually that these openings for changes were narrowed and finally closed. We can picture the course of things thus: During the active lifetime of the Founder and his men, these held themselves free to teach their message and accessory teachings quite in their own words. Now and again we read of a disciple, man or woman, referring to what the Bhagavā, the Satthar, had said; more usually there is no such reference. That is, supposing we have in the Suttas in question a faithful record. Next, with the old age of the Founder and the death or departure of most of the first men, the need would arise of putting such teachings as were yet remembered, and taught where he was living—namely, at Sāvatthi—into a fixed wording, both in prose and, for even better preservation, into verse. With respect to the prose, I do not suppose that complete Suttas were yet so fixed; only those *uddesas* of which I have spoken. Had the whole discourse been then fixed, we might not have these "outlines" here and there left in. Next, when the Order was completely orphaned, with all the first men gone, the influence of new men and tendencies to schism increasing, there would gradually grow strong the need of fixing the talks handed down as talks, and not as secondary exposition on the explaining of *uddesas*. And original poems, too, not metricized prose, may have been accepted by the metropolitan Sangha at Sāvatthi, such as the Anthologies, called Dhammapada, Sutta-Nipāta, Thera-Therīgāthā and the Peta- and Vimāna-vatthu's. But some of the Thera-Therīgāthā, the Iti-vuttaka and Udāna I incline to place at the end of this period, the period between the Second and Third Councils, or approximately from 400 to 230 B.C. It will then have been only in the "talk on the matter, or meaning—namely round about it, the "Attha-kathā" as the Commentaries are called—that the right to word in his own speech will have been left to the teacher or preacher.

But we have nothing whatever to tell us how far this increased fixing in the sayings or discourses was being done at one centre only, or at several. I incline to think the latter is the truer conclusion. Such centres seem to me indicated, if faintly, by an exceptional way of beginning a Sutta; not in the well-beaten way of "At one time the Bhagavan was staying," or "Thus has it been heard for me," but simply with the words *Sāvatthi nidānaṃ*, or *Kapilavatthu nidānaṃ*. I have found six such towns, and have discussed the term *nidānaṃ* as conceivably meaning deposit, depôt, or, as we should say, library. The six towns are Sāvatthi, Kapilavatthu, Benares, Sāketa, Patna and Rājagaha. The order I use is in accordance with the frequency of occurrence. But Sāvatthi far exceeds all the rest put together. The mother-settlement, Rājagaha, occurs but once in this way; the latest ecclesiastical metropolis, Patna, only twice (*K.S.*, iii. & iv., Introd.).

Incidentally I find it significant that Vesālī is not among the towns thus mentioned; we find no "Vesālī nidānaṃ." Vesālī was linked with much of the earliest history of the mission; some fifty-seven Suttas are recorded as having been Vesālī episodes; the Founder made his painful way to it on his last tour, and it is impossible to see no significance in his singling it out for a farewell look and valediction—matters which found pious memento in a cairn or "shrine" of sorts, still standing over a thousand years later. But we see also that Vesālī maintained the teaching of the reality of the very man or self, and we know that this was, in newer centres such as Patna, grown more and more discredited; so much so that the Vesālī or Vajjian teachers were among those "suspended" as such at the Third Council. It is possible, therefore—we can say no more than that—that "Vesālī nidānaṃ" was voted as non-existent. It is true that there are a few other places whence we might have expected to find "nidānaṃ." There was Kosambī, also place of Sutta episodes. But Kosambī had won an evil repute as a home of bitter quarrelling. As to that, Why, you may ask, is the mother-settlement as nidānaṃ referred to only once? Here will surely have been a live library of old repeatings. Yes, but Rājagaha had shared the fate ecclesiastically of Calcutta politically. Patna had become to Rājagaha as Delhi now is to Calcutta. The once monarch of Magadha, whose capital was Rājagaha, was become the emperor at Patna.

It is clear that if my supposition be right—namely, that the Sutta- (or connected talk-) fixing was done, not at one, but at several centres—we can see that there could in that way be *no final and complete standardization.* Even supposing that many or most of the Suttas were the common property of those centres, there would still be a likelihood of versions differing somewhat in word and phrase, or even in more than that.

I do not think that local apartness had anything to do with the specialization in repeating, that we see in the Commentarial terms Dīghabhāṇaka, Majjhimabhāṇaka, Saṃyuttabhāṇaka, Anguttarabhāṇaka. These bodies of Sutta-repeaters are never found associated with a particular place. Specialization in interest about this and that topic of doctrine was among them, for this we see in the varying degree of attention paid in each Nikāya to such topics. In the Dīgha, *e.g.*, the moral basis of the "Godlife" is paramount, awareness of other worlds has waned but little, the "Man" is still real, and the layman still "counts." (The one talk on "causation" reads like a curious freak-interpolation, taken with the rest. We wonder it was not relegated to the collection of cause-suttas in the third Nikāya, or at least repeated there.) The Majjhima, with over four times as many Suttas, is more catholic in its interests, but it betrays, among these, later values as to the very man, as to the influence of Sānkhya mind-study, and in the emergence of breathing practices. Equally catholic are the assorted Suttas of the Saṃyutta. "Karma," on the one hand, and Upanishadic survivals are mainly, though not only, to be found in the Anguttara.

I should judge that the bhāṇakas of one Nikāya knew as a rule very little about the contents and emphasis of the other three. Else the apparent devolution of subjects would have been better carried out. Thus we should not have in two Nikāyas versions differing in amplitude of the same Sutta, as, *e.g.*, the Satipaṭṭhāna Sutta in the two first Nikāyas. Further, with respect to these four and the

Anthologies, it is hard to reconcile mutual knowledge with the repetition of the Sela and Vāseṭṭha Suttas in both Majjhima-Nikāya and Sutta-Nipāta. It is probably only later revision that has reduced these to mutual consistency and coincidence respectively.

Into the facts (5) and (6), of the influence exercised by two great changes, religious and intellectual, monastic and Sānkhyan, I have previously gone. The religious conception of, and outlook for, the very man was no longer what it had been three hundred years previously. The intellectual conception of the very man became one, not of a knower, valuer, purposer, experiencer, doer, but of the *processes* only, the "proceeder" being knowable only *in* these, as, still later, he was held to be *only these*. It was thus become imperative that, with the older teaching of the "proceeder" being still maintained here and there, the Order, as represented at the metropolis, should take steps to secure a greater unity in doctrine.

And there was another pressing need for a more united front. In their day there had arisen the first political unity on a great scale that India had ever witnessed: the fusion of many kingdoms into a hegemony under the Mauryans. There had, late in the preceding, the fourth century B.C., been a great mobilizing of war forces in North India to oppose the sudden inroad of Alexander of Macedon. He had conquered and annexed territory in the North-West, but on his sudden death, the invasion petered out, and it was left to the first best adventurer, Chandragupta, to profit by the released war material and secure his own rise to power, avenging himself on his kinsman Nanda, King of Magadha. Bindusāra, his son, succeeded him, and probably extended his annexations far into the South. Both were on terms of amity with the Greek house of the Seleucidae governing the remains, mainly in Baktria, of Alexander's conquests. Asoka Vardhamāna, son of Bindusāra, enlarged his empire still further in the South-East, and appears, by matter in his rock edicts, to have by "messengers" (wrongly, I think, called missionaries; they were envoys or ambassadors; for missionaries a different word would have been chosen) established friendly political relations with the rulers of the states into which Alexander's empires had been divided. Here, then, was a new political unity; the old legend of a Chakka-vatti, a turner of the wheel of governance, was now incarnate. To win the support of such a head was all-important. He will have had brahman chaplains about him, but he had apparently not openly declared himself a supporter of any one cult. To win his especial patronage it was obviously wise to show a religious, an ecclesiastical unity, as impressive in its way as Asoka's in its way.

This could only be done by a very great gesture of purgation and revision. And this is recorded under the name of the Third Council, literally Thorough-Chanting (*sangīti*). Doubt has been raised whether this Council took place; the Pali records of it are not in the Piṭakas, but in Commentaries only, and in the two "Chronicles" of Ceylon, belonging, it is thought, to the fourth and fifth centuries. Buddhist Sanskrit literature ignores the event. But this does not invalidate the truth of the Pali records. It only shows that this effort at Patna, of supreme importance for the Sangha there, and for the monastic centres elsewhere acknowledging allegiance to that Sangha, was not of the immense importance it will have been for just these. It might almost be likened to the new Christian metropolis at Rome, in the reign of Constantine, ignoring a Council held to purge and revise at Jerusalem. Do not say that a later Rome will have well chronicled the secessions in North Europe from the Roman headship of the Christian church. In that later sixteenth century we had not only the written record to facilitate the taking note, but also the printed record. We know this much: that the Mahāsanghika "church" of and about Vesālī, and the Sarvâsti "church" of Nepal and further east were already of considerable importance, and became yet more so till well into our era. In so far as there were representatives of their teaching with its specific values at Patna, they will there, at the Council, to judge by the Kathāvatthu debates, have been condemned and—shall we say?—suspended. From that day *those* "churches" will have ceased to hold the Patna Sangha as a proper authority, or to be much interested in their doings and decisions.

But, then, the Patna Sangha it was that won the patronage of Asoka, and was instrumental, as emissaries of his, whether directly from Patna or by way of his South Indian domains, in working the "conversion" of Ceylon. And it was Ceylon that became the first headquarters of "Buddhism in exile," when it crumbled away in India; it was Ceylon that made a *recorded* writing down the Piṭakas in full; it was Ceylon whither Buddhist divines from Conjevaram, such as Buddhadatta and Buddhaghosa, went to build up a purely Pali-speaking, Pali-writing religious metropolis. Hence whatever the mother-metropolis at Patna had done was in Ceylon carefully treasured and recorded.

To the Third Council, then, we come back as being, like its two predecessors, an extremely likely event, because the need for it will have become so great. It was a colossal task to "bear" in mind the Vedas, compiled for solemn ritual, and petrified in metre though they were. It was an even more colossal task to bear and keep in oral concordance a heterogeneous mass of mixed prose and verse sayings, dealing with so wide a range of subjects as rules by the hundreds, episodes with popular homilies, interviews, catechisms, categories with expositions and so on. Equally colossal must have been the revising. Collation of MSS. such as we have known over the Bible, such as Poona knows over the present Mahābhārata revising, is a simple task in comparison with the collating the utterances of one group of repeaters after another, noting variants in the repeating, and selecting which was to be the choice, whether any varying versions were to be retained side by side (you often see this has been the case), whether a clause containing an idea come into discredit was to be dropped, or whether it was better to replace it by a term or clause come into high repute, whether a gloss enhancing the present value of a point in some verse should be introduced.

How interesting and significant, too, are what I would call the "left-ins," that we come across! Passages that breathe the very teaching of the Upanishads, and that one would think the Third Council would never have "passed"! To me they suggest that revision was not carried on by one central council, but was devolved upon individual Theras (seniors), to each of whom some section was entrusted, and among whom there may have been one or two covertly in sympathy with, say, the older tradition about the Self, as we read it was maintained at Vesālī. Compare, *e.g.*, Anguttara-Nikāya; 147 f., § 40.[1]

What openings for change have we not seen! What changing values to be brought forward in exploiting those openings were there not! And all done from very worthy motives: the will to lead aright, the will to magnify the "dhamma" as the teaching was coming to be called, the will to exalt the wisdom and superhumanity of the founder, the will to impress and edify. But never the will to get at the working of what had come to be so stoutly maintained: the *necessity in everything of change*; never the will to get at what we now call *historic truth*! Yet Buddhists and writers on Buddhism still go on speaking and writing about these Piṭakas as being the Buddha-word, and that because he is said therein to have said this and this, and that he certainly did say it just as it stands.

Liberally minded lay-Buddhists will protest that they do

[1] See *Gradual Sayings*, I., Introd. xvii.

not pin such faith in the Piṭaka sayings as *ipse dixits*. None the less will they listen to what their Sangha authorities teach, and for these those sayings count as "gospel." Thus I read in an article by a Ceylon monk: "In the Anguttara Nikāya the Buddha says . . ." This is a typical sentence, save for this, that it cites at least a (large) "collection" for the saying. More usually we are simply told: "The Buddha says . . ." Even scholarly writers will be ever telling you the same thing in French, in German, in English. It is true that they are quoting what is stated in records, are aware that these are little more than venerable *on dit's*, and that they cannot be always reminding the reader that this is so. But that they spare him (and themselves) the constant *caveat* has the effect of *checking the critical attitude* in the average educated reader. Either he swallows all that is virtually only alleged, or he holds all to be mere legendary tale, unworthy of credence. If such writers would only substitute, for "the Buddha said," "Buddhism says," then would all be relatively well said. But on to the shoulders of that idealized image "Buddha" is piled a responsibility for any and everything that "Buddhism" has here, and there, and now and then, been adding to and taking away from the original mandate. When we read in a venerable, once very popular English poem of the thirteenth century, called the Proverbs of Alfred, that among other wise sayings King Alfred (he is called Alured) said:

And eueruyches monnes dom
to his owere dure churre
(*and every man's doom returns to his own door*)

—a rune as Buddhist as it is Christian—we should be content to see in it a current adage, ascribed to the sayings of a king of old, because he made *an impressive figurehead* for the collection. We might probably quite as truly call this book Proverbs of Old English Wisdom. But when we come to so-called scriptures, Bibles, Piṭakas, Kuran, etc., we are up against a much more dogmatic, undiscerning belief. I am not saying that the average educated reader is on this point where he was fifty years ago or less, when it is a question of scriptures with which he is by tradition familiar. But when it is a question of *unfamiliar scriptures*, he tends to resume the attitude he is outgrowing; he tends either to take all at its own face-value, or to hold all as unworthy of belief. He is intellectually lazy.

It may here be asked: How much, then, and how little are we to take, in the Piṭakas, as historically true? Is anything to be so taken?

I write here and now for the reader who does, or who can know, as reader of English, much more about my subject than could such a reader when Rhys Davids wrote his Manual. And for the former reader the question now is, not What can I read? but, How should I read? This is the question I wish to have him raising.

Let him first consider this, that scriptures are monuments of values held by men here or there in the past. They are the work of men in the past, hence their present worth is relative, historic, rather than absolute worth. Chiefly will this be shown if, as a whole, they do not show perfect mutual consistency. Where he finds inconsistency, he will see he is up against a work of joined pieces, giving values differing in time and place. When, *e.g.*, he finds, on the one hand, a teaching, divergent from the teaching of India of the day when that former teaching is said to have begun, and, on the other hand, passages conforming to that Indian teaching, he has this interesting historical problem—How did the passages get left in, since the whole trend of the teaching may preclude their being included later? And he may find no sign of recrudescence of their Indian teaching in any records. So he may conclude—those left-in inconsistencies must be of the more original Buddhism. How they got left in, I have suggested above.

Then let him note that the early Indian teaching laid the

utmost stress on the reality and possibilities of the very "man," or self, while the trend of the Pali books is a pushing away of him, a teaching a "Less" about his reality and his ultimate destiny.

Next let him read, mindful of the working effect of those two growing vogues, monasticism and the study of the mind and its tendency (as with us) to usurp the place of the "man." Thus guarded in outlook, there may arise in him a conviction that, in these three Piṭakas, and, more, in each section of them—nay, in each section of a section—he has a portion of a venerable web that is like that of Penelope, or of Elaine, one that has come into being as the work of many years, of centuries even, not a thing ready-made, the work of any one period of man's values. And more: that this "web" has not been left to display its slowly changing growth in those values, but has been, time and again, pieced and rewoven to *adapt* its earlier device to the later tastes of the after-weavers, even as Penelope might have taken needle and thread to work over her earlier weaving.

Or let me shift the parable: "Let the reader have ever in mind that he is pacing the streets of an early mediæval city, where the older city lies beneath his feet, or is seen as a fragment of wall enframed in later walls. For the most part it is the city of the monk that stands about him. Yet is the old city not wholly dead. In the ways and the walls he may yet witness the surviving spirit of the first architects in the repeated injunctions to make-become the very man, the real man, in conduct, in character, in progress."[1]

It was a great work to have achieved so much consistency as we find. But steady reading in the Suttas will show you that, as a whole, these reveal occasional inconsistency, not so much in mere matters of detail—that would be of scant importance—as in things of the highest value. Look, *e.g.*,

[1] *Gradual Sayings*, I., Introd.

at Saṃyutta-Nikāya, iii., XXII., § 33, where mind as well as body is said to be not really "you," the self of you, and is to you as are faggots to the wood with its trees. Then look at Dhammapada, verses 1, 2, where in each the first line, which is a very obvious gloss, reflecting later mind-values, the mind is assigned a value belonging, in India, only to the very man, and superseding the man. And compare the sayings depreciating and denying what India meant by the "self," in many Suttas, with Chapter XII. of the Dhammapada, and with the sayings in the Devadūta vagga of the Anguttara-Nikāya—teachings some of which are purely Upanishadic.

Hence to the question, how far we can impute anything approaching a true record of anything taught by the Founder and his men to a Piṭaka passage, I would suggest the following for guidance. It is guidance on one point only, but a point so important in religion that I let other suggestions, for brevity, go unsaid. Does the passag show the *very man as real*, and as having in and before him a *More, in nature and life*, leading him on *towards a Most?* If it does, then look upon it as of the genuine Sakya teaching. First, because it is thereby shown to be offspring of the loftiest level reached in Indian religion just before the Śakyamuni taught. Secondly, because it is thereby shown to be, by the nature of such a mandate, a genuine world-religion.

As to the latter reason, you may not agree. You may claim that world-religion may be, not of an inspired original message to the Many enlarging his manhood and outlook, then slowly declining as borne by a weaker vehicle down the ages, but of a weak feeble beginning, expanding in time to a mighty noble tree of doctrine. Herein it is for you, reader, to decide.[1]

[1] On the lamentable lack of reliable records of the 4th Council connected with the name of the N. Indian king Kanishka (second century A.D.), see Rhys Davids, *Buddhist India*, ch. xvi. and Eliot, *Hinduism and Buddhism*, III., ch. xli.

CHAPTER XV

AN EVERYMAN'S GOSPEL

I HAVE seen, twice at least in the last few years, the opinion put forward that Buddhism—that is to say, the Buddhism of Indian religions—" really consists of two parts": one for monks and nuns, one for householders; "one clerical and mystical, one popular and pious." This is as you will find it, with more details, in L. de la Vallée Poussin's *Nirvāna*, published 1925. A similar assertion has been recently published (I know not if it be for the first time) in B. C. Law's volume *Buddhist Studies*, in an article on "Asoka and his Mission," by D. R. Bhandarkar. It is put forward in criticism of certain writers, but without reference to the earlier statement just cited; indeed, it too may be seven years old, or more.

I do not know whether any "Southern" Buddhists would subscribe to this opinion. But I would judge it as not incorrect for present-day Buddhism, nor for mediæval Buddhism, nay, we can see the distinction emerging even in the Piṭakas. There is, in the last few Suttas of the Majjhima-Nikāya (No. 143), a Sutta called "Anāthapiṇḍika-homily." Here this faithful and generous merchant-patron of the Sakyan missioners lies mortally ill, and sends word to the Bhagavan and also to Sāriputta, professing his loyalty and begging the latter to visit him. Sāriputta and Ānanda go, and the former, after learning how grave was the malady, proceeds to give a homily how the dying man is "to train himself" so that he may not, through sense or imaginary concepts, "be clinging to this world or to other worlds."[1] It is fairly amazing talk to

[1] Cf. above, p. 177.

be giving a dying man, and this one is said to have shed tears. Not, however, over any unfitness in it, but because neither the Teacher nor any "mind-cultivating monk" (note the epithet [1]) had ever talked like that to him. He is told: "Not to white-clothed housefolk is such dhamma-talk revealed, but to those who have left the world." The dying man rejoins: "Then let it be revealed to the house-folk!" And in the very words assigned to the *deva* who entreated Gotama to begin his mission—words which in fixed form will have become of great importance—he is made to add: "There are men with little dust in their vision; from not hearing dharma they are perishing; as coming to know they will become." No response of any kind is added; the two disciples get up and walk out; Anāthapiṇḍika dies and from the happy world of the *devas* revisits the Teacher. Gotama psychically sees and hears and tells Ānanda a *deva* has been and spoken affectionately of the Jeta Wood he gave and the worthy company now there. Ānanda infers this will have been the reborn merchant, and is told his inference is right.

Without the homily the Sutta is thus told, better told, in the Saṃyutta.[2] As told here it gives a valuable *aperçu*. I do not admit for a moment that we have in it a true record of what Sāriputta will have done or said. Putting the homily on one side, as being for him out of the question, I cannot conceive a first Sakyan talking about a distinction between layman and recluse that smells of an ecclesiastical growth of centuries. For Sāriputta, as for his Leader, there were no such external distinctions in the religious fitness of the "man." Man was not *first* lay or monk; he was "man" first and last. There were, of course, different stages in the man's becoming: he is fit or not fit, ready or not yet ready for this or that in religious "training." But these differences will have been independent of his being "without," in the world of man's

[1] *Mano-bhāvanīya.*

[2] *K.S.*, i., 79 f.

work, or in a world *within* that world. "Not as householder nor as home-leaver do I rate a man in conduct," runs a Sutta of earlier stamp,[1] "but according as either of them strives after the Way, after dharma, after the moral life, or does not."

I am not, alas! able to show when this curious embroidery on the simpler Suttas was inserted; whether it was at the Patna Revision or later or earlier. But it is a witness, unquoted by either Western or Eastern scholar named above, that what it is usual to call an esoteric teaching as such had crept in before the Canon was closed.

Where I find their assertion inadequate is in the fact that they speak of "Buddhism" as, *once and for all*, a dual gospel. *Once* it was no such thing! What we should see, if we would see history, is, not a primal gospel preached as dual, but a second later specialized set of values emerging out of and on top of the unitary primal message. Much will here depend on the seer's value which he attaches to the inspired nature of that message. If he looks, from a Christian or Hindu or sceptical standpoint, upon Gotama the Sakyan as a wise, energetic pundit, teaching a stressed worth in the moral life, on the one hand, and a new worth in an ideal of world-waning, on the other, so as to be in a way all things to all men by a new social cleavage, then is the theory, of a dual gospel as from the first, tenable. If he looks upon Gotama the Sakyan as a man fulfilling, not only his own will, but a Divine Will in him, by giving to his world for "the world" a mandate of the very man, as able to grow in a Divine nature as Becoming "That," then is the theory of a dual gospel *as original* untenable, unthinkable. In either case, we must, we *must*, when we write of Buddhism, write of it as history, and not as all foreground. And to say "Buddhism" *is* a dual gospel, and that thereby all has been said about that, is to have a blind spot where should be historic vision.

[1] *Anguttara-Nikāya*, I., p. 69 (2nd Nip. 4, § 9); *Gradual Sayings*, I., 64.

Of the two writers, the first draws the contrast, the better to expound the values, which I call emergent. He depicts, namely, (*a*) the monastic outlook, bred of segregation from the common life of man, from all human relations save that of friendship, from dependence upon the outer world for bodily maintenance, from the growing idea, not that he was in retreat the better to help mankind, but so as the more to speed up his own welfare, with this sole exception (also an emergence) that he was so far helping the slower pace of the laity by conferring his surplus merit upon his maintainers. Then (*b*) the outlook on life, bred of intercourse with fellow-men in the "common lot," in the many relations; the need in it of (1) *sīla*, or moral habits, or "decent" living, not hurting the others so that he might not be hurt, together with the worthier expansion, in some, of a more positive will to "ward" the others, in a way more akin to his domestic and comradeship relations; (2) the felt need of certain fasts and feasts as linking him up with things unseen; (3) the hope that by such conduct he would win a happy awakening from the bed of death into a worthier world, an exemption from dreaded "falling" into an unhappy "bourn" (*gati*) of suffering; (4) eventual rebirth on earth in lucky circumstances. The writer speaks of this outlook as "above all, a *bhakti* or devotion, a *pūjā* or cult"; and of the support looked for hereafter in "merit" from ministering to monks. But all this, which is of a *growth more or less later*, is lumped together with that general "lay" outlook on life and should not be pictured as in the same perspective with it. The *bhakti* implies a Buddha-cult, which had made but little progress till the fourth century B.C., *i.e.* after the Second Council. The *pūjā*, for "Buddhism," is the cult of the trinity—Buddha, Dhamma, Sangha, a very long after-growth. A distinctive term for lay worshipper: *upāsaka, upāsikā*, and his ministry to clerics, as having both an ethical and a saving efficacy, *grew up with the growth* of a segregate clerical world, a new non-conformist Brahmanism, so to speak, over against that older institution. Finally, as to having an idea that at a very distant date "Nirvāṇa" was also for him, but only when he too might be monk—this, too, is for me of much later values. Nirvāṇa only became a *summum bonum*, even for the monk, at a later date. Your layman of Gotama's day never thought of it as that. For him it was a way of describing freedom from bodily ill health.[1] When first used as a religious term, it meant the waning, the making to wane of vicious disease—lust, hate, dullness; a new departure that brought up the questioner with, "What is this *nibbānaṃ* that you talk about?"[2]

No, Buddhism as a dual gospel is an assertion that needs historical qualification. If the asserter accepts the present edited contracted version of the First Utterance as a talk to and for monks,[3] his assertion does but follow from that acceptance. If you, reader, agree with me, that this edited version hides the greater world-gospel underneath, you will be no more content with the unqualified "duality" than am I.

The way of the other, the Eastern writer, should have of itself shown him how clearly right it is to make no assertion about Buddhism as "really consisting of two parts," without the qualification that one part has not from the first coexisted with the other, but is an excrescence on it. He shows, and shows rightly, that there is harmony between the teaching enjoined in a Sutta expressly for laymen and that enjoined in the Edicts of King Asoka. The Sutta is the "homily to Sigāla" (No. XLI. of Dīgha-Nikāya). Bhandarkar calls it "perhaps the only one of the Suttas," but this is not so. Very far have Sangha editors gone in dropping into oblivion the many talks to Everyman, and not only to the man-as-monk, that will have been uttered by the Sakyan missioners, but things are not so bad as that.

[1] See above, p. 112. *Majjhima*, Sta. 75.
[2] *Kindred Sayings*, IV., p. 170. [3] See above, p. 113.

And now that it has become so accessible for the English reader to look up such Suttas, I will here name more of such, that he may refer to them.

There is the talk on the cleansing of the inner, the real man to Visākhā, the amiable lay-patroness.[1] There are the talks to Chitta house-father, and those to village headmen, contents of the 42nd and 43rd. Saṃyuttas, on a variety of topics.[2] Here, as I have commented, though we still see through a monastic medium, we are now contemplating the facts in the life of man-as-becoming, of life with unsuppressed faculties, of death, of the hereafter, of the man as choosing, willing, working, growing. True, there is no clear call anywhere, that any one stage of life is just an *opportunity for growth* in the great Way of the worlds. But it is saner than the monastic atmosphere, and we are in the open air. Here we do not find that body and mind are "ill," and the stopping of their recurrence to be devoutly hoped for. Here is the Founder shown urging men to believe, that "This world *is*. The world beyond *is*. . . . Parents are facts; beings of the next world are facts; so are teachers who are realizing both worlds . . . and I, if I live wisely and well, shall be reborn in the happy beyond. . . . But if I do not so live here, nothing that well-wishers may say to or of me will bring me there." Here do we feel near to Gotama. Here is his Way, here is man the Wayfarer, here, in the midst of the gospel which is asserted to be one half only of his teaching. Again, there is the little Saṃyutta, the "Mother-World" (meaning woman's world).[3] Here, after many little talks, largely the alleged answers to queries put by Anuruddha, the Sakyan disciple, and containing, not without sympathy, much crude monastic valuing, we find a precious saying of what is for me pure Sakya, such as we very rarely find. "Growing in five ways a woman becomes a core-grasper, a better-

[1] *Gradual Sayings*, I., pp. 185 ff. Above, p. 230.
[2] *Kindred Sayings*, IV., pp. 190–255. [3] *Ibid.*, pp. 162–9.

grasper (*sār'ādāyinī var'ādāyinī*), namely, by growing in faith, in moral habit, in what she has learnt (*suta*), in generosity, in wisdom.

Who while e'en here by faith and virtue grows,
by wisdom, liberal giving and by lore,
a virtuous votary such as this lays hold
e'en here on what most real is for the self.

It is difficult to render well *sāra*—the "heart-of-oak" in the tree—often used for the essential, the heart of a thing. And I regret that the Pali versifier has omitted the fine term "layer hold of the better." Conceivably *vara* may here mean "elect (lady)"—Christians know that term—but so meaning, it is to be found more usually as affix. It may also mean the "best," in the comparative way we see superlatives used—so be it; it matters nothing here. The *sāra* here is the fact of growth in the very "man," male or female, in that "self" who, in "becoming," is slowly beginning to reveal divine origin and identity. Very possibly the first utterer was a woman, for who is so preoccupied with "growth" as the mother? And further it is a woman who is, in the Nuns' Anthology, preoccupied with this in her son, the woman called only "mother of that son," Vaddhamātā, or Vardhamātā.

I say not that herewith the Sayings expressly for lay folk are exhausted, but hunting for them is needed. Their rarity makes monastic Buddhism stand condemned as the vehicle of a literature of a *world-religion*, so immensely more is it interested in the world-within-world of the monk. To return to the Sigāla homily—that the Commentary in conclusion calls it the "houseman's Rules" (*gihivinaya*) is well known, though whether this be from the old Sinhalese Commentary, or a terminal flourish of the Pali recast by Buddhaghosa, no man knows. It says, that "nothing laymen ought to do is here left unsaid, and that from one practising it, growth, not decay is to be expected." This is a worthy echo of the "Mother"-Sutta quoted, albeit the important assigning of the growth to the "self" is, as we might expect, omitted.

I am not here raising the question, for readers of the Homily, how far its "ought to do" for men and women, so exhaustively sufficient for the Commentator of the fifth century A.D. in Ceylon, will seem so at the present day. I am only concerned, in following Bhandarkar's point, to come from the Homily to its harmony with the injunctions to his "lay" subjects in the Rock and Pillar Edicts of King Asoka. This harmony is shared by the other "lay" talks I have quoted.

To go into the Edicts here were too long; the reader will find them in several English books. It must suffice that they, as religious advice, stress three points: (1) the positive satisfying human worth of the good life *in the world*; (2) the interesting nearness of the next step, the "beyond" in that good life—the bright world (*svarga*) awaiting such livers; (3) the all-importance, in the good life, of the human (not just bodily or mental) fact of growing, of becoming.

The first two have been worthily pointed out by writers; the last has been generally ignored. This is an astonishing blindness to emphasis, an emphasis that is the easier here to weigh, since by book measure the Edicts make short reading. In this short "Book," then, there are some *eighty references*, not to Asoka's subjects "being" this and not "being" that, but to their growing and becoming such and such, and to their making to grow, to become this and that in their welfare. He has even the compound *bhavaśudhi* and *bhāvaśudhi*. You will find it woefully mistranslated as I think, by the French scholar Senart as "purity of soul," by the German translator Hultzsch as (in English) "purity of mind." I confess to having failed to find the word noticed in other books on the subject, but I venture to render it as salvation by, or through "becoming" or growth. *Śudhi* (Pali, *suddhi*) is a common Indian expression for "salvation" or "saving religion." And *bhāva* can mean becoming no less than being. Now whereas I saw in the compound *bhava-magga*—way of becoming—the original term in the First Utterance for which "eightfold way" was substituted,[1] I have not found *bhava-* or *bhāva-* used, with *appreciation*, in early compounds, Prakrit or Pali. But here, where no editor could tamper, we do meet such a compound; and coming as it does in a set of exhortations, where the very atmosphere is one of "becoming," it is the most plausible of readings to see in it that identity of becoming with religious endeavour and hope which is, for me, not a specific lay gospel of Gotama Śakyamuni, but the very heart and "core" of what he gave the world. It is true that, so far, we have not in any inscription—more may yet be found—met with the figure of the Way in the very word. Yet the very frequent reference to the good life as a *charaṇa* or *chalaṇa*—a walking, in the Old Testament sense—is proof that the religious life is never conceived in a static shape, as a state. He goes further: he gives us a word for wayfarers, if not for way. His desire, he writes, is that all denominations should learn much and be goers-in-what-is good (or lovely: καλὸς κἀγαθὸς, *kalyāṇa-gama*) much as he tends to speak of his actions as "a going" in this or that.

And there is another feature about his references to growth (*vadh-*): he takes us in his emphasis back to the very first things recorded of the Founder at the crisis of his resolve to teach. In the 4th Girnar Edict we read: "This verily is the best work: the teaching of dharma; for the immoral man walking according to dharma comes not to pass (*na bhavati*). In this aim (*artha*) growth and not decay is excellent; for this aim this has been written; let (men) study both growth and decay." What an echo is there not here of that scene of the Hesitation!

You will not find those first two points so passed over, so cloaked in English terms betraying a lack of insight into this most vital teaching, as is this third point. That (1) a good

[1] See above, p. 125.

life in work in the world is held to be all-sufficient for growth, and needing no inner life of world-withdrawal, is made clear in the English. So too is (2) the looking forward to life in a worthier world, from which the monastic teaching turned away: "What," we read (Girnar IX.), "is more desirable than this: the winning of the Bright World?" His whole life, he declares, is given to bring about the worthier life of men here and their winning then of that.

There is one more point, not overlooked, but possibly misconstrued, which nearly a score of years ago was the subject of discussion. I refer to the words in the Rupnath IV., Maski IV., Brahmagiri III., Bairat IV., Siddapura VII.: "At the present time men of India (who had) not been mingling with devas are mingled with them." Many scholars have been puzzled by this, and Hultzsch has connected it with the reference in another Edict to certain "religious shows" which the king had performed, doubtless in suitable halls (IVth Rock Edict). But the idea of "mingling" or "mixing" or associating is obviously something of a different kind. It is what the early Buddhist sought to train himself for and, if it might be, attain in Jhāna.[1] Not in the later monastic Jhāna, which favoured either mere detachment from all earthly awareness, or vague abstract quasi-trance of the kind we class as "mystic." I refer to that communion of the worthy man with the worthy man of another world, by the exercise of what we now call clairvoyance and clair-audience; such communion as we find the Founder so often attaining even before he began to teach and no less afterwards. I refer you to what I have here said on this matter (pp. 186 f.). If you will remember that, for a Buddhist of that day, *deva* did not mean anything more awful than what those three Men who came and talked with Abraham meant for him in his day, you will

[1] I am glad to say that this interpretation occurred to Dr. A. K. Coomaraswamy independently, soon after it had been revealed to me when poring over Hultzsch's noble edition.

not find that Asoka's words need further explanation than this. If, in the coming latter half of this century, we imagine psychic converse of this kind become a channel of new knowledge and inspiration for priest and minister, we can also imagine some A.D. 2100 record of *our* century mentioning that "Men of other worlds were now become accessible to converse with us as never before."

The man as (*a*) capable of More (*b*) as amenable to a teaching in the More, (*c*) as seeking and finding a More, here and hereafter, not through seclusion, but in carrying out his duties in the life of the world, as (*d*) capable, either directly or through the more gifted few, of learning how to grow in that More, and to make his fellows grow in it—this is man as conceived and taught by the founders of Buddhism. And this is man as conceived and taught by Asoka far better than by the monk, who believed in monkdom as a better way of life than life not "in the cloister." No one sympathizes with the lover of the lone more than I; lover of the lone have I ever been. But the Alone has a way of saying, after converse, that which Elias heard in the cave: "What doest thou here, Elias? . . . Go, return on the way . . ." The Sakyan founders knew that monition; the Rāmakrishna monks of to-day know it. But the long formula of the Suttas of the going into the alone is devoid of any reference whatever, except by an inclusion of a wide, compassionate feeling, to the work, suspended only temporarily, in the welfare of anyone save of the solitary one alone.

The chronic recluse has contracted his life from a relative fullness to a relative emptiness. Nor was the cenobitic monk a much more. He had life contracted for him from one of many human relations to one of a minimum of such. Repressions are not healthy, and, as his language testifies, his life was a complex of repressions. Life for him was mainly summed up in negatives: *anicca* (impermanent), *dukkha* (ill), *anattā* (man as not persisting), with a waning out, from this and every other vital opportunity of growth by a way of the worlds, as *summum bonum*. *Bhava*, as meaning "lives" and "worlds" was condemned. *Bhāvanā* (making to become) was true, not of himself—that was nonentity—but of certain ideas about "himself." Of *bhavaśudhi* he never spoke. That there is nothing of life as thus monk-valued in the Edicts is a true comment. Less true is the comment that there is nothing in them "about God and the soul."

Thus wrote the man to whom I owe the will to measure things, not only by historical, but also by alien standards. Careful was he to banish from his own maturer writings terms that we associate with scriptures of different lands, different times, and to deprecate application to Pali scriptures of them. Yet here he writes as if pointing to a surprising omission, and one that, for him, undermined the necessity of such terms as being vital to all religions. This is much as to say that, in the Hebrew prophets, there is nothing about the self, nothing about *dharma*. Your rejoinder to that would be unhesitating—the traditions of their religious teaching were different; they were Semitic, not Indo-Aryan. The India of Asoka's day had been steeped in an immanent theism for three or four centuries. The "man," religiously considered, was no longer man over against God; he had the God within; he was as God more or less unawakened, latent, a tiny shoot. His "growth" in a More was a stage in that awakening, that becoming patent, that evolution. And he *was* soul; the very word *puruṣa* was not, as alas! with us, a name mainly for what we see, with an inner "mental" world somehow going along. The man did not "have a soul," as we absurdly say. *He was*, as self, spirit, *soul*. And the more he gives himself to divine growth, the more will he show this growth in acts of body and of mind. By Indian standards then, there is *nothing atheistic, nothing anti-animistic* in the Edicts; they are pregnant with the teaching of a divine Becoming in that

More whereby man, each man, will ultimately find the way to a yet inconceivable Most.

But there is more yet of "God and the soul" in Asoka's Edicts: there is the constant allusion to the spiritual ideal named *dharma*, not used save in one of the latest Edicts, in the sense of "doctrine" of a formulated, fixed-worded kind, but used in the sense in which we saw it taken over by Gotama when he began his mission, and made the object of his own worship. The sense, I mean, of the inner monition we all know when up against the call of "duty"; the feeling of an "ought to be done" or ought not to be doṇe, the "voice of conscience." Let me add at once that when he seeks to define it, he does not use any one of these expressions. Let us have his own words (so far as he may have dictated them, and not just indicated what was to be carved):—

The Pillar Edict called Second.

"Dear-to-Devas Piyadasi King thus has said: *Dhaṃme* is excellent, now how much is *dhaṃme?* Few evil tendencies, many virtuous (deeds), kindness giving truth purity."

He then goes on to speak of his own efforts to reign worthily, and then concludes: "This *dhaṃme*-writing was caused to be written that they might walk in accordance and that it might long persist. And he who will thus ever walk will do good deeds."

Here is no proper definition of *dharma*, but only what walking according to it involves and brings to pass. Nor is he anywhere else concerned to say just what *dhaṃme* is. He was, as Rhys Davids rightly reminded us, urging his people, not to accept a New Word in religion, but to live up to the religious essentials which had been taught, and were being taught in India, by brahman, Sakyan (Buddhist) and Jain alike. It was the godly life known as *dhammachărāṇa*, "walking according to *dharma*," that he was urging upon them, ensuring peace on earth and happiness—luck, it was often called—hereafter. It was this: the voice of the God-within, which had become for Asoka the one great secret of strength and security, the guarantee of welfare now and hereafter, the leading motive for everything in thought, word and deed needed by men. Round this all the Edicts on rock and pillar centre; you will find in this brief "literature" some 184 occurrences of the word, either simply or in compounds; and since there are only twenty-six Edicts as yet deciphered, this gives on an average seven times per Edict in the use of the word.

No, you will not get the Asoka of the third century B.C. if you render his dharma utterances by "morality" and moral this or that, and see in him a staunch Victorian Agnostic. That he looks steadfastly beyond life on earth —this separates him in spirit from such. That he distinguishes dharma from moral code does so no less. This he calls *sīla*, as we should expect. A man must walk by dharma if he would become *sīlasa* (moral). "In one who is immoral there is no walking by dharma." "The king, persisting in dharma, in *sīla*, will teach dharma." It is greatly to be deplored that Hultzsch spoilt his translations by using "morality" for dharma. Senart's older work is herein better, that he calls dharma "religion." This is far nearer the right meaning, yet is religion too weighted with external implications to coincide with dharma as Asoka used it.

The one later use is that occurring in the Bairat Edict, where he first makes reference to the Buddhist Sangha. He salutes them, professes faith (*prasāde*) in "Buddhasi Dhammasi Sanghasi," approves of whatever the "bhagavā budhe" spoke, and advises monks and nuns and the laity to listen and reflect upon certain *dhaṃma-paliyāyāni*, i.e. expositions of doctrine. He gives names to these, and they have been a pretty puzzle, most of them, to scholars. They are:

Vinaya-samukāse . .	estimation of the Rules.
Aliyavasāni . . .	ariyâvâsā (*Sangīti Sutta, Dīgha,* and *Khp*).
Anāgatabhayāni . .	fears as to the future (*Anguttara* III, pp. 100 ff.).
Munigāthā . . .	*Sutta-Nipāta*, verse 207 ff.
Moneyasute . . .	*Iti-vuttaka*, 367 ?
Upatisa-pasiṇe . .	Questioning Sāriputta (*Majjhima*, Sta. 43).
Laghulovāde musavādam adhigichya . . .	Homily to Rāhula on conscious lying (*Majjhima*, Sta. 61).

In the Rupnath and Maski Edicts—in the latter he at last calls himself " Asoka "—he confesses to being a Budha-Saka, or, upāsaka. And since " the rest is silence," it is very possible that, like certain other Indian kings of which we read, he abdicated and entered the Order. Centuries after, the Chinese pilgrim records having seen a statue of a monk, said to be of Asoka. He had done his work for India and for the testimony to a religion more like that taught by the first Sakyans than the dual doctrine of the Sangha to which he came. But he entered retreat as an old worker seeking rest, and here, too, it was the Indian ideal of the past that he was upholding; not the monastic ideal, that a man did well to leave his duties to the world and enter an Order of monks while yet young.

And there is not a word in his Edicts to lead us to suppose that at whatever time in his reign he became a Sakyan layman, he was influenced by the monastic ideal of the waning out of the man in the beyond. His faith was in the very man, as distinct from body or mind, as seeking and finding his salvation in growth, in becoming ever a More, so only he lives according to dharma-monition. Herein for him was " God." And as to " soul," this man-in-the-becoming was " soul."

CHAPTER XVI

THE EASTWARD EXPANSION

We may not leave the greatest of early Buddhist laymen without mention of that other genuine Sakyan feature shown in his Edicts: the will that all men in and beyond his great empire should be stimulated in religious growth. After deploring his earlier assay in "making roll the wheel of conquest," in his defeating with much carnage the Kalingas, who threatened, as he judged, the safety of his eastern borders in India, he turns to that other equally traditional "making roll the wheel of dharma,"[1] whence arose not mourning, but joy. He sent envoys about in his empire called *mahā-dharma-mātras*: chief judges of dharma, after he had made many dharma-tours (*dhamma-yātrā*) himself, "visiting brahmans and monks, making them gifts, visiting and endowing the aged, visiting and teaching the people generally." He claims that these officials were a new institution, begun in the fourteenth year of his reign, and he describes their duties as adjudging between servants and masters, visiting the poor and aged, the incurably ill, and prisoners, and concerned with the inculcation of dharma and morality in general. It is clear from this that nowhere is he found engaging, or co-operating with, monks of the Sangha, to carry out any work that we should call mission or evangelizing work.

Asoka also records other envoys sent by him to other kingdoms, and only to such as lay westward of India, and were the new political growths resulting from the great upheaval wrought by the conquests of Alexander the Great;

[1] On both traditions see *Dialogues*, Sta. XXVI.: "The Lion's Roar of Wheel-turning."

kingdoms of the Ægean Sea and Persian Gulf, governed by the new men, Alexander's satrap-generals. The famous Edicts, Kalsi XIII. and Shahbazgarhi and Mansehra XIII., tell how he claimed dharma-conquest over all his border provinces, even as far as where reigned the Greek king Antiyoka (Antiochus 1st or 2nd), in North-west India, yea, " beyond this, where are the four kings Turamaya (Ptolemy of Egypt), Antikini (Antigonos of Macedonia), Maka (Magas of Cyrene) and Alikasudara (Alexander of Epiros): likewise down to Chodas and Pandyas as far as Tāmraparṇi (South India and ? Ceylon),[1] likewise here in the king's territories: Yonas-Kambojas, Nabhakas-Nabhapanktis, Bhojas-Pitinikyas, Andhras-Paladas, everywhere are conforming to the king's instruction in dharma. Moreover they to whom the messengers of Him-dear-to-devas do not go, they too having heard of dharma-duties . . . are conforming to dharma and will conform. This that has thus far everywhere been won has the taste of joy, firm becomes that joy, the joy of dharma-victory."

There is at first sight a splendid assurance, a large optimistic complacency about these words that provoke, that have provoked, smiling sarcasm. And did we rightly see in them an assertion that under *dūte* (messengers) Asoka was referring to missioners preaching a cult, we might be similarly provoked. But I do not for a moment believe that Asoka's *dūte* were sent out with such an object, either in or beyond India. Nowhere do we find a trace of *cult-propagation* in his Edicts. Where he does refer to denominations—and he often does—it is to enjoin these to live in mutual toleration and at peace. Or if to the monks and nuns of his own newly adopted cult, that they carefully study their own oral teachings. Had the *dūte* been brahmans or samaṇas (Sakyans), he would certainly have called them so, as he does elsewhere, and not

[1] Tāmraparṇi may refer to the watershed of the river so-called in Tinnevelli, not to Ceylon. Cf. Geiger, *Mahāvaṃsa* (1912), p. xvii f.

just *dūte* (envoys). Asoka's *dhamme* was no cult, but a faith in and a drawing out of the More that is in man, the very man. And the promotion of friendly relations between border provinces and capital, between foreign neighbours and the Indian empire was vital to that *dhamme*, the establishing such relations to be counted as *dhamme*-conquest. A ruler red-handed from warring on a neighbour and publishing remorseful confession thereof was ill-fitted to pose as head of a missionizing church. But when we see in his envoys the expression of his own reaction to his former hostile relations—as we do in just these three Edicts—the desire, namely, to establish *relations of amity*, then can we spare our sarcasm, and substitute sympathetic appreciation.

And there is other evidence. In the Ceylon chronicles we read of the Sangha at Patna sending its missions to Kashmir and other northern provinces and also to Ceylon. Here we get the right word: not *dūte*, but *theras*, or senior monks. And recent excavation near Sānchi bears out the probable truth of this undertaking.[1] But nothing whatever is recorded about theras being sent *beyond* Asoka's boundaries. The King of Ceylon sends gifts to Asoka by a political embassy, and Asoka supports the missions already begun in Ceylon. This is all. Yet what a feather in the cap of the Sangha it would have furnished, had there been a royal mission of monks to other lands! We have only to read about the monk-mission to Ceylon to be assured of this. Here is no question of ethical or social fraternizing; the one object of the mission is seen to be a bringing of the majority of hearers into the Order. A first "sermon" brings a few hundreds into the first stage of the Way; a few days later these ask for ordination: 500 court ladies, fifty-five brothers of the king; five times 500 from five villages; soon there are 30,000 monks, world-duty shirkers, alms-feeders to impoverish the island!

[1] See Rhys Davids, *Buddhist India*, pp. 299 f.

All this, compiled centuries later, may of course be only pious fairy-tale; anyway, let us keep Asoka's friendly *dhamme*-victories far from it. I am not saying that Buddhist influences may not have found their way abroad in the wake of both political *dūta* and of the merchant. In Egypt, for instance, such influence has been suggested for things in the philosophy of Basilīdes (A.D. 117–138).[1] And the exotic birth of Christian monasticism in Egypt may have been inspired by Buddhist samaṇas there, particularly in that it was not of the Franciscan kind, now practised also by the Rāmakrishna monks—a release from worldly ties the better to tend the ailing fellow-man—but of the more truly Indian kind, which is sole absorption in the salvation of the individual recluse, the "other man" only deriving "merit" from the recluse's nearness and dependence upon him. But beyond such very uncertain evidence I have come across nothing entitling us to say, that the central Buddhist Sangha in India carried out any foreign missionary work beyond that which is recorded in the apocryphal chronicles of Ceylon. Very curious is the contrast, the silence between the early sending forth of the first sixty missioners as they are clearly shown to be, around Rājagaha, and the mission of Mahinda and his few helpers some 300 years later in Ceylon (the only *records* of the same dating centuries later than that); between the first missioners, with a message (like Asoka) of just dharma and the God-life; and the later missioners, recorded as reciting certain formulated sayings in prose or verse, with the First Mantra of Benares, almost as it were thrown in as tenth and last, not put first.[2]

There is something wrong here, and much do I wonder we have been so long finding it so. "Buddhism" has the credit, just because it did in some form or other spread to the eastern confines of Asia, maybe even further east

[1] See J.R.A.S., "Buddhist Gnosticism," 1902.
[2] *Dīpavaṃsa*, XIV., p. 46; *Mahāvaṃsa*, XV., p. 199.

across the Pacific, of being, or rather of having been, a great missionary religion. I have even seen its addiction to categories and schedules explained as having its origin in a zealous preparing an apparatus for propaganda ! Yet we find in neither Commentary nor in Chronicle any traces whatever, Ceylon excepted, of enterprise in foreign missions. What was wrong with the Indian Buddhist church ?

I believe it was an impoverishment resembling that which befell the Church in France after the revocation of the Edict of Nantes. England and Holland thereby won an increment of worthy men and women, who preferred exile to reinstating certain religious beliefs and practices which had become distasteful to their conscience, to their dharma. If the records of the Patna Council be true, a very great number of monks, who were not in conformity with the Vibhajjavādin or "Analytic" majority—the monks, that is, who sought and found the very man or self in mind or mental processes, and not as the minder or mind-proceeder in and with these—were "suspended," or expelled. That this was the orthodox view you will find treated with much detail in the long debate on the man (*puggala-kathā*) in the Kathāvatthu which, I repeat, is said to have been compiled for the Third Council. You will read that it was the Vesālians, called Vajjians and men of the Great Company (Mahā-sanghikas), who upheld the distinct and unique reality of the self or man. These, together with the men of the school called the Sabbatthivādins, or Sarvâstivādins, who were also upholders of the man's reality, maintaining that his past was in a way ever present with him (how like Bergson's "past bending over the present" !), were defrocked and considered as mere laymen.

Now that these and other dissentients were turned down in the Patna Sangha does not permit us to conclude that their zeal for what they held was the true, the mother-teaching suffered any abatement. On the contrary, men who held it worth while to dissent would hold it worth while to turn their released energies along other channels, where they would be free to teach according to their conscience. And I believe it was through these Nonconformists, and not through the orthodox Analysts, that Buddhism became a great Eastward-flowing stream.

The expulsion of them by the Patna Sangha must have been a terrific blow for the expelled. But the anæmic state in which it must have left that Sangha was for the latter a yet more dire calamity. You may say: But do we not read, in the Ceylon Chronicles, of Moggaliputta-Tissa sending out those missions to North India? True, but there is no reason to believe that the expulsions had then been decreed. The theras he sent may have been of those who, a little later, suffered expulsion. You may say: But was there not the mission sent to Ceylon? True, but that mission was conducted by a thera who was either son or brother of Asoka himself, and thus there was royal patronage at the back of it. And I have said what I think of the genuine worth of it as a true and worth-while religious mission.

Once more you may say: Do we not read of the tradition, in a (later) Chinese record, that "eighteen Buddhist monks were brought to the Chinese capital in 217 B.C.?"[1] Yes, and the date conforms well to the time it would take, in those days, for such missionaries to reach China after the upheaval at Patna. For, after all, there is nothing in the record, so far as we have been told, to see in these eighteen, not delegates from the Patna Sangha, but members of those bodies of monks who had been expelled, had reformed themselves into "Reformed Churches" and were carrying out the Founder's ideal of exercising "compassion for devas and men" beyond their own borders. When next we hear of Buddhist monks visiting China is in 2 B.C., when ambassadors are said to have returned to China with

[1] Cf. *Ency. Religion and Ethics:* Missions (Buddhist), by M Anesaki.

Buddhist scriptures from Central Asia, from Yuechi. Again, there was the expedition sent by Emperor Ming to find the golden man of his dream, resulting in the messengers bringing both Buddhist scriptures and statues and two named monks from India, Kaśyapa Matanga and Dharmaraksha, who found the way had been prepared for the new religion. Even then, however, I find nothing to identify these men or these scriptures with the members or works of the Theravāda Sangha, which came to be named Hīnayāna.

Years of patient translation from Chinese records must pass before we can get nearer any certainty about this. That work has been well begun, and has already given us results beyond those disclosed in the Pali Canon. But we can already see that, if they possibly did not form the vanguard, men of the Theravāda *followed* on the Eastward trail. For we actually find, in Dr. Behrsing's translation of the Chung-Tsi-King, or Sangīti Sutta of the Dīgha-Nikāya that, whereas in Pali the famous Eight Angas of the Way are unconnected with that Way, in the Chinese they are so connected, as now in the Pali.

Time will show, but till then the whole history of Buddhism, between the time of Asoka and the fifth century A.D., can as yet be one of mere conjecture. And we have to conjecture from three results emerging in literature of, and from the latter date. They are these: At the end of the fourth century A.D. there begins the notable literary feature of Chinese records purporting to be diaries by a succession of Chinese Buddhists pilgrimaging westward to visit the cradle land of their faith and to obtain not only adventure and new experience, but also copies of Indian scriptures, in particular the Vinaya. These men: Fa-Hien, then after two centuries Hiouen Chwang and I-Tsing, coming, the former by a route south of the great Tarim Desert, by Lob Nor, Yashkend and Kashgar, the other by a route north of the same over Turfan, Tashkend and

Samarcand, are not only in themselves witnesses of the spread of Buddhism, but have recorded how they came to and passed a number of Buddhist vihāras, where resided monks belonging to one or the other of the two main sections of the faith into which, in their day, the one original Order had become divided—namely, into Hīnayāna and Mahāyāna, *i.e.* the great and little or low Road respectively. Yāna may also mean "means of road-faring," such as a horse or carriage or elephant: a "vehicle," but as "road" (lit. going) it is, as we have seen, a very ancient Indian term, preceding *marga*, for the way to salvation.

Now it is not at all clear how far it was correct to speak of the offshoots of the Patna expulsions as branches of the Theravāda, Sanskrit Sthaviravāda, *as still Hīnayāna.* For my own part, I venture to think this is not correct. For these Seceders, the *Patna central majority* had rightly gained the name of the Low Yāna—whenever, we know not when, they did gain it. For they had lowered, they had contracted the lofty, the broad Everyman's gospel of the Śakyamuni. The main Seceders—the Mahāsanghikas and the Sarvâstivādins—would have stoutly maintained that this world gospel had suffered no such lowering, no such contraction at their hands. We find them, in the Kathāvatthu debates, insisting on such tenets as belonging to the Founder's teaching: (*a*) that the man was always recognized as an entity seeking his own welfare or that of others, or the reverse—in other words, he was not resolved into "states" of body and mind; next (*b*), that the man "runs on" (transmigrates) from this world to another and returns thence hither; next (*c*), that the man was taught as the feeler or experiencer of this and as doer of that—in other words, he was not merely the experience or the deed; he was worth-er of both, valuer of both; next (*d*), that "the man survived in that he was in (not being, but) becoming"—because, that is, he was not remaining self-identical, static, but was by nature becoming a "more";

lastly (*e*), in acts of supernormal (as we should say) will there must be a "man," a chooser, willer, and not merely a mental mechanism, to effect such acts.

You will find these arguments and more in those debates. But you will also and ever find that the defender of the Man is being tripped up by some dialectical trick; he is made to assent to a term or thesis meaning this or that, and is then shown that this meaning involves a refutation of his standpoint. Thus, in "becoming" he is made to admit—a needless and fatal admission—that whatever becomes also decays: a fact that is ***true only of material things***, and of ***mind*** in so far as it is process bound up with a material, *i.e.* nervous, mechanism.[1] The defender is thus ever being shown at a disadvantage by the special pleader, who alone has had the compiling of the debate. Far too long have the sympathies of writers on Buddhism (and readers of them) been all on the side of this specious partisanship, regarding all so-called "sects" other than the Theravāda as mere heretical mushroom growths. The hour is now at hand for better vision, and for discerning that it is in this Patna Analyst majority, exercising most mischievous mutilation on its best elements, that we ought to see the cancerous growth of changed and decadent values.

The mistake we make in this matter of Hīnayāna is to imagine that Mahāyānists look upon "primitive" Buddhism as "hīna." Ignorant Mahāyānists may possibly so think; those who are wise will mean, that it was the monastic régime before and after Asoka who, by their contracted outlook on man's nature and destiny, distorted the original teaching, and so deserve the name Hīnayāna, but that the original teaching by no means deserves to be so called. I have good reason to impute this view to cultured Mahāyānism, for I have been for some years eye-witness of the zeal with which, *e.g.*, the Japanese, who call themselves Mahāyānists, are taking up the study of the Pali scriptures, and the

[1] *Points of Controversy*, I., p. 1, esp. § 228*a*. Cf. above, p. 98.

generosity with which many have helped our work in purveying these to them, both financially and by gift of time and labour in contributing to our editions. They have yet, it is true, as we all have, to study the Piṭakas and Commentaries critically, *historically*, to elicit what in them is left of the "primitive" teaching. For all we yet know, Chinese libraries may contain more genuinely primitive matter in translations than almost anything we have in the Pali books. But none the less is it necessary to compare any such discovery with what the Pali books, as yet the oldest we have made accessible, put before us.

I am not assuming, in saying this, that China and Japan were necessarily first converted to Buddhism, as the last reach only in the wave of its eastward-flowing missionary efforts. Another way is conceivably possible, possible at least in China, as having a religious and general culture much older than the day of the birth of Buddhism. The older a culture, the more varied will tend to be the wants of the cultured. It may be, it is not material commodities only that will be in demand. It may be that need will arise, to use our own phrase, to learn "the wisdom of the East." The East may in one case be wrong; the West is the word.

There survives in a Greek chronicler a quotation from a Greek historian: of how Asoka's father, King Bindusāra, requested his Greek neighbour Antiochos Sotēr, ruler over what was left in N.W. India of Alexander's conquest, to procure for him from Greece some figs, some wine and a teacher, a "*sophistēs*." The reply is quoted as, "Figs and glycos we send you, but trade in teachers is for Greeks not lawful." Did ever chronicler of old throw in one sentence more interesting historic light? India the bookless was asking for "the wisdom of the West" through oral teaching from a land which could have exported its "books," but which looked on the live book, the teacher, as a request for a slave-chattel.

Now we can easily imagine a cultured Chinese commissioning a merchant to procure "books" from India, and on learning there were none, to have instructed him to import a teacher who could be maintained, till he had learnt Chinese and expound his native lore in that tongue. And if such a demand only began about Asoka's time, it might well be that the supply was found, hardly in a brahman—we know how they still handicap themselves in the matter of travel—but in a Sakyan teacher. And if Sakyan, why not one of those so ruthlessly unfrocked by the Sangha? Here, then, is a possible way in which we can imagine China first coming to know a teaching which was so greatly to affect her religion, and to learn it in a truer form than that in which it would have been taught by any Sangha-deputed missionaries.

My first "result," then, in our conjecturing about the history of Buddhism, is, that somehow, and over some period "Buddhism," in one shape or another, spread from India eastward to the Pacific.

My second result is this: Speaking for myself only, I have yet to find in Pali literature, the signs of any interest taken in making other lands acquainted with the teaching professed by the Buddhist Sangha. It is inconceivable that had there been such interest it would have been left unrecorded. Let me say at once, my knowledge of Pali literature is of the most incomplete. But I have found no reference to it in other better-acquainted writers. And where we should chiefly look for it—namely, in the work held by Hīnayāna to be the quintessence of its early mediæval learning, Buddhaghosa's Visuddhi-Magga—I find not a word! Indeed, there is in it *only one chapter*, where we find ourselves not wholly and solely in the world of the local monastery and its doings: the ninth chapter, on the teaching of the Brahmavihāras or Divine Moods. And even that teaching was, I hold, not, in origin, Buddhist! [1]

[1] See above, p. 200.

Can we assign a reason for this? That there has been, in our day, a little stirring of the still waters in Southern Asia to propagate has been mainly due to a zealous monk here, a pious layman there, and there has been no solid growth. Not for a moment am I denying intercourse, mediæval and of course modern, between Sanghas in Ceylon, Burma, Siam, and now, on educational lines, in Pali, etc., between the Buddhist countries of extreme South-east Asia. But I speak of earlier days—days when the initial enterprise shown by the Founder seems to have been so neglected by his followers in the succeeding centuries, in all that they show in their scriptures. Why is it that we never see in that literature their vision, their will, their aspirations bent towards a continuous carrying out of that early summons: "Fare ye in a tour that may be for the good of the many, out of compassion for devas and men; teach dharma beneficent at the start, in the middle, at the end"? Why do their efforts this way seem ever limited by such pious lay-votaries as come with or without offerings, to listen on feast-days, but *to whom* they go little? And I might add: Why is it we who have to *supply words* for "missions," for "propaganda"?

In reply I would repeat that word "impoverishment" of the Sangha by the Sangha, inflicted by those expulsions. By expulsions I am not only referring to men of conscientious will; I refer also to the essential *faith in man* which the expellers had rejected, and to the pitiful dummy which had been substituted for that faith. What had they come to reject? A belief in a gospel of growth and of hope for the very man, not for man as a mere complex of body and mind, but for the user of, the valuer by, these. If the very man be held to be a fiction of the mind, if the growth, the becoming in him be only a becoming in so many ideas about him, the will for a More in such becoming will concentrate on these ideas, *e.g.* "love, joy, peace, longsuffering," and the like, but not on other *men as having those ideas*. Where the man, whose are, or can be these ideas, is held to be the *truest of true things*, then it is the *becoming-in-other-men* that the benevolent man wills to help bring about. Not his to be content with developing the ideas only; it is the fellow-man, real as he is real, that he will be seeking with outstretched hands, —the fellow-man, not as real only in this earth-life, but as fellow-wayfarer in other worlds, other lives. Here again was impoverishment, in that such prolonged wayfaring had become, not opportunity for becoming, but protraction merely of suffering. Herein it is that I find ample reason for the mission-silences in Pali literature.

Nor is my reason rendered invalid by modern propagandist attempts on the part of Buddhists, even though theirs are Hīnayāna views of the man as unreal and as not personally persisting. There has been another long wave of Expansion from a more central nucleus, sweeping both Westward and Eastward, Northward and Southward, expansion of a religion in which there has been no faltering in missionary zeal, if we reckon by its life as a whole, nor sinister silences in its books. And the example of this religion has ever been a powerful stimulant. They who reacted to it did not ask, how much its incorrigible will to help the world was due to its firm faith in the very man as real in the deepest sense, both here and hereafter, yea, even in the concept of the Highest. I have seen Hīnayānist writings quoting Christian scripture to justify the crudest denial of the man as being real. How have they not twisted the sense! How could not they here be smothered in Christian testimony to man's persistent reality, were it seemly here to do so!

The fact remains that, since the second century of the Christian movement, Asia has had the object-lesson of religious missions moving across it, the Nestorian missions reaching China in the fifth century, leaving traces, material and immaterial, along the routes where also passed those Chinese Buddhist pilgrims, and affecting, as we can scarcely doubt, the temple rites of Tibet.[1] How interesting, too, is it not? that here, too, the original Nestorian missionaries were of those who, like the Mahāsanghikas and Sarvâstivadins, had suffered expulsion from a Christian Sangha at Ephesus, expulsion not because they had held views contrary to *anattā*, but because of their *maintaining* the dual personality, human and divine, in Jesus!

I come to my third result on which to base conjecture about the history of Buddhism. Mahāyānism differs in important features from Hīnayāna: what are these? And whence the difference? If you will consult the very clear article on Mahāyānism by an eminent expert in it, De la Vallée Poussin, in the *Encyclopædia of Religion and Ethics*, three chief points will be given you, distinguishing it from Hīnayāna, that is, not from the original teaching of the Śakyamuni—I would have you omit the writer's "Buddha has said" as unworthy of a historical scholar's terminology—but from the teaching of the Indian Sangha, *when the founders of Mahāyānism seceded* from that Sangha. The three are: (1) Substitution of the "career of a *bodhisattva*" for the short way of an arahan; (2) belief that the human complex at any given moment, the much-taught five aggregates (*skandhas*), or body and mind, are void of ultimate reality; (3) worship of the Man "Buddha" under this or that aspect of a Divine Providence: "he who has infinite life," "who has infinite splendour," "has compassion," "protector of the world," "lord who is looked upon," or however this last much-discussed title Avalokitêshvărā be rendered. Note that *all* the titles should be rendered as agent-nouns, not some only; not with Western writers, as *e.g.* "infinite life" or "splendour" only, but *with the Man*.

In the first feature, *bodhisattva* means "wisdom-being," one who is, through many lives in many worlds, training himself in certain "perfections" (*pāramitā*) or virtues, ten

[1] Cf. the testimony, often cited, of the Jesuit Fathers Huc and Gabet.

in number: giving, morals, renunciation, wisdom, energy, patience, truth, resolution, amity, poise. It is the dominant idea in the evangelized mass of folk-lore stories called Jātaka, of the Sutta Piṭaka, made credal.[1]

On all three points there is the one vital matter to be noticed: we are here in the teaching of the very Man, and the Yāna, the Way of the man, as real and as persistently real. Not the man-as-complex—the "complex" is now in its turn *resolved into the unreal*—but of the man-in-man ever becoming in the More on his way toward Man the Most. Can such a teaching as this have been started by any "Buddhists" save by those who, precisely for a faith along these lines, were rejected of men at Patna?

Consider for a moment the basis of the *bodhisattva* belief, and in particular that great *bodhisattva* "biography": the theme connecting all the Jātaka stories. If we are not to see in these the age-long advance of one man, as persisting individual, in the Way of Becoming ever More towards a Most, a More-as-man towards a Most-as-man, the very *raison d'être* of the whole collection collapses.

It may be said: Yes, but the Jātaka name of that man—the Bodhisat, or Buddha-to-be—was but a label for an ever-changing complex. And we shall hear the similes of the all-but-canonical Questions of Milinda trotted out, similes fatally ill-fitting, because beside the point, the point being the Becoming *in the man*. That which the objector ever evades is the express and reiterated attestation, by the alleged Teller, the Founder, to his own persisting identity as Bodhisat, when concluding a story: *A* was *X*, *B* was *Y*, but so-and-so "was just I." And more, we have in a Sutta a very *caveat* against error: "Now it may

[1] On the confusion between Bhagavan and Barlaam and between Bodhisat and Joasaph . . . Josaphat, characters in Eastern legend, see Rhys Davids's *Buddhist Birthstories* (Broadway Translations); *E.R.E.*, "Josaphat," and E. J. Thomas, *op. cit.*, p. 288.

occur to you, Ānanda, that the youth Jotipāla (of whom I have been telling) was a different person. But you must not see it thus. *I* at that time was Jotipāla."[1] The emphasis with "I" explicit is in Pali very strong. There is nothing here to suggest that a merely popular way of talking was used, such as may be claimed for the Jātaka talks. The Founder was seated alone with his companion, a noble and his devoted pupil, and verbal recorder. Long after, when Buddhaghosa was writing Abhidhamma Commentaries, it was felt necessary to assert that the Founder used a double way of teaching: a popular way admitting the "truth" of the individual, and a learned way, recognizing only dhammas, ideas about him.[2] But he is singularly unsuccessful in the citation in support of this, and the distinction, which first peeps out in the *Milinda*, was clearly unknown, when the text commented upon was compiled, viz. at the Third Council. The Jātaka itself twice affirms that a Bodhisat at least holds back nothing that he can teach, "has not the closed fist." (*Dial.*, II., 107).

When once the Hīnayānist has discerned in the original teaching, which accepted the man as persisting, not in a static fixed identity, but in a growing, a becoming identity, using body after body as a means whereby to become, it may be that this unhappy harping upon an irrational, impossible theory of unreal man will cease. Then, too, will the Mahāyānist no longer try to combine a not-man (*nirātma*) notion of his own with that vindication of the man advancing in his growing manhood in other worlds, but not yet finished (as the arahan was held to be), that we have in the *bodhisattva*.

That he says *nirātma* rather than *anattā* is interesting, and may be significant; it may be it is a true derivative from Upanishadic teaching, brought by men who were opposed to the Analysts' *anattā* doctrine; the selflessness, namely, of the Maitri, due to "the vision of the Great Self

[1] *Further Dial.*, Sta. LXXXI. [2] See above, p. 276.

by the self"—a very different thing from a rejection of both.

We cannot know. More interesting yet is the belief in Becoming as seen in the *bodhisattva* on the threshold of divine consummation, but resolving to wait that he may yet be helping mankind. Surely one would say, As consummated in Deity he could yet more supremely help? But have we not perhaps failed here to understand? What if, in persisting in his Becoming, he may yet win to a higher worth in conceiving That Who is the Highest? It is usually held that the *bodhisattva* ideal excels that of the arahan in ethical concern for human welfare. The arahan concept is by its own threefold formula [1] concerned with the arahan's own salvation. I would not do monastic Buddhism the injustice of calling this preoccupation a Buddhistic divergence. It was, it is, yet, an Indian ideal. A wave of ethical reaction is now perceptible in the Indian religious world, yet still one can generalize to this effect, that India has ever favoured in the saint that self-preoccupation, seeing only altruism in the benefit the bare fact of saintship confers on the less worthy by a transferred "merit."

Who, knowing India, has not seen this? Sir Francis Younghusband has told me how, when he went in a queue to pay respect to a sannyāsi sitting crosslegged, and expressed appreciation of his absorption in high matters, he was answered by an accepting grunt, but when he added "And with the welfare of others," the reply was a burst of laughter and the words: "What have I to do with the welfare of others? It takes me all my time to mind my own welfare."

With such a hoary ideal still prevailing, we may perhaps better understand the consent of Buddhist India to the arahan ideal. And we may the more do justice to the new spirit in the movement that shines in that first mis-

[1] Cp. *Saṃyutta-Nikāya*, Index-vol., p. vii.

sionary mandate of the Śakyamuni, in those first missions abroad by the men who maintained his teaching, and by the form it took in the Far East, that to go on growing in becoming *be interpreted* as a will the better to help the fellow-man.

Here, with so much unsaid, I bring this brief word on the Eastward Expansion to an end. It were indeed premature to try to compress all that a decade hence, if then, may have become compressible. We have in our Museums a very mass of material, accumulated by the research of men like Sven Hedin, Sir Aurel Stein, A. van le Coq and F. W. K. Müller along those highways from India to China indicated above. And then we are, it may be, on the eve of beginning to learn what Tibetan libraries may not always hold sealed from us. For that matter, it is only to-day possible to read, in English, that which most of us have believed was till our day a very unknown land: the Report on Tibet, its people, language, etc., composed while there in the second decade of the eighteenth century, by the Jesuit Father Ippolito Desideri, a time when Tibet was governed, not by Lamas (its Buddhist monks), but by a king, till Tartars overran the country, a time when Tibet was the hunting-ground of Capuchin missionaries.

Even were the attempt not premature, to write the whole history of Buddhism is not within the scope of a modest manual like this. Its utmost ambition is to help bring about a truer, sounder view of the New Word in Indian religion that was offered to the Many by the sons of the Sakyas, and to arrest the mistake that is still everywhere made, of seeing that New Word in the contracted gospel which was evolved out of it by and for that monasticism which became its vehicle.

This mistake is ever confronting me in nearly every book, every article on Buddhism that is published. The scholar still fails to grip the subject historically and see the change in values coming between him and the original message, change infecting all the editing the texts have undergone in oral and then in written recensions. The general reader has now, as never before, an opportunity of wide reading in complete translations, and not only in the false guides called Selections. But here he may be in two ways off the right track. He may not discern, any more than does the scholar, the changing values, and he may be misled by much in the rendering chosen by similarly undiscerning translators.

To take a case where I was myself the undiscerning translator: in the second volume of the *Book of the Kindred Sayings* [1] (Saṃyutta-Nikāya), p. 40, I have made Sāriputta say: ". . . by deliverance from self . . . I live with a clear mind . . . and I admit no soul." It is an important Sutta, where Sāriputta is said to have made "a lion-roar" on the causal nature of things. Now the first phrase, *ajjhattaṃ-vimokkhā*, is wrongly rendered. It should be "because of self-freedom." *Ajjhattaṃ* (*adhi-attam*) is, as *we* say, of our "inner kingdom"; in this the wise man is ever free. "Up-on-to the self"—it was a new word at the birth of Buddhism in Indian thought, and always have the Piṭakas respected it, even though it tells of a belief they came to reject. I was probably misled by the emphasis in the last clause. Here, I should *now* say, we are up against a deliberate alteration made to suit the changed values. Sāriputta knew that these were already afoot, hence his asseveration, which had not been needed when the Sakyan mission was first begun. What he will have said was: "*And I do admit the self.*" In *this way only* will his first clause and his last be concordant. For the Commentator there is no discordance, because the inconvenient *ajjhattaṃ* had been etiolated to mean "what isn't outside me, external to me" (*bahiddhā*).

How does not the reader non-conversant with Pali need

[1] Translated eleven years ago.

much taking by the hand with such difficulties! And yet how much can he not now do in self-guidance, if only he, mindful of those changing values, lays one passage beside another and compares. Lays, for example, this alleged, "And I do not admit (or allow) the self," beside that first advice ascribed to his Leader, "Were it not better, gentlemen, that you sought the self?" and then looked at the Dhammapada, Chapter XII., on the self, and seen how highly rated was the "having the self established, having the self-made-to-grow." But how few do this! Men read a little monk-formula here, a little verse there, much in little books about it all, and then—Heaven help them! set to and write something "on Buddhism"!

Such have I seen, both before and after publication, have seen and marvelled. Would anyone, with so relatively simple a historical problem before him as to how much of the famous Dialogues is Socrates, how much Plato, have dreamed of writing about it with no knowledge of Greek and, let me add, of Greek thought before either? Yet this is what some deem themselves capable of attempting, when the problem is the immensely more complex one of disentangling original and derivative values in the history of early Buddhism, and when their knowledge of Pali, of Vedic, of the Upanishads is nil! Nil, too, the sense that it is the *history* of ideas, the *history* of a man, of men, with which they are dealing.

But one man only has there been who undertook such a task with no Pali and no Vedic Sanskrit, and brought out in the main a successful, because a true solution. But, then, he had more insight than have all the rest put together. I refer to my venerable friend Edmond Holmes.[1] *He* began with setting out the gulf between Indian tradition and our own; he began with seeing, in the former, the "self" or soul as "the supreme and fundamental reality," divine and human. And his conclusion was, that the "Buddha's

[1] *The Creed of Buddha*, 2nd ed., 1919.

message to man is an appeal to him to find his true self with all that this can give him." It was a great achievement to see this, when he does not even appear to have known the admonition, of Upanishad and of Gotama, to seek the self!

Well, the writings by the less discerning have gone on appearing. Not yet do we seem adolescent enough to grasp a movement historically. If in any way this book may help the reader to do this, the while he lays his hand, with Job, upon his mouth, putting away his pen; if it may check the frustrating of our slow progress in the true knowledge of a great world-religion caused by such irresponsible authorship, then will it have wrought a good work. I pray it may so work.

INDEX

ABBREVIATIONS

Dialogues, *Dialogues of the Buddha*, S.B.B., II.–IV. (p. 19).

E.R.E., *Encyclopædia of Religion and Ethics.*

Further Dialogues, *Further Dialogues of the Buddha*, S.B.B., V.–VI. (p. 19).

Grad. S., Gradual Sayings (*Anguttara-Nikāya*), p. 26.

H.O.S., Harvard Oriental Series.

Jātaka, *The Jātaka, or Stories of the Buddha's Former Births*, Cambridge, 1895, etc.

J.P.T.S., *Journal Pali Text Society.*

J.R.A.S., *Journal Royal Asiatic Society.*

K.S., Kindred Sayings (*Saṃyutta-Nikāya*), p. 26.

S.B.B., *Sacred Books of the Buddhists* (p. 19).

S.B.E., *Sacred Books of the East* (p. 16).

Vinaya Texts, *Sacred Books of the East*, XIII., XVII., XX.